D1757584

100 521 137 04

THUNDERBOLT

THUNDERBOLT
Memoirs of a World War II Fighter Pilot

MARVIN BLEDSOE

VNR VAN NOSTRAND REINHOLD COMPANY
New York Cincinnati Toronto London Melbourne

To my wife Harriett, our "Little Princess" Marva, our other two daughters Barbara and Janet, and our grandchildren Kirk, Kathryn, Jennifer, and Jeffrey. To these wonderful people I owe everything.

Copyright © 1982 by Van Nostrand Reinhold Company Inc.
Library of Congress Catalog Card Number
ISBN 0-442-21355-7

All rights reserved. No part of this work covered by the copyright hereon may be reproduced or used in any form or by any means—graphic, electronic, or mechanical, including photocopying, recording, taping, or information storage and retrieval systems—without written permission of the publisher.

Printed in the United States of America
Designed by Sylvia DeMonte-Bayard

Published by Van Nostrand Reinhold Company
135 West 50th Street
New York, NY 10020

Van Nostrand Reinhold Limited
1410 Birchmount Road
Scarborough, Ontario M1P 2E7, Canada

Van Nostrand Reinhold Australia Pty. Ltd.
17 Queen Street
Mitcham, Victoria 3132, Australia

Van Nostrand Reinhold Company Limited
Molly Millars Lane
Wokingham, Berkshire, England

16 15 14 13 12 11 10 9 8 7 6 5 4 3 2 1

100521137
940.544973 BLED

WARRNAMBOOL PUBLIC LIBRARIES
19
W.S.C.
C

Library of Congress Cataloging in Publication Data

Bledsoe, Marvin V.
  Thunderbolt: memoirs of a World War II fighter pilot.

  Includes index.
  1. World War, 1939–1945—Aerial operations, American. 2. World War, 1939–1945—Personal narratives, American. 3. Bledsoe, Marvin, 1916–   . 4. United States. Army Air Forces—Biography. 5. Fighter pilots—United States—Biography. 6. Thunderbolt (Fighter planes) I. Title.
  D790.B53   940.54'4973   82-2732
  ISBN 0-442-21355-7   AACR2

CONTENTS

FOREWORD

In relating my experiences during World War II, I have made no attempt to portray the vastness of the conflict. This is one man's observations made during a participation that began on December 7, 1941, and ended some three and one-half years later.

I have touched upon my training period as a Flying Cadet in the Army Air Corps. In doing so, I have been critical of what seemed to me to be a system that valued paperwork over the preparation of the student pilot for the day he would meet a formidable enemy. In fairness, however, I must say that the inadequacies I experienced in this training may have been the faults of an individual flight school or uninspired officers in charge, rather than that of the overall program.

This book revolves around the first one hundred days after June 6, 1944, D-Day on the European Continent. Following that invasion, there was no day until the end that did not bring an encounter with some German ground gunner who lay in wait for us.

This work is factual with the exception that some names of individuals have been changed. The incidents I have related come from my own experience, my own knowledge, and from the reports of my fellow pilots. The combat was violent, yet exciting and fascinating. Pilots pitted their skill, their wits, and luck against the enemy in order to survive.

The frequent tragedy, the nervewracking tensions, and the terrifying days of combat that seemed endless, made those months the most tremendous trial of my life. Death rode along with me on every flight.

In this book, long after the events, I hope to create a feeling for the combat fighter pilots who served during this brief span of history. I want *Thunderbolt* to take the reader into the cockpit of my single-engine plane as I flew my seventy combat missions during those crucial days of World War II.

MARVIN BLEDSOE

Oceanside, California

THUNDERBOLT

PART I

More Than Two Years

PROLOGUE

June 9, 1944: An Air Base in England

The target for the day was a railroad tunnel that the heavy bombers had been unable to destroy. The Germans were rushing reinforcements toward the beachhead at night, using this particular railroad track. The fighters' job was to go in low and destroy the tunnel.

The air was charged with excitement when we entered the briefing room. I was nervous, my insides kept whirling around, and I was scared as hell. The instant the briefing was over I raced for the latrine, where I felt my stomach turning inside out.

As we headed to our planes my mouth was dry. I found it hard to breathe and almost impossible to swallow. My stomach was doing flipflops; I was terrified.

In the cockpit of the Thunderbolt I felt somewhat better. How I loved to fly that airplane!

This takeoff of our fighter squadron was a thrilling spectacle. Every engine started at the same moment in one huge roar. The planes taxied out toward the runway in close formation, then seemed to pause and huddle together at the extreme end, wing tips and twirling props bare inches from the ships next to them. Each squadron lined up on a different runway, waiting its turn to take off. When the last plane of the first squadron started down the group operations officer fired a flare from the tower, signaling the second squadron to give their engines the gun. They crossed the intersection an instant behind the last ship that had taken off on the other runway.

My flight leader's ship taxied by and I moved into position alongside him. My ground crew gave me a final "thumbs up" as we headed out to the runway.

The frightened feeling had passed. I felt a surge of pride that I was a member of a combat fighter squadron and was flying the most powerful fighter ship in the world.

CHAPTER 1

The Wild Blue Yonder

My long, sometimes almost intolerable journey to Raydon airfield in England began on December 7, 1941.

The light of dawn that day found me at a Los Angeles airport, spinning the propeller of a rented Piper Cub. I had soloed just the week before; after two hours I already felt as though I was master of the air. The propeller began to spin, I revved up the engine, charged down the runway, and took off to greet the rising sun.

Minutes later, I was over empty fields. Suddenly, I felt an impulse to get down on the deck and take a crack at hedgehopping. It was irresistible. I shoved the stick forward and headed down.

A startled calf looked up, then raced for cover. But when it came to the end of the rope I hadn't seen, it did a ground loop, fell on its side, and lay perfectly still. Quickly I zoomed away, feeling foolish and brutal. I wondered if the calf had broken its neck.

All the way back to the airport, I worried about being reported for buzzing. Disciplinary action could include revocation of my student pilot license; I could be grounded on the spot while awaiting a formal hearing by the Civil Aeronautics Authority.

As I landed, one of the field crew ran out to meet me. "Get out of that goddamn airplane!" he shouted.

This is it, I thought. My buzz job has caught up with me.

"All ships except military are grounded," he yelled.

"What's going on?" When would I be chewed out for buzzing?

"The Japs have bombed Pearl Harbor!"

"Pearl Harbor? Where's Pearl Harbor and why would the Japs be bombing it?" What I didn't know about the world could have filled several volumes.

As I climbed out of the plane, I could hear a car radio blaring away. The news sounded grim.

"They must be nuts, trying to start trouble," the field crewman snorted when my feet hit the ground. "We'll wipe those Japs off the map." I heard that boast often—for the first six months of the war.

Because I wanted to avoid being drafted into the infantry, I had planned to enlist as a Flying Cadet in the Army Air Corps. Now I wondered how this bombing of Pearl Harbor would affect my plans.

I had my problems. The Army Air Corps program required two years of college and I was only a high school graduate. But I couldn't picture myself serving in any capacity in the military except as a pilot, so I had already quit my construction job on a tunnel for the Los Angeles Metropolitan Water District. I had enrolled in an accelerated program to cram the two years of college into six months. I was twenty-six years old, which was the maximum age for Flying Cadets. With luck, I could just make it.

Three days before the completion of my college courses the Army changed its entrance requirements: written examinations would be accepted. I took the exams and passed—barely, but I passed.

The following day, I was sworn into the Army Air Corps at March Field, California. Anxious to start, I waived the usual furlough and reported for active duty at Williams Field, Arizona the same day.

Williams Field had been developed under wartime conditions and the entire base was proof of it—organized confusion. I arrived with only the clothes on my back; four days later my civilian shoes were worn out and my clothes were grimy and thin. Nothing looked better than the G.I. shoes and uniform I got six days after reporting for duty.

The ten days spent at Williams seemed endless. Apparently the commanding officer didn't know what else to do with us, so we marched from dawn to dark. I wondered if I'd ever see an airplane. I was afraid I'd spend the rest of the war eating the dust on the drill field. And then it happened. "Aviation Cadet Bledsoe, report immediately for primary flight training at Thunderbird Field," my orders read.

What luck! Thunderbird Field, located a few miles outside Phoenix, Arizona, was the "country club" of the Air Corps training schools. But the moment I entered the gate at Thunderbird, I was braced by upperclassmen. All newcomers were hazed under the Air Corps class system, which was based on the service academy tradition. We were the "plebes." We were taught to "sir" every human being and salute anything that moved.

The hazing went on during days busy with ground school and flight training in Stearman Primary Trainers. Competition was fierce, and cadets were washed out by the score; in only three weeks nearly forty percent of our class was eliminated.

All this while I was confident; the love of flying consumed me. I couldn't wait to take my turn in the air. I felt one of my life's greatest thrills when my instructor said, "Okay, Bledsoe, take her around on your own. I've wasted enough time on you."

Although it was strictly against regulations, a week later I had that urge again—to get down on the deck and churn up the Arizona desert with my prop wash. Whenever possible after that I'd sneak off to do some hedgehopping. I was hooked on buzzing, and the closer I got to the deck the more I enjoyed it.

On graduation day eight weeks after we arrived, only a third of our original group remained to go on to basic training. The other two-thirds had been washed out.

I was assigned to Minter Field, about a hundred miles north of Los Angeles. The so-called country club days at Thunderbird were gone, if they ever existed. Every day it was ground school classes and flight training in single-wing basic trainers.

When we did get time off, my barrack buddies went girl hunting around Bakersfield. But I had different ideas. It was only a two-hour drive to my home town of Los Angeles, and I had sneaked my 1940 La Salle sedan onto the base. On every weekend pass I'd head my car south.

On my first leave, I made a date with Harriett Hurlen. She was a girl I had known in high school. I had a crush on her then but after her graduation I had lost track of her whereabouts. It was only during my stay at Minter Field that I learned of her address and telephone number from a mutual friend.

I still had that glow inside when I thought of her and was looking forward to seeing her again. She hadn't changed a bit, except to become prettier. We spent most of the night dancing at the Casino Ballroom on the beach. It was a wonderful evening. I fell in love with her that same night and jokingly asked her to marry me. To my surprise, she didn't completely reject the idea. On our second date, I asked again. She evidently thought I was coming on too strong because after that I wasn't able to get another date with her. I did convince her to write to me, though, just before I left Minter Field.

Graduation from Minter Field found our original group whittled down once again—to about twenty percent of the one that had started together at Thunderbird. My roommates, Hillary Blevins and Wayne Blickenstaff, had survived with me. We were now headed for Luke Field, Arizona, for advanced student training in AT-6s. We expected emphasis to be placed on preparing us to fly combat aircraft and that hazing would have no place. We soon learned how wrong we were.

We arrived at Luke Field in the middle of June 1942. The temperature was 120 degrees in the shade, and there was no shade. We were met by administrative officers—"groundpounders," as nonflying Air Corps officers were called. They were second lieutenants enormously impressed with their new gold bars. The officer in charge let us know what we could expect during the next eight weeks.

"You men are at Luke Field now and things are going to be different. You've had an easy time at primary and basic. We're here to make men out of you. No foolishness. Follow orders. No back talk if you want to stay out of trouble. Now, we'll start you out with some marching, calisthenics, and a little run around the field," he announced.

As a warmup, we were marched two miles with luggage in hand. Then we did calisthenics. Then we ran around the base at double time. The temperature took its toll. More than one cadet passed out from the heat.

In the several days before we reported to the flight line to start flying, we were briefed by the upperclassmen. They warned us that Luke Field was a hell hole. "Even the flight instructors will give you trouble," we were told. "Most of them are as bad as the most chickenshit groundpounder. They blame the students for keeping them here instead of in a combat outfit."

Other bases ordinarily dispensed with the usual military

courtesy and the formalities of saluting while at the flight line, and it was a refuge from the groundpounders. But not at Luke Field!

Flight instructors kept us braced in the hot sun while they lounged in the shade. Two in particular made our days miserable. They seemed to delight in making everyone stand at attention while they chewed out individual cadets. They warned us *ad nauseam* about filling out the poop sheets correctly, the poop sheets being the records kept of our flight training.

Life was a little easier for me than for some of the others. though. I got along fine with my instructor and I took to this new advanced training like an old hand.

"How much time have you had in the AT-6, Bledsoe?" my instructor asked on our first flight.

"This is my first ride in one, sir."

"You seem to know what you're doing. I'm going to turn you loose. It'll give me more time with students who're having problems."

That gave me almost a month of free flying time, and I took complete advantage of it. I flew every chance I got, and whenever possible, I'd be down on the deck getting the feel of the cactus and brush scraping the belly of my ship.

After that month my poop sheet showed I had been checked out in high- and low-altitude flying, and that I was proficient in formation, acrobatic, and instrument flying. What the poop sheet failed to reveal was that my training in these procedures was totally insufficient; only by breaking the rules did I have some real idea of formation and low-altitude flying. Besides that, neither Blevins nor I did well in the Link Trainer, a machine to simulate flying by instruments. Yet according to the poop sheets we were both qualified to fly in bad weather. "Who's kidding who?" I asked him when they gave us our instrument pilot rating.

As the unhappy days at Luke Field continued, the mail became our main diversion. I was getting along better with

Harriett in our letters—until I asked about marriage again. Her answer said she was going steady with someone else and suggested I not write anymore. That seemed to be the end of that romance.

I left Luke Field with an intense dislike for most of the groundpounders and instructors. I also felt contempt for the poop sheet system. Two months was just not long enough to train us in the various maneuvers and procedures outlined on those poop sheets. It disturbed me greatly that such importance was placed on making it appear that we were proficient when we were not. What I did not realize was the great pressure for pilots and air crews from combat commands in Europe and the Pacific and the urgent need for them. I had wondered why, in all my days at Luke Field, the war being fought overseas was never alluded to. It probably meant that the brass there had no more idea at the time than I did of the reasons for the pressure they were under.

Anyhow, it felt great to walk out the gates of Luke Field. I had silver wings on my chest and was a commissioned officer in the Army Air Corps, the best damned fighting group in the world.

CHAPTER 2

Mitchell Field

My orders sent me to active duty at Mitchell Field, New York, where I would fly P-47 Thunderbolts. Blickenstaff would be based at the Municipal Airport in Baltimore, Maryland, where he too would fly the Thunderbolts. But Blevins almost cried when he read the orders sending him to a bomber base. He was bitterly disappointed at having to fly the "Big Birds." I didn't blame him. It would have been a crushing blow to me if I had been assigned to anything but a single-engine fighter. I did not see Blevins again until 1946.

When I arrived at Mitchell Field on September 10, 1942, I was sent to the 90th Fighter Squadron, 80th Fighter Group, stationed at La Guardia Field in New York City. What luck! I'd be flying a brand-new fighter at a civilian airport, right next door to where American Airlines was training stewardesses for commercial flights.

Pilots were the toast of New York City. We were welcomed with open arms everywhere; our uniforms were an "Open Sesame." The Hotel New Yorker adopted our squadron and gave us the VIP treatment. Everything was on the house when we went there, and we went there whenever we could. It was a cheap way to impress the stewardesses.

The P-47 Thunderbolt was the hottest American fighter plane. More of them were produced during World War II than any other fighter. Mayor Fiorello La Guardia wanted New Yorkers to know we were available to protect the city, so he encouraged us to fly at low altitude and in tight formation to impress the civilians. Each day, crowds lined the spectator gallery at La Guardia Field to watch our squadron in action. The brass ordered us to put on a show for the people who came out, and we were more than anxious to comply. We even taxied in battle formation.

It didn't take long for our inadequate flight school training to show. The experienced pilots in the squadron worked hard to get us in shape. They put us through the wringer; they flew us as if we had had hundreds of hours in this new 14,000-pound fighter, including all the "bugs" that inevitably go along with something new. It was no place for the faint-hearted. Several of the inexperienced pilots were killed; many others asked for transfers.

The more I flew the Thunderbolt, the more I liked it. My confidence in the plane increased after I was involved in a midair collision with John Brighton, a classmate from Luke Field.

The group always kept one flight on alert, ready for immediate takeoff should any unidentified aircraft be sighted at sea. On this day it was our flight's turn. The alarm sounded. "Bogies"—unidentified aircraft—were reportedly approaching the coast, and we had to intercept them as fast as possible.

We raced to get into our ships and then roared down the runway. I was in the number two position. Brighton would fly on my wing as the third man in our flight of four.

At eight hundred feet I began closing on my leader. I kept my eyes riveted on his ship as I prepared to slide into position on his wing. I was unaware that Brighton was bearing down on me from behind.

Suddenly there was a tremendous crash. Brighton had made an error that caused him to overshoot and ram into the belly of my P-47. I felt my ship catapult high in the air. My prop cut off Brighton's tail assembly. What was left of his plane surged into the air, then started a violent spin toward the ground.

With the first shock of impact, my engine began making a furious noise. The plane vibrated as though it would fly apart. My immediate reaction was to bail out. At eight hundred feet, I had just time to go over the side and pull the ripcord—and hope that my chute opened before I hit the ground. My bail-out training was nil, but instinctively I jerked open my canopy and released the safety belt. Before I could hoist myself up, the plane went into a stall. I'll give this baby one chance to respond, I thought, and if it doesn't, over the side I go.

I rammed the stick forward to get out of the stall, kicked the rudder to start a turn toward the airport, and held my breath. The plane straightened out and started a gentle glide toward La Guardia Field.

The immediate pressure off, I looked down. Below was a sea of apartment houses. I shuddered at what would have happened if I had bailed out and seven tons of metal had come crashing down into that congested area.

But so far so good. I couldn't maintain altitude but I could control my direction. With luck I would glide to safety at the end of the airport.

I got on the radio. "Mayday! Mayday! La Guardia tower, Mayday. Midair collision. I'm coming in with a damaged P-47 for an emergency landing! Heading for Runway 27."

The tower came back: "Roger, P-47. We saw the collision. Emergency crews are alerted. The field is clear. Come on in . . . and good luck to you."

I heard my landing gear snap into place; that meant I wouldn't have to risk fire in a belly landing with a full tank of gasoline.

As I came in I could see the ambulances, fire trucks, and emergency crews racing for the spot where I would put down. I prayed I wouldn't need them.

My immediate concern was the strong cross wind. I was having to slip and slide to stay lined up with the runway as the wind buffeted my ship, but my luck was good. The 800-foot glide to the field worked just right.

My plane rolled to the end of the runway. The emergency crew swarmed around the plane to get me out. Fire was still foremost in everyone's mind. The moment the P-47 stopped, I jumped out and ran. It did not burn.

The undercarriage of the P-47 was battered and bent. Large chunks of metal had been torn off the belly and both wings. The supercharger was crushed. The big four-bladed prop was twisted like a corkscrew, and the lower engine fittings were jammed together. Yet that P-47 had held together and brought me safely home. I wasn't going to forget that.

Poor Brighton! He had gone in with his ship, but at least no one else died—by skill or through a miracle he had crashed in the only vacant lot in that heavily congested residential area.

Following an old Air Corps custom, my CO wanted me in the air again before I had time to dwell on the accident, and within the hour after my landing I was ordered to take off on another mission. I was extremely nervous and kept a wary eye on the pilot behind me who would pull up on my wing. Involuntarily I cringed as his plane closed in tight. But by the time I got back to the field my nerves were under control. My commanding officer's psychological trick had worked: I was ready to continue flying close formation. I would be thinking of Brighton every time someone closed up to join me from the rear, but I could go on.

The news media reported the accident nationwide because I was the only pilot who had survived a midair collision in one of the new Thunderbolts. As a result of the publicity, I was deluged with mail. I was pleasantly surprised to find a letter from Harriett Hurlen; she had read about my accident and expressed her concern. The letter filled me with "that old feeling" about her all over again.

I bombarded her with telephone calls and telegrams telling her of my love for her and asking her to marry me. Before too long, the campaign was successful. She came to New York and we were married at the Mitchell Field base chapel on Long Island a few days later.

Marriage changed me almost immediately. I wanted to get out of the Air Corps, settle down in southern California, and start to raise a family. Even the flying seemed less important. Constant rumors that our unit was going overseas didn't fill me with the old wild urge to get into combat with all guns blazing. When headquarters started emphasizing combat formation, gunnery, weather flying, and especially high altitude maneuvers, Harriett and I began sweating out the wait for that inevitable day when orders for combat duty would separate us.

We fliers had lots to discover about this new Thunderbolt. It was almost like learning to fly all over again. At thirty thousand feet the thin air caused the controls to feel mushy and loose. Superchargers sometimes exploded in midair if not handled correctly. If the plane was flown upside down for more than a few seconds, the engine froze up. The tail assemblies were weak, and when the plane reached high speed the tail seemed to jump up and down. But despite these bugs, most of us loved the big brute.

We were all scared as hell about diving from high altitude and reaching the speed of sound, where rudder and ailerons locked and the pilot lost all control of the ship until altitude was reduced and the aircraft slowed down a little; we knew nothing about the sound barrier. Some pilots came back with stories of wild rides. It took time before we all realized that once the plane left the rarified high-altitude atmosphere, it would automatically slow down to a point where the pilot could take control again.

As we stepped up our high-altitude flying, I developed problems with my ears during the descents. One day, on a combat training formation flight, the CO peeled off in a dive at about 35,000 feet and started a "rat race." The object was to stick close to the ship in front of you while trying to lose the pilot behind.

The more rapidly we lost altitude, the more clogged my ears became. As the plane screamed down toward the ground, I could feel the pressure building in my head. I gulped, swallowed, yawned, yelled at the top of my voice, did all the prescribed moves to release the pressure. Nothing worked. The top of my head felt like it was going to blow off. I broke away from the rat race and headed back upstairs, where I found relief in the thin atmosphere.

I came down slowly. When I landed, the flight surgeon checked and found my eardrums were badly inflamed. He grounded me on the spot. A few days later, a medical board restricted me from high-altitude flying. Since my squadron was ready to be transferred overseas and combat flying was ruled out, I was sent to Mitchell Field for a new assignment.

"I've got a good job for you, Bledsoe," the CO there said. "General Woodbury down at Norfolk needs a flying aide."

Harriett and I headed for Virginia on May 5, 1943, happy at the thought of being together for a while longer, particularly since by this time she was pregnant.

Right away General Woodbury spelled out the future for me. "As my flying aide, you'll be about as much use to me as a chicken. But the book says I have to have a flying aide, so that's that. You'll sit around on your butt till I whistle, then we'll go on a trip somewhere. If you think you're going to do the flying, get that out of your head right now. I've been pushing these ships around for twenty-five years, and I don't intend to let some junior birdman auger me in."

The general was being frank. "It's a stinker of a job for a guy who likes to fly," he said. "On the other hand, if you're interested in quick promotion and if you like to hobnob with the brass and polish their buttons, you might enjoy it. What do you say, Bledsoe?"

I didn't like it. Since he had put things to me straight from the shoulder, I did the same to him.

"General, I joined the Air Corps to fly in a fighter squadron, not to be with the brass. I think I'd like working with you, but I'm afraid I'd be a complete fizzle at the job itself. I'd like to get out of this assignment."

"I don't blame you one bit, Bledsoe. They ought to give this job to some groundpounder bucking for a promotion." The general had a twinkle in his eye. "But since you can't fly in that fighter squadron, just what the hell do you want to do, Bledsoe?"

"Sir, my wife is expecting a baby. That's the most important thing to me now. If I can't do any real flying, I might as well get located somewhere and settle down for the duration. I understand instructors are stuck with their assignments. I'd like to go back to the West Coast to some flying school as an instructor and stay put until the war ends."

"Okay, I'll see what I can do," the general said. He had new orders written to send me back to Mitchell Field. "Tell them Bledsoe's services have been requested by the West Coast Training Command," he told the clerk. "I'll clear it with a pal of mine on the West Coast later. Now, when you get to Mitchell, go see Colonel Davis, an old buddy of mine. Tell him I said to fix you up. He knows the wheels in Washington."

When I returned to Mitchell Field, I saw the general's friend. Within minutes, I had a three-day pass to travel to Air Corps Headquarters at the Pentagon. The object of the trip was to see a friend of the colonel's.

I expected to see another colonel. Instead, I found myself before a busy two-star general. When I told him my story, he didn't bat an eye. He opened the office intercom and spoke briefly. "Major, I'm sending in a young lieutenant to see you.

See to it that he is transferred to the West Coast Training Command right away." Then he turned to me. "Okay, Bledsoe. That will take care of it. Now, you'll have to excuse me. I've got work to do."

And that was that. My orders were cut and Harriett and I were on our way to California.

I reported to the West Coast Training Command and brashly asked the officer in charge to send me to any flying school in his command—except Luke Field. The memories of my tour there as a Flying Cadet were still bitter, and I didn't want any part of it as an instructor.

"I hope to hell you know what you want, Bledsoe," he said. "Luke Field is the only advanced training school in the West. If you don't go there, you'll be stuck flying primary or basic trainers. Frankly, I don't know where to send you. You're the only qualified fighter pilot in this branch of training." He was almost thinking out loud. "But if you don't want to go to Luke, I'll send you up to Merced. There's a basic training school there. I'll let them figure out what to do with you."

I went to Merced Field. The CO took one look at my file and said, "With your Thunderbolt flying experience, you should be at an advanced training school." I answered that I didn't mind flying basic trainers and was satisfied to be assigned to Merced.

"I don't give a shit what you don't mind," he snapped back. "By God, you're going to go where I want you to go. I'm sending you to Luke Field. You ought to be able to handle a job there. And, Bledsoe," he added curtly, "you're supposed to stand at attention when being addressed by a superior officer."

I had forgotten. In a fighter squadron, rank didn't prevent frank talk with superior officers. The major hadn't wasted any time in straightening me out. I knew then that I was back in the training command with all its pettiness.

When I arrived at Luke Field a few days later, I found the same old hell hole, but I still had hopes. Now I had a silver bar on my shoulder. As a first lieutenant, I could be more independent and would be treated differently from before, I thought.

Since I had been ordered to report to Luke Field without delay there would be no time to try and find a place to live near the base. Furthermore, the temperatures could reach 120 degrees in that dry Arizona desert which can really be rough on someone not acclimated to such weather. We decided it would be best for Harriett to remain in Los Angeles, where relatives were available in the event of problems, until the baby arrived.

A few weeks later, Harriett phoned to say that her time had come and she was on the way to the hospital. I got an emergency leave and drove the 400 miles in a frenzy to be on hand when the baby arrived. The rush was in vain as it was several hours later that we were blessed with an 8-pound baby girl on October 31, 1943. She was christened Karen Anne but resembled me so much we had her name legally changed to Marva to go with my first name, Marvin. But in no time at all we were calling her our Little Princess and the nickname stuck.

CHAPTER 3

Luke Field Again

Six students were assigned to me at Luke. I began teaching them some of the important things I had learned with my New York fighter squadron. I tried to reach them on a man-to-man basis and impress them with the importance of learning as much as they could in preparation for combat.

But in a short while, I was called before a senior officer. "Bledsoe, we don't want any accidents around here. You forget your fighter tactics and follow the poop sheets," he ordered. "Your job is to get your students qualified for graduation without problems."

"But isn't Luke Field an advanced training school for combat pilots?" I asked.

"Damnit, you do as you're told," was his answer. "The poop sheets outline what you're supposed to teach. Don't you try and improve on them. Everytime we have an accident around here, we have to explain it in triplicate to headquarters."

The poop sheets were sent each month to Training Command Headquarters as progress reports of the Cadet Training Program. If Luke Field instructors could demonstrate through the sheets that they had given a certain number of hours of dual instruction with a minimum of accidents, headquarters would be happy and the boat wouldn't be rocked.

I tried to explain to the CO what our students would face after Luke; I described the midair collision that had been caused by lack of training and told him about the numerous accidents and fatalities among the new pilots. But it was no use.

"That's enough, Bledsoe. You heard what I said," he interrupted me. "And another thing—it is Goddamn time you learned to say 'sir' when you speak to a superior officer!"

"Yes sir." I saluted and left the room.

A few days later all instructors were called to an "important meeting." We were ordered to bring our poop sheets along. First, one of the squadron commanders chewed out an instructor because a student of his had been involved in a minor accident while taxiing. Next, all the squadron commanders bitched about the fact that some instructors were not being careful enough in filling out all the little boxes on the poop sheets.

No one had said anything about teaching the students as much as possible about flying or how to prepare them for combat. The war? It was never mentioned. Poop sheet procedure came through as the important activity at Luke Field.

After an hour of this chewing out, the major in charge asked: "Any questions or statements? If anyone has anything to say, now is the time to get it off your chest."

There wasn't a sound. The various instructors who had bitched to me in private were silent.

I found myself on my feet.

"Sir," I began, "I've only been here a short time and I'm new at instructing, but I think we're losing sight of our goal and getting snowed under with paper work."

The officer was taken aback; he nearly fell off his chair. It was clear that he had not expected anyone to take him up on his invitation.

"What the hell do you mean, Bledsoe?"

I was determined to speak my piece, but I also knew I had better put my "sirs" in the right places. "Sir, everyone is too interested in making the poop sheets look good. But as I understand it, we're supposed to be sending out pilots ready to take their places in fighter squadrons."

I hadn't gotten the last word out of my mouth before all the brass in the room were on my back. They acted as if I was trying to start a mutiny. To them I was a troublemaker, someone to be stepped on—hard.

When the hubbub had quieted down, the officer barked at me: "What the hell are you talking about? Are you another one of those wise guys who thinks he's a hot rock just because he's had a little time in a fighter squadron?"

I had known this officer during my student days. He used to make us stand at attention, withering in the hot sun, while he slouched in the shade. Now he was taking pleasure in disciplining me in front of a hundred instructors, fully aware I had to be limited in response.

I repeated what I had said.

"Bledsoe, you talk like a man with a wooden head. How the hell can you stand there and make a statement like that?" another major demanded. This one had been at Luke Field since it opened. He was an accepted kingpin on the base. "You'd better dig up proof of your charges, or sit down and keep your mouth shut."

"Sir, this morning my squadron commander told me to take nine students on a training flight for an hour. He ordered me then to certify on the poop sheets that these nine students were proficient in twelve-ship, high-altitude formation, high-altitude cross-country, low-altitude formation, and low-altitude cross-country flying. I made the entries as ordered after the one flight. It looked great on the poop sheets. But the truth of the matter is that I was also ordered not to let the students get higher than ten thousand feet or lower than five hundred feet. We all know you cannot get the feel of high-altitude flying at ten thousand feet. We also know that the students haven't the slightest idea of low-altitude flying when they remain above five hundred feet. They have to get down on the deck and do some hedgehopping to learn anything about the low-altitude flying they'll do in combat. Also, sir, although the poop sheets reflected cross-country maneuvers, we hardly got out of sight of the field. How can we expect students to become efficient combat replacements with training like that?"

For a few moments there was dead silence. The brass sat there glaring at me. It was apparent the major found it hard to speak. Finally he responded.

"Bledsoe, you've admitted your students were not proficient in the maneuvers you checked off on the poop sheets. That means you're admitting to falsification of official Army records. That's a court-martial offense." His tone was triumphant, as if he had found just the right way to deal with my insubordination.

"Sir, I did what I was told to do. But I don't want to falsify official Army records," I replied. "So I'll change the records. I will then certify that those nine students were not given enough time to be proficient. And, sir, you can rest assured that I will not falsify any more poop sheets by certifying that students are proficient when I know they are not!"

I could see that the major was regretting his words. A recalcitrant instructor who refused to certify his students unless they were actually proficient in the maneuvers outlined by Training Command Headquarters could really put a crimp in the instruction schedule. Also, some other instructors might start having second thoughts about falsifying official Army records, since he had made it plain that's what they were doing.

When it became apparent that I would not back down on the position I had taken, the meeting was adjourned. I had gained the respect of my fellow instructors but incurred the animosity of my superior officers.

From that day forward, my name was "Mud" at Luke Field. I received many extra details and was harassed by the brass constantly for following my convictions.

I was later officially assigned to the Instrument Training Group under the officer who had given me so hard a time. I heard he had been told to make me fall into line; it began to be obvious that I had been transferred so he could work me over.

Unlike the other instructors, I flew two shifts—eight to ten hours a day in the air. I had twelve students instead of the usual six. But I made it a point not to complain about the extra work as I knew the brass expected. I taught my students everything I possibly could and worked them and myself hard, all in the attempt to get them through the course honestly. As a result, my students were much more capable than the average. But even though they could outfly most of the other cadets, many of them still could not meet the requirements. I refused to certify their proficiency even though I knew another instructor would make the certification in order to get them graduated.

The double duty, the endless hours of instrument training in the air, working with twelve students each day, had its reward for me in a very direct way. It became second nature for me to rely on basic instruments to get through bad weather.

At the end of instrument training, students were passed on a wholesale basis regardless of their proficiency. An impressive-looking official instrument rating card stated the pilot was qualified to fly in bad weather. Without that card, a pilot was not allowed to fly unless he could have visual contact with the ground at all times.

I thought it almost murderous: weather could kill—and was killing—experienced pilots, let alone these newly graduated cadets going off with a false sense of security. An instrument rating card in the pocket didn't help when the weather socked in and the plane was being buffeted by a storm. The newspapers were full of stories to prove it: "Pilot trapped in bad weather killed in routine flight."

I knew it was not entirely the flight schools' fault. It was absolutely impossible for them to make the students proficient in the two months allotted for advanced training. It was my contention then, and still is, that the flight schools should have told headquarters the schedule could not be met. To do otherwise was a disservice and dangerous both to the students and to the units they joined. I didn't advocate more time; I knew the time was simply not available. All I wanted was that we teach the students everything we could in the two months we had them, and then report their proficiency honestly without trying to fool or cover up for anyone.

Upon graduation from flight school, students were assigned to tactical squadrons. The records they took with them included reports on their training and proficiency. Those in charge of the tactical units were inclined to rely upon the reports. As a result the newly assigned pilots engaged in a type of flying for which most of them were not prepared.

Had the commanding officers of the tactical unit been made aware of the fact that the records were inaccurate, the new pilots would have received additional training at their new base.

I had a particularly rough time with one batch of students. Their regular instructor became ill and I inherited them during the final stages of training. None of them were able to meet the proficiency requirements. I had no alternative but to fail every one. This meant they would be held back until the next class—unless some other instructor certified them as proficient.

I was not surprised to be called into the office.

"Goddamnit, Bledsoe, what's wrong with you now?" a superior officer roared. "You've flunked every one of your students."

"Sir, these students simply did not have the ability. I couldn't qualify them."

"You know damn well we've got to pass them anyway," he shouted. "Now, get the hell out of here and change those grades. We're having enough trouble making the schedule. Get going and do as you're told!"

I had to speak up. "Sir, if you want to make that a written order, with full knowledge that these students are not proficient in their instrument flight training, I will change the grades. Otherwise I will not put my name on those instrument rating cards and be responsible for someone getting killed the first time he finds himself lost in bad weather."

He started to rage. "You're really laying yourself open for trouble, Bledsoe. What the hell do you think you're supposed to be doing in that airplane? If those students can't find that radio beam, then by God you find it for them. We have a job to do here and we have no time to do it, and you damn well know it. I'm telling you again. Get out there and pass those students!"

"Sir, I understand the situation. But why don't you flunk most of the entire class and call a spade a spade? Let headquarters know. If we lay it on the line, they would have to eliminate some training requirements from the schedule. I don't believe they know we're passing students who can't make the grade."

My commander was furious. "You aren't here to tell me how to run this outfit! Your job is to pass those students! Now get the hell out of here and do it!"

"Sir, I refuse unless you make it a direct order in writing or in front of a witness. As I said before, I'm not going to falsify official Army records. This is a very serious matter to me, sir. I am standing pat on those grades. Anything else, sir?"

He was not about to give me a direct written order to falsify records. He curtly dismissed me.

I had been standing at stiff attention during the entire affair. Once outside his office, my shoulders sagged. There was no blacker list then the one I was on now. Soon, events revealed just how true that was.

Double flying duty became routine. My ears buzzed all night long from listening to radio signals nine hours a day. When I wasn't in the air, the brass found extra work for me to do on the ground. My CO continued to give me the icy treatment. I knew he was waiting for the day I would make one complaint or a single mistake.

I was gratified to learn that my students were on my side. Each time I had to flunk a cadet I would explain that he was just not ready to fly instruments in bad weather. I also had to explain, of course, that he would be passed by another instructor and that my flunking him would not hold him back.

"You'll graduate and you'll get that instrument rating card," I told them. "But I want to emphasize that you had better not rely on it. That card isn't going to help you a damn bit when you find your life depends on those instruments."

I felt obligated to preach; I just had to get the point across. I didn't want their deaths on my conscience.

Most students took what I said in the spirit in which it was meant. They admitted they were not qualified, did not deserve the instrument rating card, and promised they would not fly in bad weather until they received adequate training at their next base. Not once did I ever regret flunking a student or make an enemy of one for doing so because they were not held back by my actions because they were "passed" by other instructors.

A rumor started: there would be a call for volunteers for a fighter squadron to go overseas. Then came an order for another special instructors' meeting, "one of the most important meetings in Luke Field's history."

As we assembled, the long-time instructors went through their usual routine of saying how much they wanted to leave Luke Field and get into combat. I'd heard the same talk from some of them when I was a cadet; their words sounded just as hollow now as they had then.

The base commander gave us the news. "Men, this is the big

chance you've all been waiting for. Headquarters has decided to allow instructors to volunteer for combat duty in single-engine fighter ships!"

A tremendous roar went up. The CO had to quiet the excited instructors down before he could go on.

"Now, I know you all want to go," he said. "But Luke Field has been limited to thirty-five volunteers." A groan went up from someone. "I realize this is a small quota," he added. "Therefore I'm going to restrict volunteers to captains and first lieutenants. They've been here longest and deserve first crack. Of course, key personnel will not be allowed to volunteer," he concluded.

Being "key personnel," my squadron leader and some of the other brass went through the motions of saying how they longed to get into combat. I didn't think they fooled anyone.

I was the first to get my name on the list; I would have volunteered for the Luftwaffe, if necessary, to get away from "the battle of Luke Field." I was not surprised when the full quota of thirty-five was not filled. Even when the offer was opened to allow key personnel to volunteer, the quota still was not met.

The senior officers retreated into their offices. All talk of wanting to get into combat ceased. The CO finally had to appoint instructors to fill the quota.

My volunteering wasn't exactly braggadocio, but I was confident I would never see combat: after all, I had already been assigned to a fighter squadron and washed out for combat because of the ear problem. Without a doubt, I thought I was unfit for combat duty.

The way I had it figured, the brass at Luke Field would be so glad to get rid of me they would close their eyes to the flying restriction in my medical record. I figured when I got checked out at an embarkation station for final approval before being sent overseas, I would be turned down. Once I got away from Luke Field and was turned down for combat flying, I would get a new assignment—somewhere in the states, I hoped.

When I got home that night and told Harriett I had volunteered for combat, she thought I had lost my mind. She didn't have much confidence in my reasoning. I couldn't convince her that my medical record would prevent me from being shipped overseas. How right she was.

CHAPTER 4

On My Way

I arrived in Perry, Florida for accelerated fighter training at Dale Mabry Field in April 1944. I tingled with excitement again at the sight of the Thunderbolts. Our thirty-five volunteers from Luke Field joined two hundred other instructors. It became quickly apparent that we were being given special training; the usual six-month preliminary course was being skipped and we were to be rushed into a combat group overseas.

It seemed obvious that we were being primed for the big push—the long-awaited invasion of Europe.

I kept waiting for some flight surgeon or groundpounder to discover my medical record. When the day for physical examinations came, our entire group of over two hundred was marched naked past a flight surgeon, who barely looked at us as we trooped by. I could imagine him filling in his own poop sheet and certifying that we all qualified. Just like Luke Field! I passed the physical along with the 234 others.

At the end of the month we were declared to be ready for combat. From Mabry we went to Camp Kilmer, New Jersey, and from there to the port of embarkation—New York. On the train to the harbor the impact of what was happening seemed to hit everyone at once. A hush fell over the lot of us. I already missed Harriett and the 'Little Princess.' I wondered if I would ever see them again.

Everything went off without a hitch after that, except for one thing that had us all laughing. The nature of our unit was supposedly a deep secret for security reasons, yet the band on the deck played the Air Corps song till the last of our group was aboard ship.

The crossing was uneventful, although one destroyer escort claimed an enemy sub on the seventh day out. We made the trip in eleven days, good time for a large convoy. No one told us where we were going. We were not even sure we were bound for the European Theater of Operations until we reached Liverpool.

When we arrived in England, I got in touch with Wayne Blickenstaff, my former roommate at flying school. I knew his group was flying Thunderbolts and that he was now a captain and operations officer of the 350th Fighter Squadron, 353rd Fighter Group, Eighth Air Force, stationed at Raydon, a base in Suffolk. I told him I wanted to join his outfit.

Blick seemed impressed with the amount of flying time I had logged as an instructor. He thought my instrument training was very important. His squadron needed replacements, he told me, and it would strengthen the group if he could get former instructors instead of newly graduated cadets. He asked for the names of two or three other instructors. Vernon Rafferty and Ray Carson came immediately to mind.

Blick knew where to pull strings to get us transferred, and before long the three of us were on our way to Raydon.

Soon after our train left Liverpool station, it was pulled off the main track and stopped. We grumbled, but there was nothing to be done. We bedded down for the night in the crowded car. The next morning we learned why we had been held up; all tracks had been reserved for the big push. D-Day had become a reality.

On that day, June 6, 1944, Rafferty, Carson, and I were officially assigned to Blick's squadron. The squadron CO was Captain Dewey Newhart, a former classmate of mine at Luke Field. As operations officer, Blickenstaff was second in command.

The group, three squadrons, consisted of forty-eight planes. A squadron was made up of four flights, and each flight had four ships. Our group wasn't up to full strength when we arrived because the heavy load of recent missions had taken a big toll of men and planes.

Each squadron of the air group had its own radio call sign. Ours was Seldom, while the 351st was Lawyer Squadron and the 352nd was Jockey Squadron. The group flight leader was known as Jonah. Individual flights within the squadron were identified by colors. The leading flight was White Flight, with Red, Blue, and Yellow Flights following. Enemy aircraft were dubbed "EA" or "bandits." This arrangement made it possible to identify pilot, outfit, and relative position with very brief radio communication.

Newhart had just finished one combat tour. He was scheduled for a furlough and was awaiting promotion to major. When the D-Day plan was revealed, he delayed his furlough to remain with the squadron until the Normandy beachhead was securely established.

The Eighth Air Force backed up the ground invasion, and the group was operating at maximum. It flew seven missions on D-Day, nine on D-Day plus one, and three missions on June 8 before bad weather kept it on the ground. Some pilots flew combat nine to twelve hours out of the twenty-four. Ground crews worked night and day on damaged aircraft.

The group was too busy to bother with replacements at that

point, and Rafferty, Carson, and I were all but ignored. I kept on Blick's heels, urging him to let me fly. Pilot losses were high, and the remaining flyers were exhausted from having to fly more missions to take up the slack. I felt useless and helpless, waiting there on the ground.

Blick must have gotten tired of saying no, because he finally told me he would take the responsibility of letting me fly if Newhart would okay it. Group policy was to take new pilots on training missions around England for several weeks before putting them into combat, but there was no time for that now. Approached with the request, Newhart didn't like the idea of sending out a replacement without local training, but he was so short of fresh pilots he decided to take a chance.

The next day I was assigned to my first combat mission. It was June 9, 1944.

PART II

One Hundred Days—
A Lifetime

CHAPTER 5

A Lifetime Begins

Although the Thunderbolt was designed as a high-altitude fighter, the Eighth Air Force was using every weapon possible to support the ground forces, and our P-47s carried a thousand-pound demolition bomb under each wing in addition to the regular load of 50-caliber machine guns. We were supposed to go in low and use the bombs to destroy the railroad tunnel and track the Germans were using to rush reinforcements to the beachhead.

Blick gave me my own special briefing just before takeoff.

"You'll be flying on my wing, Marv. I don't think you'll have any trouble. Just keep your eyes open and your head moving all the time. That's the best way to keep from being bounced. Stay off the radio unless you have something important to say. Most important, stick on my tail. With you as my wingman, I'll be able to keep an eye on you if you stay where you belong."

He slapped me on the shoulder and wished me good luck.

The pilots climbed into their planes and revved the engines to life. We were ready to go.

Sitting there in the cockpit, I prayed. I had never been a religious person and had very little faith in a higher being, but I sure didn't want to miss out on any possible help. I heard my voice say out loud, "Lord, I don't know what I'm going up against, so I want you to help me over the hurdles. Just get me back to my family."

Blick moved his plane out onto the runway and signaled for takeoff.

Okay, this is it. Now get that damn wing in next to Blick's and keep it there.

Blick gave his ship the throttle. We were moving down the runway. I pushed everything from my mind except staying with my leader. As the end of the runway came into view, Blick's heavily laden ship and mine became airborne as one. When Blick turned his head to locate me, I was right with him. He grinned and gave me the high sign. He nodded his head, pointed at my wing, and blew me a kiss. It was his way of telling me how pleased he was with our formation.

It was strange to me that Blick had ended up my superior officer and flight leader in combat. The Blick I had known at flight school was such a quiet, go-by-the book type that I had never imagined him as a combat flight leader. But his months of combat had turned him into a tiger, and now he was leading a squadron into battle.

I kept trying to remember the many things Blick had told me to look out for. I also had in mind the orders Colonel Glenn Duncan had given at the briefing. I wanted to do a good job on my first combat flight; I also wanted to prove that my instructor experience had taught me something about flying.

After we got into the air and joined the rest of the group in formation, I relaxed somewhat. But at the first sight of the French coast and enemy-held territory, a tingle went up my spine. The view was so pretty that it was hard to remember death constantly stalked us. It all seemed a long way from Los Angeles.

As we passed over the French coast, I had my introduction to flak, the scourge of every combat flyer. The first thing I knew large dark blossoms were bursting all around us. Where they came from, I couldn't tell. Blick changed course, weaving through the stuff as if he knew exactly where to go. I tried to forget about the danger and concentrate on keeping in position. I was wet with perspiration and scared silly. In a moment we were in the clear again, but the sky behind us was dark with black puffs of smoke.

We flew over the Continent at twenty thousand feet for an hour or so and then started our descent. I glanced at my watch, checked my time card, and found we were supposed to be nearing the target. Sure enough, there was a large town below. We skirted the edge of it to avoid the antiaircraft guns positioned there. I almost jumped out of my seat when radio silence was broken with a sudden cry of "Flak! Flak!" Some pilot had panicked.

"Jonah here," the group leader called. "Whoever is doing the screaming shut up and stay off the radio. That stuff is miles away."

Radio discipline was crucial on combat missions. So far on this trip only the squadron and flight leaders had been doing any talking. We wingmen were supposed to keep our mouths shut unless we had something really important to report. But it was difficult for some pilots to keep off the radio. Under such great tension, they would be thinking out loud with their transmitter button down. The unnecessary chatter jammed the radio and could be fatal if we were bounced by enemy aircraft.

We were down to five thousand feet and the target was dead ahead. "Okay, Seldom Squadron," Blick called. "Let's go down in elements of two. Make your bombs count. We want to get this tunnel." Then a wave to me and an aside: "All set, Bledsoe?" I nodded and returned his wave, said another fast prayer, and followed him down, picking up speed as I went.

I was in a trail position; Blick's ship was about a hundred yards in front of me. I saw him release his bombs and watched them hit several feet from the mouth of the tunnel. *Boom!* I couldn't hear the explosion, but I could see chunks of debris hurled into the air and feel the concussion of the blast.

The wings on Blick's ship make such pretty white streamers in the misty sky as he heads back upstairs in a steep climb.

A chill went up my spine as I released my bomb. I was yelling. "Go get her, baby!" I started a climbing turn to join Blickenstaff. "Whoopee!" I was yelling again when I saw the bomb fly toward the mouth of the tunnel. Both bombs should have gotten in on that shot, but this was the first time I had ever dropped a bomb and I had been too slow.

Blick called. "Nice going, Bledsoe. That's laying that bomb in there. Wait until the rest of the squadron is through, then go down by yourself and drop your other baby."

I was elated. I tacked onto Blick's wing and got back into position. We circled at three thousand feet, acting as top cover for the rest of the squadron.

"Red Flight, all through," came the call.

"Bledsoe here, going down with my other bomb." This time I was alone. The tunnel loomed up fast. I centered the needle and ball on my instrument panel to eliminate drift and glued my eyes to the mouth of the tunnel.

As the weight of the bomb was released my ship jumped into the air. I started my climbing turn, trying both to keep one eye on Blick circling above and at the same time watch the flight of my bomb. I lost sight of it finally and didn't see it explode.

Surely I didn't forget to arm the bomb. No, I armed both bombs at the same time, I remember that.

Suddenly, a large cloud of smoke and dust poured out of the tunnel. I had skipped my bomb right inside the tunnel and it had exploded in the middle.

"Hey, who did that? Somebody blew hell out of that tunnel. Who was it? That was a beautiful job," I heard the CO say over the radio.

"That's my man, Bledsoe. How about that?" Blick responded.

I felt as though I was flying without the plane. Both bombs had scored bull's-eyes and one had really done the job. I was so excited I could have burst. Which way to Berlin? I felt I could blow all of Germany right off the map. The first trip out and I had made two good hits.

Maybe I'm a natural. Natural, hell! You were just lucky. You didn't have the slightest idea where those bombs were going.

It turned out to be the best bombing I did during my entire combat tour. I had indeed been lucky.

As we neared the French coastline on the way home, the flight leaders knew the flak gunners below were waiting for us and began evasive action. Then I could feel and hear the concussion of the flak hitting around us, but it lasted only a few moments. We were quickly over the English Channel, already starting a letdown toward home base. Our field at Raydon came into sight.

Thanks, Lord.

Blick motioned to me to tighten up the formation. I suspected he wanted to put on a show for the guys on the ground, so I tucked my wing in as close to his as I could. As we roared over the field, we were mere inches apart and less than six feet off the ground. We buzzed the runway, and I knew we were looking good. I stayed close as Blick made a sharp, sweeping turn and came in for a landing. My wheels touched the ground almost with his. We pulled off the runway together, and as I taxied off to my parking area Blick gave me the thumbs-up sign.

The ground crew ran out to meet me, waving and jumping up and down as I pulled into the revetment. I was their personal weapon against the Germans, and I had made it back in one piece. The crew chief leaped up on the wing even before I had killed the motor. The prop was still turning over when he got the canopy open and pounded me on the back.

"Jeez, I'm glad to see you, Lieutenant. We were really sweating you out. Our last pilot got knocked down on his first mission. Goddamn, but it sure looked good seeing you and

Captain Blickenstaff buzz the field in formation."

By now the other crew members had gathered around, congratulating me on coming back alive. They pumped my hand and patted me on the back. I felt like a hero.

But I only flew the plane. They kept it working. "The ship was in great shape. She purred all the way," I said as I got down from the cockpit. I couldn't have thanked them more than that.

It felt good to be moving around again. I had been cramped in that cockpit for nearly five hours, unable to move anything but neck, hands, and feet.

We all gathered in the ready room. The pilots who had flown the mission gave the intelligence officers all the information they could recall. They raised their voices as they got more and more excited remembering what happened. Before long I too was talking loud and fast, trying to tell my version of the flight. All the pentup excitement held back during the mission poured out of all of us; the ready room became bedlam. Blick reported my bombs had done the most damage and he bragged about the way I had stuck to his wing like I was glued there. He meant what he said, but I knew he wanted to prove his judgment right in letting me go along. I also knew my expert bombing was pure luck.

Three other former instructors who had come overseas on the same convoy with me had been assigned to the 350th Squadron, and they all were on hand to greet me. They had sweated out my first combat flight too. They kept saying, "Boy, I wish I had my first mission over with. How do you feel, Bledsoe?" For the time being I was a celebrity among instructors.

"Relieved, man, relieved." There was no way I could ever describe to them the terror and then the relief when the mission was over.

That day heavy overcast forced a small transport plane to seek refuge at our base. It carried three grim-looking paratroopers who had just returned from the invasion area. Their unit had been dropped at night behind enemy lines along the Normandy beaches twenty-four hours before D-Day, assigned to gather data about enemy fortifications and troop placement. Their squad had captured several German soldiers. One paratrooper told the story of what had happened with relish.

"We forced these guys into a deserted barn, tied them up, and started interrogating them. At first, they behaved arrogant as hell and so hardheaded you wouldn't believe it. We weren't getting anywhere with them until we stripped them naked and cut the balls off of this one tough character and threw them in his face. He gave a scream and passed out cold. When they got that message they told us everything they knew. The other two Krauts couldn't spill their guts fast enough."

Some of us recoiled in horror. We had all heard about the enemy's atrocities; now we realized they could happen on both sides. I was repelled and left the room. I didn't want to be around those paratroopers any longer than necessary. I had learned something about the war. It wasn't a case of good guys in white hats fighting bad guys in black hats. Not anymore.

CHAPTER 6

Combat Zone

I had that first mission under my belt. Now I was eager to finish a quick tour—three hundred hours of combat flying. Finishing those missions was the sure way to get back to the States.

I missed Harriett and the Little Princess fiercely. Yet I felt a strange excitement at the thought of another mission. I had to tell myself not to go nuts and start enjoying this stuff, to remember my responsibilities back home, that the most important thing in the world was to get back to my family safe and sound!

Blick and Newhart had told me that the squadron was having problems. Some pilots didn't want to fly the double missions and they were getting sloppy. The 350th Fighter Squadron needed fresh pilots desperately.

Three regular flight leaders—Willie Price, Carl Mueller,

and Robert Hart—were in the States on leave and would not be back for several weeks to start a second voluntary combat tour. Many of the pilots in the squadron were young, out of flying school only a few short months. At twenty-seven I was the "old man" to most of them. Even Blick at twenty-three seemed old to many of those nineteen-year-olds.

Most of the "kids" did not fly tight formation, and as a result they lagged behind on combat missions. Blick was worried their ragged flying might become contagious and have an adverse effect on the entire squadron.

I reminded him that their training probably discouraged any kind of flying that might increase the accident rate. "When you and I graduated, we were lucky enough to be sent to fighter squadrons with the time to train us before they were sent overseas as a unit. Replacements now just haven't had that extra stuff. All they've heard before coming over is: 'Stay above five hundred feet and don't get too close to the ship next to you.' "

Blick couldn't disagree with that. He said, "I've got a feeling it's going to be up to you instructors to help this outfit shape up. If you guys keep tight formation and don't lag behind and demonstrate some ability, then maybe we can get some pride of flying back into the squadron. Once we operate as a team, it'll save lives and we can do a hell of a lot better job."

Since he and Newhart had been satisfied with my performance on my first mission, he persuaded Newhart to let me start flying regularly. Next mission I would fly as Dewey's wingman.

It seemed as if I had just dozed off when I woke up and checked my watch. It was 3:00 A.M. on June 12, 1944. Blick's alarm whirred. He groped in the dark to shut it off.

· "Kind of early, isn't it?" I asked him.

"Huh? How come you're awake?"

"You said we had to get up at three A.M. The clock in my head woke me up. Kee-rist, but it's cold!"

We piled into the mess hall to gulp hot coffee and huddle around the stove. The damp English air always chilled me through and the warmth of the mess hall stove felt good. The mess sergeant was pouring cooking oil on the coals to keep the fire going. I was amused at the thought of Harriett at home, saving waste fat for the war effort.

When we assembled in the ready room a little later, CO Newhart tried to give us a pep talk.

"Hell, I know you guys who have been flying regularly these past couple of weeks are tired. I'm tired too. But there isn't anything we can do about it.

"Being tired isn't any excuse for being sloppy on a mission. Some of you guys go haywire whenever flak shows up and take off for parts unknown. Goddamn it, you're supposed to stick with your flight leader. You all know that. Don't get so damn scattered around when the shooting starts. For everybody's safety you've got to stick together and not get separated from your leader. And, for Christ's sake, close up on your formation flying and don't lag behind. The Jerries hesitate about bouncing an outfit that's sticking together and flying good formation. And they love to catch stragglers. So if you want to save your ass, then tighten up formation. Okay? Besides, you bastards, we look like hell when we come straggling back from a mission. That's it for now—let's get to the briefing."

I had kept so busy getting my gear ready and listening to Newhart that I hadn't given this next mission much thought. Now, as we filed into the briefing room I could feel my stomach starting to churn again. I had to use all the control I could muster to keep from bolting for the latrine.

Colonel Duncan, our group commander, began the briefing. "A strafing mission today, men. Now, yesterday we had trouble on the radio again. You wingmen—and that goes for you flight leaders too—stay off the radio unless you have something important to say. One of these days it's really going to cost us because the air is cluttered up with chatter. Okay,

Hank, give us a time check." (Hank was Major Henry A. Bjorkman, the group intelligence officer.)

"In six seconds it will be exactly 3:43," he announced. We all set our watches to 3:43 and held the stems out to keep the hands from moving as Hank counted off the seconds. The room was completely silent. The scene seemed unreal.

"Five, four, three, two, one, *now*—3:43 A.M." At the "now" we pushed in the stems of our watches in unison. The butterflies in my stomach were turning flipflops. As soon as we were dismissed, I made a beeline for the latrine. I made it just in time.

The takeoff was delayed and I had a chance to talk to our flight surgeon, Doc Joe Canipelli, about my diarrhea.

"Nervous tension," he concluded. "Each man is affected differently. I'd say it's a normal reaction, under the circumstances." He chuckled, then grew serious again. "By the way, Bledsoe, I just got a chance to check over your medical record. What's this crap about you being altitude-restricted?"

I explained what had happened back in New York. I also told him I had figured that as soon as a medical officer at the embarkation station checked my records, I'd be prevented from being sent overseas. We both laughed at that physical examination where 235 naked pilots marched four abreast in military order in front of a flight surgeon.

But Doc surprised me. "Well, here's your chance to get out of combat. I can ship you to headquarters where you can get some desk job or routine assignment. It's up to you. In fact, I might be taking a big chance by not having you transferred. What do you say?"

In the few days I had been with the squadron I had gotten very friendly with Doc. He and Blick were buddies and any friend of Blick's was a friend of his. He had the bunk next to mine in our Nissen hut. Doc and I were the same age, like me he was married with one child, and he wanted to get out of the military and go home like everyone else. He was giving me the chance to play it safe.

But by now I felt a part of the 350th Fighter Squadron, as much as I missed Harriett and the Little Princess. I realized I also wanted to be a part of the squadron's effort. I found myself fascinated at the life-and-death challenge of combat.

I declined the opportunity to sit out the war in England. The quickest way for me to get home was to fly a combat tour, and with luck I could do it in about three months.

"Suit yourself, Bledsoe," Doc replied. "It's your funeral. You sound crazy to me. But at the first sign of ear trouble, I'm going to ground you."

While we were still waiting to take off, the CO gave us some bad news about the 78th Fighter Group stationed nearby. On the mission yesterday they had been bounced.

Loaded with bombs, the planes were down on the deck looking for targets of opportunity, which meant anything that could help the enemy. They were attacked by a reported hundred yellow-nosed German ME-109s. This, Newhart warned us, was the Luftwaffe's latest strategy: hide on the ground for days, then put everything that would fly into the air in one concentrated area. The idea was to surprise small forces of American planes intent on strafing targets on the ground. Their strategy was working. Those ME-109s were Germany's best fighters: the 78th Group lost eleven pilots almost before they knew what hit them. Two of those shot down were Luke Field instructors on their first mission—which was to also be their last flight.

Our squadron was assigned to targets of opportunity in the general area of Paris. The Germans were still moving a stream of ammunition and supplies to the front lines. Bad weather had hampered Allied beachhead operations, so it was vital that enemy rolling stock be prevented from getting through. Knocking out transportation vehicles and enemy tanks took first priority from our bombs and 50-caliber machine guns.

The weather was threatening, the sky dark and gloomy. The ceiling was low, with faint streaks of blue trying to break through the overcast. I was flying on Dewey Newhart's wing.

Two thousand horses controlled by the throttle in my left hand, eight 50-caliber machine guns waiting for the squeeze of a finger on my right hand, a thousand-pound bomb on each wing ready to blow hell out of an enemy target. What a wonderful feeling!

This is a long way from Luke Field.

I clung tightly to Dewey's wing as we hit the overcast. It had become so thick I couldn't see his cockpit. We were only inches apart when we broke through the clouds and pointed the noses of our planes into the bright sky as we sought altitude.

The cloudy overcast had caused some of the pilots to straggle behind. Dewey made a wide circle in an attempt to get them back into formation. Once the squadron was reassembled, we stayed on top of the overcast until it came time to let down through the soupy weather into the target area.

The clouds were thick. While Newhart flew on instruments, I concentrated on keeping my ship tucked in next to his wing. I had flown close formation in clouds many times, but this weather was worse than any I'd ever encountered. I could barely see the tip of Dewey's wing. I couldn't see the canopy of his ship as we charged on through the darkness. I worried lest the pilot who was supposed to be tacked onto my wing ram into me.

That midair collision with Brighton in New York. I had to keep my eyes on Dewey's wing and couldn't take time to glance over my shoulder to see how close the guy on my wing was.

Finally we broke through the overcast. I eased off Dewey's wing and looked around. There was nobody there. The squadron had scattered.

"Looks like we're all alone, Bledsoe. I guess the weather has separated the whole damn group," Dewey radioed. "Let's start cruising around near the deck and see what we can find to shoot up. Keep your eyes open for EA. This is the kind of weather those bastards like."

We spotted a column of enemy trucks and tanks speeding

down a road toward the front lines. The clouds were hovering only a few hundred feet off the ground, so the Jerries evidently felt safe in making a daylight dash. We dropped out of the clouds and caught them by surprise.

Dewey pounced on the lead unit, blasting away with his guns. It was a fantastic sight, watching the drivers and the soldiers come pouring out of the trucks and diving for cover on the side of the road even before the trucks had stopped rolling.

Dewey and I set up a regular gunnery pattern, diving down on the target, pulling up, and circling back for another pass. I squeezed the trigger as another truck came into the bull's-eye of my gun sight. The Thunderbolt seemed to come alive. The smoke rolling off the guns and back over my wings looked beautiful.

Yippee!

A truck burst into flame. Power surged through me. What destruction I could bring with these guns!

It wasn't all one-sided. The soldiers on the ground were shooting back at us. The tanks had now unlimbered their guns as they rolled down the highway and were blasting away at us. I had been hit a few times by small-arms fire without apparent damage, but those white puffs of smoke from the tanks' 20-millimeter shells were coming too close to suit me.

On our next pass, we concentrated on the tanks. Our bullets seemed to bounce right off the armor plating and we didn't even slow them down.

"Bledsoe, let's try shooting underneath the tanks and see if we can skip our bullets into their bellies. They won't have armor plating underneath," Dewey called as he started another pass.

I saw his bullets striking the pavement underneath the lead tank and it ground to a sudden halt. I poured a burst under the next tank and watched with satisfaction as it too came to a stop.

"Bledsoe, we've only damaged the tanks so I am going to

drop my bombs on the other ones to try and destroy them. You save your bombs in case we run into another target later on," Dewey said as he got into position.

After two more passes, the tanks were out of commission. Dewey had made two good hits with his bombs and had destroyed two tanks. The shooting had stopped, the tanks were silenced. The caravan was now a trail of wreckage.

"That's a job well done," Dewey called out. "Let's stooge around and see what else we can do for Hitler."

We were cruising around on the deck, looking for something else to shoot up, when twelve German ME-109s suddenly dropped out of the clouds directly in front of us. They were the first enemy aircraft I had seen. They passed directly above us, going in the opposite direction. They were so close, I felt as though I could reach out and touch them.

My heart was in my mouth. I salvoed my bombs and pushed my throttle forward to pick up speed. The swastikas looked twenty feet tall.

My God! Brother, here it is. This could be it!

The ME-109 was one of the best air-to-air combat planes on either side during the war. I thought of that as I watched them wheel around like a pack of hungry wolves closing in for the kill. Those twelve German ships looked wicked.

I was scared stiff.

Dewey Newhart called, "Okay, Bledsoe, let's get these guys! I think they're part of the bunch that bounced the 78th yesterday."

"Roger, Dewey. Let's have at them." I was trying to sound calm.

Scared as I was, I found myself rarin' to go as we turned to meet them head-on.

Talk about eager! We were outnumbered twelve to two, yet Dewey was making the initial attack with me in a trail position to cover his tail.

The first pass was merely a feint. Dewey was trying to maneuver to get on the tail of a 109, while the Jerries were trying to get on our tails. It was going to be a real rat race. Within seconds we were flying in a circle. Dewey was shooting away at a Jerry in front of him, while the rest of the Germans were trying to get lined up for the kill behind me. We were half in the clouds, half out, darting, twisting, zooming all over the sky between the ground and the overcast.

My job as wingman was to cover Dewey's tail while he did the shooting. We tightened our circle. This made it harder for me to cover Dewey and watch my own tail at the same time, and the bad weather made it even more difficult to keep an eye on him. For a few moments, I forgot about everything but sticking with him. It was an almost fatal mistake.

I looked behind me and almost jumped out of my skin. There were four 109s lined up. They were pouring 20-millimeter shells out of their wings in my direction. I could see the flash of their guns. It looked like signals blinking at me. Tracers were bursting just a few feet off my tail, a little to the right. I was in a fairly tight left turn, following Dewey. The Jerries were not allowing enough lead and it threw their aim a little off.

But the Germans were in perfect position and were correcting their aim in a hurry. I could see the tracers marching closer. It seemed as if the shells were climbing right up my fanny. What a sight! I had to get the hell out of there.

I pressed the mike button. "Break, Dewey! Break to the left! There's a raft of 109s on my tail. Do you read me, Dewey? Break left!" I didn't need to ask if he had heard me. Before I got the last words out of my mouth, Dewey broke to the left and pulled up.

I followed Dewey's tracks and fairly leaped into the clouds in my haste to escape the 109s.

Dewey disappeared in the soup. There was too much distance between us to see which way he went.

Lord, watch over me.

I kept in the clouds for about five seconds, then decided it would be safer on top of them. I climbed through the overcast,

hoping to find Dewey when I broke out. It was then that the battle really started. Instead of Dewey, I found a pack of 109s milling around. I could imagine the German pilots who had bounced us below alerting their comrades waiting above the overcast: "Two Thunderbolts coming up! Close in for the kill!"

As I broke through, several of the enemy aircraft immediately dove on me. Tracers again seemed to envelop me. I kept expecting to feel slugs tearing through my body. I found myself trying to hide in the cockpit, bending over to make my body a smaller target.

I horsed back on the stick, trying to lift my ship above the bullets. I had been in a climb when the new attack began. Yanking back on the stick and holding it there threw the ship into a stall, then a spin back into the comparative safety of the clouds. I stayed in the clouds awhile, hoping I wouldn't collide with another plane.

I could hear some of the other pilots in our squadron calling for help. The radio was jammed with cries of distress as the Germans pressed their attack. Some seconds later Dewey called: "Are you okay, Bledsoe? Newhart here. Come in, Bledsoe. Are you okay?"

"I'm okay, Dewey, How about you?"

"I'm okay too, Bledsoe," he answered. "The squadron is so damn scattered there's no chance of joining up, so it's every man for himself. Good luck, Bledsoe, and give 'em hell." Dewey's voice indicated he was still full of fight.

Suddenly, it dawned on me. I was a greenhorn on my second combat mission, deep in enemy territory, with no fewer than fifty Germans very intent on killing me, and I had just been made dependent only on myself. Something close to terror struck deep in my chest. It didn't help when I heard one of our pilots crying desperately over the radio: "Help me, somebody, help me. There's a dozen Jerries on my tail, shooting hell out of me. For Christ's sake, won't somebody give me some help?"

"This is Seldom Red Leader. Hit badly. Going over the side," was the next message I heard. The voice was calm and quiet, as if this were normal procedure.

"Jonah here. Take it easy, you guys. Keep your heads. Hide in the clouds if you have to, but keep your heads. Where's that man crying for help?" Group Leader Duncan asked.

"I'm about two o'clock from that large factory, Jonah. Can't last much longer. I'm shot to hell," came the reply.

Ships were diving in and out of the thousand-foot overcast. Most of the planes I saw were enemy 109s, but occasionally I spotted one of our Thunderbolts trying to get away. There seemed to be at least a hundred of their planes ganging up on our dozen. The Jerries had really caught us with our pants down.

The viciousness of the German attack was terrifying. But it was with confidence that I entered the cloud cover. I thanked my lucky stars for those hours spent teaching and practicing instrument flying at Luke Field. It didn't bother me to fall into the overcast in a stall or a spin. I could hit the clouds in a twisting, turning climb or dive, then immediately straighten up my ship by instruments. This instrument skill was saving my life—at least for the moment.

I let down under the clouds again, and this time found myself facing four more enemy 109s. They were too startled to get in more than a short burst at me before I zoomed back up into the overcast, looking for a place to hide. The thought of a midair collision made me break out into a sweat, yet I had to hide in the safety of those dark, foreboding clouds if I was to escape being shot down. They were my sanctuary.

Even though I had broken underneath the clouds for only a moment, it was long enough to see another Thunderbolt crash into the ground. Fire and debris scattered over hundreds of yards. It was a horrible sight. I didn't know whose ship it was.

I hope to God he bailed out.

When I stuck my nose out of the clouds again, I found three

109s in front of me. I squeezed the trigger and saw signs of a few bullets finding their mark in the trailing plane.

Now it's my turn, and tail-end Charlie is going to get his.

But before I could get close enough to do any good, I found more 109s lined up on my own tail. I wasn't about to close up on the Germans in front of me at the risk of letting the ones behind get in a better position. It was back into the clouds.

I was so scared, I didn't think about taking the offensive. When I wasn't flying blind in the clouds worrying about a midair collision, I was busy trying to shake a flock of Huns off my tail.

Change tactics.

Still in the cloud cover I flew straight and level for several seconds with my throttle wide open. At full speed, I hauled back on the stick, kicked rudder, and started a steep, fast, climbing spiral, heading upstairs like a homesick angel. The action put my Thunderbolt to the test, calling on it for maximum performance.

I knew the Germans couldn't get a good shot at me in a tight turn, so I held my spiral until my altimeter showed ten thousand feet. I cautiously cleared my tail before leveling out and for the first time in fifteen minutes, which had seemed like fifteen years, I took a long, deep breath. I was above the melee below. It was strangely peaceful up where I was.

Then I heard Dewey Newhart on the radio. "This is Newhart. Caught a bad burst of 20-millimeters. I'm heading out!" There went my leader. I was supposed to guard his tail; now I was sitting up here not doing a damn thing while he was having to go home with a crippled ship. I knew if the Germans caught him he wouldn't have a chance.

"Dewey, this is Bledsoe. Can you give me your location? I'll join up and escort you out if I can find you. Come in, Newhart."

A second later his answer came. "Newhart again—need help! I need lots of help. Twenty 109s ganging up on me."

"Jonah here. Where are you, Dewey?" Duncan asked.

"Jonah, this is Newhart. These guys have got the range. My controls are shot up. I can't maneuver my ship. I need lots of help, fellows, or I'm not going to make it."

I could have wept. His voice was strong and clear, yet his message was a prayer. Someone murmured over the radio: "The sons o' bitches. . . ."

Duncan tried to contact Newhart again on the radio, but there was no response. Dewey Newhart had either been shot down, or was out of radio range by now and streaking for home base across the Channel.

A moment later I had to make the decision: hightail it for England, or stick around to fight the enemy 109s. I was in the clear and could make it home safely if I held my altitude and went full speed all the way. But I thought of what Blick had told me: "If you ever get split up, try and team up with somebody else. Don't abort and come home unless it is absolutely necessary."

I wanted to leave for home so badly it was painful to stay. Yet I couldn't bring myself to desert someone below who might need my help.

You have no choice. You've got to stick around.

I did a wingover and headed downstairs.

I saw two ME-109s some five thousand feet below me, heading for the overcast. Once again, I made sure my tail was clear, said a little prayer, and started after them. I had been so outnumbered before, I felt sure I could take care of these two.

When I was still not quite in range I could see the two Huns beginning to let down into the overcast.

God, if I could just get a little closer!

I had my throttle wide open trying to catch them, but it was no use. They were going to be in the clouds before I could get close enough to do any good. I gave them a long burst, but I was too far away to tell if I had done any damage. The smoke from my guns curled back over my wings and made me feel better. At least I was spouting a little flame from under for a change, instead of being on the receiving end.

"Duncan here. Can one of you boys come down and give me

a little help? I've got a couple of these bastards cornered." Then a moment later, breaking the rule of staying off the radio, he said: "That's right, you son-of-a-bitch, bail out and save your ass." Duncan had chalked up another victory. He was an aggressive, experienced combat pilot, one of the leading aces in the ETO.

"Duncan again. Six of these bastards trying to box me in. Might need some help, if anyone's around to give me a hand." Duncan sounded cool and confident. In the fight that followed, he didn't get boxed in. He ended up shooting down one of the six Germans who tried to do him in.

I came down through the overcast, wondering if I'd see the two 109s I had been chasing, but the sky seemed deserted. I kept close to the cloud cover, cruising around to join up with another Thunderbolt or to take a potshot at a 109. When I didn't find anyone, I decided to go back on top of the overcast.

Just as I poked my nose through the clouds, I could see tracers hitting a few inches below my wing. Damn, but they were close! I strained to pull back the stick, trying to lift the ship above those deadly streaks of bullets by brute strength alone. I fell back into the overcast with my plane upside down and never did see who was shooting at me.

The next time I dared come out of the clouds, it was to find two flights of Thunderbolts from another squadron. I didn't know if they were coming in to join in the battle against the 109s or if they were on a mission of their own. They were on a different radio frequency and I was unable to communicate with them.

It had been nearly an hour since Dewey and I had been bounced by the EA. God, but that new flight of Thunderbolts looked good to me now. I poured the gas to my ship and tucked my plane in with theirs like a baby chick snuggling up under an old mother hen.

The Thunderbolts cruised around for another half hour or so looking for a target.

Let's go home, let's go home. I'm scared to death and I don't have much gas left.

I was petrified at the thought of heading out alone. I felt on the verge of panic. I couldn't stick around much longer if I was going to have enough gas to get out of enemy territory.

The leader of the squadron I had joined must have read my mind because he decided to head for home base. The Germans were still firmly entrenched all along the coast, but even the usual flak that greeted us at the coastline looked good to me. It meant we were leaving those 109s. Once we evaded the flak, then all I would have to worry about was running out of gas over the English Channel. My fuel warning light was on, indicating I had fifteen minutes of flying time left, and I was going to have to sweat out my gas.

I knew without being told that our squadron had been hurt badly. Eleven of us had started out on the mission together and I didn't see any one of them around at the finish when I headed home. I had seen two Thunderbolts crash and had heard the cries of several pilots being attacked.

England came into sight, and thank God for once the weather was clear.

I didn't have enough gas to search out a landing spot in soup. I waved goodbye to the pilots I had joined and headed for home. My fuel gauge was on empty when I neared the field so I went straight in for a landing. I had drained her dry but I had made it.

The ground crew was overjoyed as I pulled into the parking revetment. They thought for sure I'd had it. I was every bit as glad to see them. "It was a really rough trip," was all I could manage to say to them. I knew I couldn't explain what caused the bullet holes in the ship or what I had been through. Emotionally, I was drained as dry as my gas tanks.

Blick came racing up in a jeep and threw an arm around my shoulders. "Goddamn, am I glad to see you, Marv. We'd all given you up for good. Where in hell have you been? We figured you would be out of gas by now and we never expected to see you again!"

I told Blick how Dewey and I had been caught flatfooted on

the deck strafing the truck and tank convoy, that a dozen of EA had bounced us and we were separated in the ensuing battle. I also confessed how scared I was. I told him how badly I had wanted to come home after hearing from Dewey, but that I remembered what I had been told and stuck around in spite of my desire to leave.

Happy as Blick was with me, he was obviously just as fed up with three of our pilots who had turned tail for home at the first sign of trouble. "These other guys should have stuck around like you did. They've been home for nearly two hours," Blick said. "Ben's ship was all shot up and he had a legitimate reason for coming home when he did. He was lucky to make it. But the other three guys don't have a scratch. If they had stuck around to help, we might not have lost the men we did."

I thought of Dewey again, trapped up there alone. "Blick, I feel awful about not sticking with Dewey. I lost him when he pulled into the clouds. When we got bounced, I fell in behind him to cover his tail while he went after the 109s. But once he broke into that overcast, the clouds were so dark I couldn't see him. If I could have found him, he might have made it okay."

"Forget it," Blick said. "You did your best."

When we counted our losses, we found we had lost our squadron commander, three flight leaders, and two element leaders, to say nothing of six good ships that were badly needed. We learned later that First Lieutenant Edwin Peters, one of our flight leaders, had a foot cut off when he bailed out over the Channel. While in his dingy in the icy water, he had used his belt for a tourniquet. Luckily, he was picked up by an English patrol boat and rushed to a hospital in time to save his life.

Our intelligence section estimated that the 109s that bounced us numbered around one hundred. They were the same bunch that had jumped the 78th Fighter Group the day before. These yellow-nosed 109s were flown by experienced combat veterans, Hermann Goering's prize group, the cream of the Luftwaffe.

Group Leader Duncan was so furious about the ruthless attack that he went to Wing headquarters to get permission for a fighter sweep in the same area.

A fighter sweep meant just what it sounded like. It was a mission designed to sweep any enemy fighters out of the sky. This particular mission was for one reason only—revenge!

The losses on this morning's mission had so weakened our squadron that only three of our pilots were able to join the fighter sweep with the other two squadrons. Two of them, Blickenstaff and Joe Furness, who only had three missions left to finish his tour, were the only experienced men left in our outfit.

I watched the group take off and felt left out. Yet I was still so scared from my narrow escape that it was with a sense of relief that all the available ships were assigned and I remained at the base, safe.

This was not to be a normal mission. Bombs and belly tanks were left behind. The group was seeking a dog fight and needed all possible maneuverability.

Duncan planned to keep a lower flight at around a thousand feet as a lure. Our strongest force would be waiting several thousand feet above. A top flight, high above the main force, would afford cover for the lower squadrons.

Everyone at the base was tense and jittery as we waited for the group to return. There was a shout from all of us when we caught sight of the first returning aircraft. We spotted eight ships. The fact that they were in good formation signified everything was okay with them. When they landed and taxied by, we could tell from the pilots' hand signals and the pleased looks on their faces that they had met the enemy with success.

Blick told me what had happened. The ME-109 pilots had taken the bait just as Duncan planned. The Jerries had come up when they saw the weak-looking flight of Thunderbolts about a thousand feet above the ground. They probably figured it would be more easy pickings and another score of victories. They were so intent on ganging up on our lower flight that they failed to notice our main force waiting above.

Our group flying cover streaked down from out of the sun just as the 109s were closing in on the decoys. The enemy was caught totally by surprise.

Even though they outnumbered our group, the Germans didn't stick around for a fight to a finish. After the first skirmish, they streaked for the deck, abandoning the 109s still engaged in combat with our Thunderbolts. We figured they didn't have planes or pilots to spare and were following orders not to get involved in a dog fight when the outcome was in doubt. Blick and the other two Seldom pilots shot down four 109s. In a few short minutes, the fracas was over.

In all, the Jerries lost fourteen of their yellow-nosed 109s. We didn't lose a man or a plane!

Blickenstaff and Doc had a long and serious talk in the hut that night. What could be done to strengthen the squadron now that we had lost most of our flight leaders? The losses meant some pilots would have to be shoved up to element and flight leaders before they were ready.

"One bright spot," Blick said, "is that the newest replacements in the squadron are experienced instructors with a thousand or more hours of flying time. They're also a little older than some of these other guys. With a little more combat experience, we ought to have some damn good flight leaders."

"I agree," Doc replied. "The hell of it is, some of those younger pilots who have been here a little longer are going to scream to high heaven if they have to act as wingmen for the instructors."

Doc was right. Pushing the instructors into lead roles was not going to set well with the younger men. They felt they outrated us because of the combat hours they had logged before we ever arrived. There was no argument about the importance of combat experience, but most of these pilots were just young kids who had only recently left flying school. Regardless of their combat time, neither their judgment nor flying ability would measure up against that of the more experienced instructors.

If the younger pilots were going to be passed over, it was going to require great diplomacy. It was Blick's job now. With Dewey Newhart shot down, he would become our CO. For the first time, I realized how much he depended on Doc's advice in running squadron operations.

After two days of combat, I sat down and wrote Harriett a long letter. I spoke of my intense love for her and for our Little Princess and of my dreams for settling down after the war. I said a lot more; it was my farewell letter to her. I sealed the envelope and placed it in my footlocker. Rafferty was to get it to her in case I didn't return from a mission. "In case?" By this time, I didn't really expect to come out of the war alive. The odds against a fighter pilot finishing three hundred hours of combat missions were too high.

Just before we hit the sack that night, Rafferty remarked: "Maybe Luke Field wasn't so bad after all, eh Marv? At least they weren't trying to shoot us down."

I laughed. "I'd like to see some of the brass at Luke fly tomorrow's mission. They couldn't hide behind poop sheets here."

There really wasn't anything to hide behind. Things looked rougher each day.

I had been in the Air Corps for three years. Until this very week I had never realized what the war was really like.

CHAPTER 7

The Little Princess

When I awoke in our bunk room the morning after our disastrous mission, I found it difficult to adjust to the fact that the fellows who had occupied those empty beds were either dead, wounded, or prisoners of war. The heavy toll made our recent battle seem like a horrible nightmare. Losing six out of eleven pilots in one mission just did not seem possible.

But there was no time to grieve. In this period following D-Day each mission amounted to a major encounter with the enemy. Every new day meant a new mission. Sometimes three or four were scheduled, the number depending on the length of the mission and the weather. We tried to be in the air from daylight to dark.

The process of attrition was working steadily against the Thunderbolt fighter pilots. The high percentage of losses made us all aware it was only a matter of time before percentages could catch up with each of us.

Ferry pilots arrived a few days after I got there, bringing new aircraft to replace the ones recently lost. Glory be, I was assigned a shiny new airplane direct from the factory. It was Republic Aircraft's latest model Thunderbolt and it was mine, all mine! I immediately christened it the "Little Princess" and had the name painted on the side.

I also got my own ground crew to service her. We would work together for the rest of my tour. They turned out to be great guys, and we hit it off well from our first meeting. They liked having a brand-new plane to service; it was easier to take care of a new ship than to maintain one of the older, combat-weary ones.

Before my tour was over, the ship became a part of me. I came to know every inch of her like the back of my hand. I had my guns especially synchronized to my own liking, and it wasn't long before I could make each bullet count. As long as I was flying the Little Princess, I knew exactly what to expect of my beautiful ship and how much I could push her. I was able to anticipate how she would respond to the controls in almost any given situation. I knew I could rely on her performance in the air with my life.

When the weather was clear enough to fly, my life on the ground usually consisted of going to bed a little before midnight after returning from a late mission. The long sunlight hours allowed us to fly until well after 10 P.M. Then I would climb out of the sack about three o'clock in the morning to head out on another one.

Bed? The beds consisted of three hard, lumpy, short pads called "biscuits." The damn things would slip around during the night, letting the cold air come in from the bottom. Everyone bitched about the goddamn "Limey" beds. Fortunately for me, before long I was lucky enough to buy a regular innerspring mattress from a departing pilot, and after that I enjoyed a real bed.

It was always dark when we got up. It was invariably wet with fog outside our Nissen huts, and cold as cold could be inside or out. Night and day the English air chilled me to the bone. Right after my arrival, I wrote and asked Harriett to make a flannel sleeping outfit for me with feet, mittens, and a hood for my head. She added rabbit ears to the hood, and I was teased unmercifully about my "bunny suit." But from then on I slept warmly.

The daily routine found me leaving the Nissen hut in the early morning darkness and groping my way through the mist and fog to the mess hall for breakfast. I couldn't stomach the usual G.I. powdered eggs, so I did without until Blick told me we could buy blackmarket eggs at a dollar a dozen without even having to leave the base. Our field bordered a farm and the farmer would sell the eggs over the fence. It didn't bother us that our purchases might be illegal. Those were honest-to-God fresh eggs.

After breakfast, I would head for the briefing room, ride on the back of a jeep to where the Little Princess was parked, and then I would be winging my way toward enemy territory. After the first mission of the day, I would grab a snack on the run, attend another briefing while the ground crew reloaded my ship, and then be off on another mission.

This was the usual schedule till darkness fell an hour or so before midnight and drove me back to the security of my bunny suit and cozy bed. Only when the weather hemmed us in would I get a real rest. When I wasn't flying I was catching up on my correspondence, grabbing some sleep, or seeing a movie on the base. The movies were shown in a Nissen hut that had been converted into a theater. They were shown continuously, at all hours of the day and night, to accommodate any personnel who had a little time off.

It was June 14, 1944, and I had been at Raydon only a few days; it seemed unbelievable. We were briefed on the day's mission, and it really had us worried. It was a high-priority target, a railroad bridge near Tours, France, used by the enemy every night to push troops and supplies to the front, the only undamaged bridge in the area. Heavy bombers had made two attempts to destroy this bridge. When they failed, a group of medium B-26 twin-engine bombers had tried to wipe it out from low altitude. They were driven off by the intense concentration of antiaircraft guns guarding the bridge. So fighters were given the job. Our orders were to try and fly under the flak if we could. In any event, we must destroy the bridge.

"Marv, you've been flying several days in a row. Maybe you ought to take it easy and lay off this mission," Blick said.

"I'm okay, Blick. Let one of the guys who's tired stay home instead of me. I'll let you know if I get too tired. Besides, I want to build up my combat time as fast as possible."

"None of that stuff," Doc came in. "First thing you know I'll be sending you to the flak home for a couple of weeks." The "flak home" was a country estate away from airplanes and the strains of war. Most pilots spent at least a week there after several missions.

"Okay, Doc, I'll sit on the sidelines if I start getting flakhappy," I assured them. "Keep me on the schedule, Blick. I really want to try out my new ship. How about it?"

"Okay, okay. I've got more to do than argue with you." That was that.

As I taxied into position for takeoff, I reviewed the plan for this mission. Lawyer Squadron would go in first with fragmentation bombs to work over the flak gun positions on the ground. If they were successful, Seldom and Jockey Squadrons would have a better chance to get in low and lay their babies on the bridge. It would also improve our chances of coming out alive.

We were really loaded down, with a thousand-pound bomb under each wing and extra gasoline in exterior tanks hooked onto the bellies of the Thunderbolts. The belly tanks were designed to be jettisoned in an emergency, or when we had drained the last drop of gas. Fast maneuvering was impossible when we carried the tanks, so it was a rule to jettison them at the first sign of enemy aircraft. A belly tank of gasoline also made a very effective incendiary bomb. But if they slowed us down and were dangerous, they also gave us a couple of extra hours' flying time. Each tank extended our range from 175 miles to 375 miles.

I was Blick's wingman again. By this time, I felt like an old hand. My nerves seemed to be holding up okay, except for those few minutes after each briefing. Invariably, the briefings ended with me racing for the latrine. I was still plenty scared.

We made our takeoff, climbed through the overcast without incident, and joined up with the rest of the group. A few minutes later we crossed the Channel, steeling ourselves for the bursts of flak we knew would be coming our way any second. When it did come, we took evasive action to get away from those dark puffs of destruction.

Crossing France, we avoided the cities that harbored most of the flak guns. That part of the flight was uneventful. When we came within sight of the target bridge, my skin was tingling from head to toe. "Jonah here," our CO called over the radio. "Target directly ahead. We will go right in as planned and avoid circling. No need to give those gunners any more notice of what our target is than necessary. Lawyer Squadron, make your move and lay those frags right in the laps of those flak gunners. Okay, let's go to work."

The bridge seemed like an easy target, just waiting for us to dive down and lay our bombs. Everything looked peaceful when the P-47s of Lawyer Squadron peeled off, screaming toward the ground with their fragmentation bombs. They seemed to catch the flak gunners asleep and made their pass without drawing a heavy concentration of fire. But the frags failed to neutralize the ground gunners, and the Huns were now alerted to our plan to attack the bridge.

"Jonah here. Okay, Seldom, do your stuff. You'll be the first bunch down. You guys in Lawyer Squadron start working on those flak nests with your guns. Maybe you can make those gunners pull in their necks."

Blick was in the lead and ours would be the first element to attack. He gave me the high sign. He did a wingover heading for the ground and we were on our way! I stuck close to his tail as we dove for the bridge. Our bombs were armed for instantaneous detonation, and if I lagged too far behind, his exploding bombs could blow me right out of the sky. More than one pilot had been killed that way; it was not going to happen to me. I had to be over that bridge and pulling away before Blick's bombs hit.

Down Blick and I dove and up came the flak! It was all around us. I could feel my ship shudder as steel ripped through the wings and fuselage of the Little Princess. She was really getting some initiation on her first combat mission.

Stick with me, Lord.

The gunners on the ground were aiming at Blick but they were not leading him enough. Most of the flak was bursting behind his tail and I was diving right into it. I tried to put the flak out of my mind and concentrate on keeping the ship coordinated so my bombs would drop true. Flying straight gave the ground gunners a better target, but if the ship skidded it was impossible to guide the bombs to the target.

I could hear the whoom! whoom! of the bursting flak and felt the concussion knock my ship around as the blasts came closer and closer.

My God, how can I come out of this alive?

When I saw Blick release his bombs, I sighed with relief. A second later, I let mine go and felt the extra surge of power in the Little Princess as I disposed of the ton of weight. Blick made a sharp climbing turn and I stuck with him like a leech. I looked back at the target and saw huge columns of water rise in the river. Our bombs had been carried to one side of the bridge by a cross wind. I could see the bridge shake as if we might have hit its underwater foundation. Maybe we had weakened it enough to prevent heavy German equipment from crossing the bridge. Blick and I cleared out to watch the others make their bombing runs. We were to provide top cover in case enemy aircraft attempted to bounce them. It gave me a moment to lick my wounds and survey the damage. My ship had been shot full of holes, some which were within arm's reach. But I was in one piece. I could see several larger holes in my wings, inches away from my gas tanks. Nevertheless the Little Princess responded to the controls and her engine was purring. Evidently she had not suffered any serious damage. It had been close, very close. My flight suit was already wet with sweat and the danger wasn't over yet.

The next element to attack the bridge was led by First Lieutenant Allen Lightfoot, a kid from Texas nicknamed "Chief" because of his Indian heritage. Rafferty, who was flying his first mission, was on Chief's wing.

Lawyer Squadron had silenced some of the gun positions and was drawing the attention of other ground gunners away from the bombing pilots. The flak was still intense. Rafferty was experiencing the same thing I had. The gunners were not leading Chief enough and Rafferty was catching the flak directed toward the ship in front of him. I saw his ship lurch as he dove into the wall of flak. I felt ill when he called over the radio: "Blick, this is Rafferty. I've caught it. I'm hit in at least a dozen places. I've got a big hole in the canopy, right above my head. Blick, I've been hit bad!"

"Seldom Leader here. Is your engine running okay? Can you control your ship, Rafferty?" Blick spoke in a calm voice.

"I don't know, Blick. My ship's all shot up. I'm losing a lot of oil. My ship seems to be responding okay. I hope to hell it hangs together till I get home." Rafferty was excited but had not lost his cool.

As Chief and Rafferty joined us, I could see that Raf's ship was covered with oil. It could catch fire and explode any second. A 20-millimeter shell had knocked the glass out of his canopy just a scant few inches above his head. It was a close call, and he was still a long way from home base.

As other flights from Seldom and Jockey Squadrons made their bombing runs, they ran into the same barrage of lead. But our mission had been accomplished. Through a combination of direct hits and near misses that shook the foundations, the bridge was damaged beyond repair. The Jerries would have to find some other route to get their supplies to the front.

The immediate problem was to get our crippled ships home. One of the pilots from Jockey had separated from his squadron and had joined our flight. His ship had been badly damaged, and his engine was throwing oil and smoking furiously.

"Hey, Seldom! Jockey here," he called. "I'm wringing wet with fuel. There's oil and gas all over the cockpit. I'm afraid my ship might blow up, but I'll be goddamned if I'm going to bail out as long as I can keep her in the air. Got any ideas, Seldom Leader?"

"Seldom Leader here," Blick responded. "We can make the beachhead in a few minutes. They bulldozed out an emergency landing strip there a few days ago. You better not try to cross the Channel. How about it, Jockey, you want to try and make it to the beachhead?" Blick sounded cool as a cucumber. His voice was reassuring.

"Okay, Seldom, I'll take my chances on the beachhead. Lead the way!"

"Rafferty here. My engine is missing a beat and acting up a little. I might land at the beachhead, too."

"Hang on, Raf. You'll make it," I said as a word of encouragement, hoping that he really would make it home okay.

I knew I shouldn't be on the radio but couldn't resist a comment. "Better be ready to bail out in case she quits on you."

We were a sad-looking quintet as we headed for the beachhead. Chief's plane was unscathed but Blick's ship had been hit in several places, while the Little Princess was riddled with bullet holes. Rafferty's plane looked like a sieve and Jockey was leaving a trail of smoke behind him. I knew I'd go over the side sooner than chance going up in flames.

As we neared the area where the 109s had bounced us before, I prayed our subsequent fighter sweep would keep them on the ground awhile. We were in no condition for any dog fight.

Approaching the beachhead, I could see the makeshift emergency landing strip. It looked short and rough. It had been carved out overnight by a couple of Army bulldozers. It would be no picnic landing a crippled ship.

"Hey, Blick. This is Rafferty. My ship is acting better now. Think I'll take a chance on getting across the Channel." Rafferty didn't like the looks of that short, bumpy emergency landing strip either.

I had gotten in close to check Rafferty's plane and could tell he might have some real problems. I felt compelled to speak up and try to get him to land.

"I'd suggest you land, Raf," I said. "Your ship is covered with oil. That thing's liable to blow up on you if you push it too far."

"It's your party, Rafferty. Suit yourself," Blick called. "If you want to try for England, good luck. Chief, you take Rafferty and Bledsoe home. I'm going to stick around with Jockey. How you doing, Jockey?"

"Damned if I know. I lost my oil pressure a moment ago and my engine's starting to miss worse than ever. I don't know if it'll hang together or not, but I'd rather try for a landing. To hell with bailing out!"

I pulled up on Chief's wing and Rafferty took a position behind me. We circled a moment to watch Jockey and Blick land on the emergency strip. Blick made it okay. Jockey was a different story. His engine cut out before he could get lined up for an approach to the short runway. His ship skidded along the ground, rising up on its nose for an instant, then falling on its back where it burst into flames. He didn't have a chance.

I felt sick and helpless. He should have bailed out. He might have been taken prisoner, but anything was better than being burned to a crisp.

We were flying at 15,000 feet when we crossed the coast of France. Our entire "let down" descent would have to be accomplished by instrument flying because of the lousy weather.

As Chief, Rafferty, and I headed out over the Channel we saw the weather front ahead; it seemed as solid as a brick wall and black as pitch. The farther we flew, the worse it looked. After flying on instruments for a few minutes, we broke out into a pocket of clear air that was totally surrounded by the black storm clouds. I looked over at Rafferty and shrugged to indicate I didn't know what to expect from the Chief. As we flew back into the weather again, I knew Raf was thinking the same thing I was. The Chief might be more experienced as a combat pilot than we were, but we had our doubts about his ability to fly on instruments when the going got really rough. Many pilots with even more combat time than Chief were lost by spinning into the ground trying to fly on instruments in bad weather. I thought back to the training at Luke Field and wondered if Chief was one of those students who had been given an instrument pilot rating before he was qualified.

The three of us kept letting down through the storm. I was having difficulty holding my position on Chief's wing. I tried to fly formation and at the same time cross-check with my own instruments by quick glances at my instrument panel. I wanted to make sure we were not in a turn when we should be straight, and that we were not diving fast when we should be losing altitude at a slow and deliberate rate. In bad weather, it wasn't possible to tell the position of your plane in relation to the horizon by the seat of your pants. You had to rely upon those instruments.

The altimeter showed we were at five hundred feet and that we were losing altitude at a proper rate. I started sweating when my altimeter hit the 300-foot mark and we were still flying blind. We hadn't the slightest idea whether we were over the United Kingdom or still over the Channel.

"This stuff is too thick to make our letdown here," Chief called to us over the radio. "We'll head north and see if the weather is any better up that way." Colonel Duncan heard him, and from somewhere in the blackness called, "This is Jonah. I'm north of home base. I don't know where you guys are, but it can't be any worse there than it is north of the field. Better consider making your letdown where you are and be quick about it. The weather is closing in fast and will be right down to the deck if it gets any worse. Do you read me? Come in, Seldom Flight."

"Seldom Flight, Jonah. Okay, we'll make our letdown now. Seldom out," Chief replied as he continued straight ahead, slowly losing altitude every second.

I didn't like the idea of pushing blindly ahead as Chief intended. It didn't make sense to head inland, trying to break through an overcast that might be a bare hundred feet off the ground. Chief was our leader and in command, but I had had enough. "Bledsoe here, Chief. Let's turn around and be sure we're making our letdown over the Channel. There are too many buildings and other stuff we might hit if we let down any lower over land," I said.

"It'll be okay, Bledsoe," Chief responded. "We might as well let down here as take the time to make it back to the Channel."

"Not me, Chief," I replied. "I'm not about to plow straight ahead in this soup. We're too damn low now. It will only take a few minutes to make sure we're over the Channel. The only thing we could hit there would be a naval ship and I'll take my chances on that." I had made up my mind to go it on my own if necessary. It seemed foolhardly, to me, to grope for the ground and risk hitting a building or tower hidden by the weather.

"I'm with you, Marv," Rafferty called. "What about it, Chief?"

Chief thought it over and said: "Okay—we'll climb to OK hundred feet and turn back toward the Channel. But I still think we could let down here." In a few seconds we were back up to OK hundred feet and Chief was making his turn. Rafferty and I hung on tight. Turning at that altitude in heavy weather isn't the surest way of living to a ripe old age.

Five minutes later, we knew we had to be over the English Channel so we started letting down again slowly, ever so slowly. My altimeter read 280, 250, 200, 190, 170, and we were still flying blind. I was sweating when a moment later we broke out of the overcast at about 150 feet above the choppy sea. It was a cold, unfriendly sight, but at least we could get oriented now and see far enough ahead to prevent running into anything.

As we turned and headed back toward land, here and there the clouds merged with the water. We had to skirt around such spots. It was a nightmare. At times we were flying ten feet above the water and visibility was almost nil. Suddenly we saw land looming up ahead of us. We didn't recognize the area and didn't know what part of England we were approaching.

The clouds seemed to melt right into the terrain. The ceiling was less than fifty feet at times. Though we were skimming along the ground, the top of our canopies seemed in the clouds. We flew on in, buzzing over the tops of trees, skirting around objects that rose up into the clouds. All of a sudden, we spotted a Royal Air Force Airdrome directly ahead. It looked like a welcome port in the storm to me. But the Chief was going to pass it up.

"Chief, we'd better land at this RAF base," I called in as stern a voice as I could muster. I didn't want to take the lead away from him, but common sense told me it was time to get on the ground—anybody's ground. "The weather might be even worse later on. Rafferty's ship could give out on him at any time. Let's get on the ground while we've got the chance."

"No, we'll not land here, we'll go on home. I know where we are," Chief responded, obviously irritated at a wingman telling the leader what to do. I replied, "Okay, you're the leader, but I strongly suggest landing right here."

Rafferty broke in: "By God, Chief, you can horse around in this stuff all you want, but I'm going to set this plane on the ground while I've got a chance and I'm going to do it right here. To hell with going any farther in this crap!"

Chief was furious, but reluctantly he circled back toward the airdrome. We weren't able to make radio contact with the

English base and didn't know their traffic pattern routine, so we decided to make our landing on the runway dead ahead.

We were going too fast for a normal landing. Chief overshot the field and had to pull up to try another approach. I chopped my throttle, lowered my gear, had full flaps down, but was still coming in too hot. I had no intention of having to go around again, so pulled up my nose and kicked the ship sideways to slow down my approach and lose altitude at the same time. The Little Princess responded beautifully to this dangerous maneuver. At the last moment, I straightened her out and we were on the ground.

Rafferty was right behind me and coming up fast. I pulled off the runway and watched him hit the brakes. He came to a grinding halt just before running off the end of the runway. He opened his canopy, slid out over the wing patted the ground, and hiked over to where I had parked. "Damn, but I'm glad to get my feet on something solid again. My engine quit just when I landed and I couldn't get it started," he exclaimed. "I said to hell with it, I'll walk in, so here I am. Christ, what a great airplane. Taking a beating like that and yet it kept on flying all that time! He looked around. "What happened to Chief? "

"Don't know," I answered. "No sign of his ship."

I went over to look at Rafferty's plane. It had caught a direct hit from one of the heavy flak guns. The prop was chewed up where the lead had bounced off and there were a dozen holes in the engine cowling. It made me wince to see the large hole in the canopy where a shell had exploded a few inches above his head. No wonder Rafferty patted the ground when he landed.

RAF personnel poured out of the buildings at the sound of our engines. An English pilot greeted us. "I say, old boy, you chaps are out in some pretty rough weather, aren't you?"

"Hell, this ain't so bad. We fly in worse stuff than this all the time," Rafferty said. He and some of our other pilots were teed off because the English fighter pilots were rarely seen over enemy territory these days. I knew they had done their share of the fighting and then some, but I figured if we could be out flying missions they ought to be able to do the same thing.

"We got lost and this is the first place we found to land. Which way is it to Raydon?" I inquired.

"Raydon? Oh, that's near Ipswich, isn't it? About thirty kilometers north," the Englishman replied.

We could hear an airplane circling above and thought it must be Chief trying to find the airdrome. In a few minutes he joined us on the ground. He told us he had lost the field after pulling up from his attempted landing.

"Which way is home, Chief?" Rafferty demanded.

"Hell, it's only about ten miles south of here. We could have made it to our own base if you guys weren't so anxious to get on the ground," Chief retorted.

"Bullshit. It's in the opposite direction and you would have got us lost for sure," Rafferty snorted. "It is a goddamn good thing we came in here, because my ship cut out on me before I got to the end of the runway. It's so shot up I'll bet it never flies again."

Chief was irritated at Rafferty's tone of voice but understood his concern. We were all happy to be safely on the ground with the hazardous flight behind us. Chief shrugged off Raf's remarks and the incident was forgotten.

When I inspected the Little Princess I found two good-sized holes in one wing, a larger one in the tail, and one the size of my head right behind the cockpit. It looked as if a 20-millimeter shell had hit just a foot or two behind my seat. A chill ran up my spine when I realized what a close call I had.

"Would you chaps like some breakfast while you're waiting for the weather to lift?" It was a British officer speaking. We thanked him and were led into one of the main buildings, where the RAF pilots were just having breakfast. We had lived a lifetime of experiences already that morning, yet the day had hardly started for them. "Pretty soft life," I heard Raf whisper.

We were a strange-looking trio to enter the staid old tradition-steeped dining room. Chief had a big tear in the leg of his pants and was wearing an old turtleneck sweater. One pants leg was half-in, half-out, of his fancy cowboy boots. His pockets were bulging with everything he thought he might need if he had to bail out or make a forced landing. The cap he had on was probably the dirtiest these cleancut Englishmen had ever seen.

Rafferty, who was short and stocky, hadn't shaved for a couple of days and his whiskers were way past the five-o'clock shadow stage. His coveralls and shoes were grimy with oil from his damaged engine. His long underwear was visible from his open shirt and dirty gloves hung sloppily out of one pocket. His cap wasn't in much better shape than Chief's.

I had taken time to shave and had put on a clean flight suit before taking off on the morning's mission, but my clothes needed pressing and I knew I looked far from "proper." I felt very conscious of our appearance when I saw the spit-and-polish of the British officers in their correct uniforms.

Rafferty's Irish eyes were twinkling as we strode down the aisle with our host. He didn't care what we looked like to these Limeys. Every eye in the place followed us as we walked to our table. To hell with them if they don't approve, I thought. But there wasn't an unfriendly glance.

We were given seats at a special table reserved for VIPs. "Bring these gentlemen combat rations—they have just returned from an engagement with the enemy," our host said gravely to the waiter. In a few minutes we were served oatmeal with cream, there was sugar for the coffee, real butter for our toast and, lo and behold, two fresh eggs. It was their way of complimenting us on our morning's mission. They were treating us with respect and gratitude without being overly solicitous. They were saying, in effect, "Thanks. Thank you for what you are doing." I felt pretty sheepish about some of the thoughts I had had when we entered their dining room.

When the weather lifted a few hours later, Chief and I took off for Raydon. Rafferty had to wait until someone could come over and pick him up. His ship had been pushed off the runway. It may still be sitting there.

Fighting the weather had driven the battle at the bridge from my mind. When Chief and I arrived at home base, it was brought sharply back. We learned the group had lost three pilots on the mission.

Most of the group was able to get home before the weather closed in, but those who were delayed ended up landing at any base they could find. Blick had just returned—the first pilot to take off in a fighter plane from the emergency strip on the beachhead. He told us about Jockey. "The poor guy. There wasn't any fire-fighting equipment on the strip, so all I could do was sit there and watch him burn. What a hell of a deal!"

We couldn't allow ourselves to brood over the loss of men or equipment. The war had given us our jobs to do. But it was no wonder some of us were losing weight and looking gaunt. We were getting but a few hours of restless sleep each night and we often missed meals. Our missions kept us under a continuing strain, and there wasn't a thing we could do about the endless tension and fear that gripped us.

Within the squadron, the tension showed in constant bickering and bitching about unimportant matters. Some of the combat-weary pilots made big things out of very small matters. They made Blickenstaff's job more difficult and Doc was angry as hell about "the way those kids are acting."

Doc had been with the 353rd Fighter Group for a long time. Since he had virtually no customers for medical treatment, he spent almost every waking hour on the flight line.

Doc had wanted to become a pilot, but was made a flight surgeon instead because of his medical training. He was in charge of the health of the group yet regulations prevented him from doing little more than administering pills. If anyone needed real medical attention, regulations required he be sent to a headquarters hospital. Doc's most important job was to keep a wary eye out for anyone suffering from "combat colic." When that happened, he sent the victim to the flak home for a rest.

Doc had always bunked in the same hut with Blick. He made his headquarters in the 350th's pilots' ready room instead of the base hospital, because that's where the pilots congregated between missions.

Doc attended almost every briefing and watched most takeoffs. He made it a point to be on hand when pilots returned from missions and was in on the debriefing at the conclusion of a mission. He knew everything that was going on in the 350th because when the pilots related their combat experiences, he kept his eyes and ears open and his mouth shut. When the pilots were on missions, Doc spent his time studying war reports, statistics, and monitoring the radio that tried to keep in contact with the fighter pilots.

Doc had watched the original 350th Squadron change. Many of the squadron's original pilots finished their tours and went home. Others were on long rest leaves or had been killed in action. He had more time than anyone to analyze the replacements as they came in. They were young pilots who had not been assigned to a fighter group in the States, as had the original 350th pilots. Thus they had no esprit de corps. He was disappointed because many of them seemed to take no pride in the squadron or in their flying.

"Doc knows more about airplanes and the running of a squadron than any flyer in the outfit. He would make a great combat pilot," Blick had said more than once.

Three A.M., June 16, 1944. I was having a tough time getting Rafferty out of bed.

"Okay, okay, I'll get up in a second."

I kept on shaking him.

"It's no wonder I can't get up this morning," Rafferty griped. "That damned Tuttle kept me awake all night scratching. I couldn't get any sleep."

Lieutenant Robert Tuttle was plagued with a bad case of eczema, which he scratched constantly. Pilots bunking nearby were annoyed; the nervous strain of combat made them not the least bit sympathetic.

Doc had tried everything in the book to relieve Tuttle, but nothing worked. "If I send him to the hospital at headquarters, they will ground him for sure and it would just about break his heart," Doc told me.

"But Doc, how can he concentrate on combat missions with that eczema?" I asked. "Seems like he'd get his butt shot off when he gets into a tight spot and has to think about scratching."

It was strange, Doc said, but Tuttle said it never bothered him when he was flying a mission. Evidently the excitement made him forget about everything except staying alive. The eczema wasn't contagious, so Doc let him keep flying. He told the rest of the guys they just had to make the best of it.

As we entered our mess hall that morning, I couldn't help but think about the contrast between it and the formal RAF dining room where Rafferty, Chief, and I had had breakfast. There was about as much formality in our mess hall as in a cow barn at milking time. Half the guys were bleary-eyed from lack of sleep, needed a shave, and were wearing the usual random assortment of flying gear. Nearly everyone bitched about the grub, yet those complaining the loudest seemed to be eating the most.

I was scheduled to fly again, so I cut down on the liquids. Having to urinate on a mission posed a monumental problem. It took both hands to use the relief tube. To make matters worse, you had to be careful to keep from wetting yourself, which had you concentrating on urination instead of keeping on the alert. The could prove disastrous. Sometimes the relief tube outlet would freeze and the urine would back up instead of flowing outside. One of our pilots told me about that: "There I was, at twenty thousand feet with a handful of piss when this 109 bounced me. When I turned over on my back trying to get away, the damn stuff poured all over me." More than one pilot came home with wet pants rather than resort to the relief tube. I figured if I cut down on the liquids, I could wait until the mission was over.

The briefing officer gave us the lowdown on the day's mission. "We've lost so many ships this past week, it looks as if we're going to have a breather for a change. We've drawn an escort mission this morning," he said. This brought a cheer from a number of pilots. "We'll be flying high altitude, so keep you eyes on the bombers. You never know when the Jerries will show up in full force, but this one looks to me as if it might be a milkrun. Our job is to stay with the bombers, so we won't be going down on the deck."

Fighters avoided the flak thrown at the bombers by moving out to one side, so if there was no enemy fighter attack, everyone said it would be a piece of cake.

It was evident that the pilots were relieved. This was the first time I had seen horseplay and heard relaxed chatter in the briefing room. Even I didn't feel terrified, as I had before every other mission. It marked the first time I did not have to race for the latrine immediately after the briefing.

This was my first bomber escort mission. Since some of our other pilots had never flown one before either, Blick took us aside for further instructions. "In case we run into enemy fighters, stick with your leader, and for God's sake cover your own tail. If we get bounced by EA, try not to get separated from the rest of the group. Don't get sucked into a dog fight and find yourself down on the deck alone. We'll be a long way inside enemy territory, and it's damned unhealthy for a lone man to head for home without plenty of altitude. Remember, there is usually safety at high altitude. Another thing," Blick continued. "Never get too close to the bombers or approach them head-on. If you do, they'll shoot first and explain later. Bomber crews are triggerhappy and when you see what they have to go through, you won't blame them."

While Blick was talking, I visualized getting into a dog fight at thirty thousand feet and having to make a power dive. The ear problem! If I had a problem, I'd just have to fly back upstairs and stay there.

When the jeep dropped me off at the Little Princess, I heard my crew chief, the usually mild-mannered Jackson, griping about "having to stay up all night to get the son-of-a-bitch in flying shape." I felt irritated. He looked as if he was suffering from a hangover. I didn't mind him being grouchy but I didn't like him swearing at my airplane.

I climbed aboard, and soon we were in the air.

The bombers had headed out two hours before we took off. They had to climb through the overcast and regroup on top of the clouds. Their heavy loads of bombs and fuel prevented them from getting much speed out of the B-17 Flying Fortresses, so it was an easy trick to catch up. We joined up right on schedule.

What a sight! A thousand bombers streaking for Germany with a hundred P-47 Thunderbolts and a hundred P-51 Mustangs, ready to mix it up with the Luftwaffe.

Our 353rd Fighter Group was flying top cover, so we kept weaving around and above the bombers at thirty-two thousand feet. The controls were mushy in this rarified air and it was easy to go into a stall. I remembered the argument at Luke Field over certifying students for high-altitude flying when we couldn't take them over ten thousand feet. I wished some of those "poop sheet artists" were on this mission.

The target came into view. Up came the flak. The gunners were not shooting at any particular aircraft. They simply anticipated where the bombers would release their bombs and laid up a wall of flak which the bombers were forced to fly through if they wanted to drop on target. I shuddered as the lead Flying Fortress entered this wall of flak and dropped its bombs. One of them was a smoke bomb that left a trail in the air as it went down. Other bombardiers, following in the wake of the lead ship, would use this smoke as a guide.

Once the bombers released their loads, the big ships were free to take evasive action. I watched them stagger out of the wall of antiaircraft fire, pour on the power, and get out of the area fast.

The protecting fighters swarmed around the "Big Friends." We concentrated on stragglers, some of whom were limping home with one or two engines out. The flak had not been overly severe today, but even so, it had knocked down several bombers and had damaged a score of others. But for the fighters, it was an easy mission because we were not jumped by the enemy.

For the first time since I had been with the squadron, our group came home as a unit. I was even able to complain because it had been a cold four and a half hours and my fanny was sore from sitting on the hard life raft that was the Thunderbolt's seat. My butt often hurt like hell after a long mission sitting on that thing. I would have liked to dump it, but it was fastened to the bottom of my parachute; besides, if I had to bail out and happened to be over the Channel, I would sure need that raft.

The assistant crew chief met me when I pulled in to park the Little Princess.

"Where's Jackson?" I asked.

"He's around somewhere, Lieutenant," Swanson replied. "He got some bad news from home yesterday. I think he's having problems with his wife playing around. It hit him pretty hard."

Swanson was a nice guy. Drafted at the outbreak of war, he'd had to leave a good job, a wife, and a child at home. He was about thirty-two. Being ordered around by shiny-faced lieutenants who had never held down a job was part of the frustration of Army life; he got along, but I didn't envy him.

I didn't really need to see Jackson. The mission had been a milkrun for us and I had logged several more hours of combat time on the chart in our ready room. A little later the weather got so bad we couldn't see the buildings as we walked around the base, so we wouldn't get in a second mission that day.

The next morning the field was still socked in. We had to stand by in the ready room and wait for the signal to take off. My name was on the schedule. I wanted the chance to chalk up more combat time.

The radio was playing in the ready room. Usually it was tuned in to a German propaganda station because it played popular American band music. Between numbers, Axis Sally came on to tell us our wives and sweethearts were cheating on us at home while we were overseas wasting our youth in a needless conflict. She explained how the Jews had pushed Germany and the United States into this foolish war. It wasn't worth dying for, she said. Her broadcasts were ridiculous to the point of being entertaining. We usually got a good laugh out of her. It ceased to be funny, though, when she got to the part where she warned that many of us would not return alive from the day's mission.

One of our squadron administrative officers was bustling about in the ready room, passing out situation reports that showed where the enemy was located. He gave one to Rafferty.

"Christ, we know where the enemy is located. It's easy to find out when you go out each day and he tries to shoot your ass off. Quit shoving this shit at me," Rafferty snapped.

He didn't like this particular ground officer much because he once had said that combat pilots were pampered when they were allowed to return to the States after a combat tour. Maybe he didn't know that fewer than half of us in the room that day would live through our tours and get the chance to go home.

At briefing time we were told we were to fly top cover again on an escort mission. The group was being given another milkrun; headquarters was letting us take a break from the rigors of those strafing and bombing missions that had cost us so dearly in the past week.

When I got out to the Little Princess, Jackson was working on the belly tank. We had been delayed by weather, and it was more than an hour after our originally scheduled takeoff time. The ship should have been ready a long while before now. "What's the problem, Jackson?" I asked.

"This goddamn thing won't draw gas from the belly tank," he responded.

"Try another tank. Get Swanson over here to help. We haven't much time."

It was obvious Jackson had a hangover. He was a top crew chief and I had always felt secure about relying on his work. I didn't mind the drinking, but if it was going to affect his job, that risked my neck and was a different story. I had misgivings until Swanson took me to one side.

"Don't worry about the ship, Lieutenant. I checked it over thoroughly. Other than the fouled-up belly tank everything is okay. I had a long talk with Jackson this morning. I'm sure he'll snap out of it. I've never seen him neglect his job before, and I've worked with him for a long time."

I knew I could rely on Swanson.

Five hours later, I returned from our escort mission with the rest of the group. The bombers had made it to the target and home again with no help from us. It had been another milkrun.

I was bothered again by the pain in my rear end. I had tried a cushion, but it raised me up too high. I finally accepted the fact that I'd have to put up with an aching butt or quit flying till my bruised tailbone healed, and I was too determined to finish this combat tour without delay and get home to do that.

Despite those milkruns, the threat of death constantly hung over us. The skies exploded nearly every day for someone. Wondering who would be next was a major—but unannounced—preoccupation.

At least usually, there wasn't time to brood. Each day brought two or three missions to fly. Every day usually meant the deaths of men you knew, some of the men you lived with and flew with.

But when we had time to stop and pay attention to the news, certain kinds of reports from the home front made us all sore.

The day of our second milkrun was one of those times.

News of an impending coal strike in the U.S. brought mayhem into the minds of more than one of us. "They ought to take that John L. Lewis and stick a bayonet up his ass!" one of the pilots said. (His ship had been shot up several times in the past week; his nerves were obviously frayed.)

"The first thing I'll do when I get home is kill that SOB," another pilot declared seriously. "Imagine that bastard calling a strike. Yep, I'm going to have a talk with Mr. Lewis when I get home."

He never got the chance to have his talk. He was killed mixing it up with ME-109s a few days later.

Our ground crews were bitter, too. "My God, don't the people at home understand what's going on over here?" Jackson complained. All the ground crews were working twenty hours a day, seven days a week, trying to keep our planes in service.

It was small wonder that men in combat had murder in their hearts when they heard about people at home, safe and secure, ready to strike for better working conditions. There were no strikes here.

Sometimes our situation seemed futile and all in vain. We wondered what the war was all about. Why were we laying our lives on the line? The answer was that to most of us the war had become a personalized battle because of the loss of a friend or our anger at the antiaircraft gunners.

Virtually no one understood the political aspects of the war. I didn't attempt to figure that out; I was sent to fight, so that's what I did. I prayed to God I'd live through the war, even though I had no faith in His ability to save me from the flak. Even so, faith or not, I never failed to say a prayer before each and every mission. It was comforting to think there just might be something besides my machine guns and the Little Princess to depend upon.

CHAPTER 8

Instruments and Experience

Blick and I were early birds this morning. We were finished with breakfast and on our way to the briefing room before the rest of the pilots were awake.

We walked close together, hands stuffed in our pockets, trying to get warm. The fur collars on our flying jackets felt good in the chilly English morning. The air was damp with the heavy fog and our boots made a swishing sound through the wet grass. Our warm breath created a steady stream of vapor. In the distance, we could hear the occasional hum of an airplane engine turning over. It was only two A.M., but the mechanics were already on the job.

Blick and I were silent, each involved in his own thoughts. I wished I could be home with Harriett and the Little Princess. Blick's mind was obviously on the job he had ahead of him because at last he spoke.

"Colonel Rimmerman is going to lead the group with our squadron today and I'm going to send you along as his wingman. Be sure to stick tight. He's a regular tiger about his wingman flying good formation. After another mission or two, I'm going to have you leading an element and you'll have your own wingman. Then, a couple more missions after that I'll have you leading a flight."

"If you push me ahead of the younger pilots who've been here longer they'll scream like wounded bears," I warned.

"Yeah, I know. But let them scream. I've got a job to do. I've got to use the experience you instructors have in building the squadron. We're going to have a little competition for leadership around this place."

I kept my mouth shut and let Blick talk. I anticipated a lot of discontent. After all, the young guys had more combat experience. That could be a big factor when the shooting started.

When we got to the flight line, the British air controller was on the radio describing bad weather, using the expression "the oranges are sour." They were very sour indeed when the pilots were called to the briefing room.

"Must be something hot going on to get us out in this soup," Rafferty exclaimed.

"I wish the sonofabitch giving out the flight orders at headquarters was here to fly in this goddamn weather," the Chief said.

"Somebody's got to be nuts, sending us out in this stuff. We'll be lucky to get off the ground, much less find a target," another pilot groused.

More than one of us complained when our weather officer stood up and read the weather report from the headquarters teletype message; he was jeered by everyone.

"Why doesn't the silly bastard look out the window?" Rafferty snorted.

It wasn't quite that simple, but I agreed with Raf. It seemed ridiculous to have the weatherman tell us we had half-mile visibility and a 500-foot ceiling when we could look out the window and not see fifty feet in any direction.

Colonel Ben Rimmerman took over the briefing.

"Maybe the weather's a little different at headquarters," he said. "At any rate, we can't get off the ground until this stuff lifts, so we'll stand by. Everyone is to be available at a moment's notice. When we take off, we'll pull up through this stuff and see what we can see. One other thing, I want you wingmen to stick with your leaders. I'm damn sick and tired of having flights split up by poor formation flying. Who's my wingman?" he asked.

"I am, sir. Lieutenant Bledsoe."

"Okay, Bledsoe. That last remark about sticking with the leader goes especially for you."

We went back to the ready room. I was dead tired. The recent missions and shortage of sleep had worn me out. I dozed off for an instant and was awakened by someone calling: "Mission going in five minutes." It was four A.M. To my great surprise, I had slept for nearly two hours.

Blick warned me: "When you hit the overcast, pull in close. Rimmerman wants his wingman sitting right next to him when he comes out on top of the soup."

After climbing into my ship, as usual I checked and rechecked to make sure everything was okay. One mistake was all it took to make mincemeat out of a careless pilot. I did not intend to become one of the statistics.

In a few moments, I was pulling out onto the runway alongside Rimmerman. He gave me the signal to take off. I slipped my ship in close to his, anticipating his moves as we rolled down the runway. We were loaded down with extra gas, bombs, and ammunition. It would require maximum power and additional speed to pull our heavily laden planes into the air.

I advanced my throttle normally, but found I was going faster than Rimmerman. I would overshoot him if I didn't slow down. I had never flown with the colonel before and thought maybe he liked to take his time getting flying speed. I liked to get that throttle wide open and get off the ground without flirting with the fence and trees at the end of the runway.

We were almost halfway down the runway and still loafing along. I could see the end of the runway now and my throttle should have been fully advanced, but it was far from takeoff position.

I noticed Rimmerman had looked into his cockpit a time or two, as if checking his instruments. Surely, I thought, if there was something wrong with his ship he would signal me to move out and take off by myself. He had glanced at me a couple of times and had looked at my wing tucked in next to his, but nary a signal. I hung on. If he was testing me, he'd find me with him till the last possible moment.

The trees at the end of the runway loomed larger, larger, as we lumbered down the runway. I could imagine what would happen if we piled in. I was beginning to sweat.

Come on, Colonel, get off the dime. Get that ship off the ground. Ram that throttle forward, Rimmerman!

Rimmerman took another look at my prop churning away at the end of his wingtip, and then seemed to raise his ship into the air by brute strength. We needed more speed and we needed it now! I pulled back on the stick and could feel the Little Princess struggling. She shook and shuddered as we passed over the end of the runway. We barely cleared the trees; prop wash blew the limbs back and forth. As we staggered up through the air I was still in position on Rimmerman's wing. It felt a little better when we had our wheels up, eliminating the drag. That was as hairy a takeoff as I'd ever made. We were still going so slow that the rest of the group was overtaking us. We had to move out of the way.

All of a sudden I could see smoke pour out of Rimmerman's ship. I signaled to him to get back on the ground. We had been ordered not to break radio silence until we were over the Channel, but I was ready to speak out if the colonel didn't turn back immediately. There was something drastically wrong with his plane and he needed to land before the engine quit or caught fire. With a full combat load he'd be in serious trouble if he had further problems at this low altitude.

Rimmerman nodded affirmatively as I gave a thumbs-down gesture, the warning to land. He peeled off quickly and headed for the field. I circled, watched him land okay, then joined another flight.

The mission turned out to be a waste of time. For three hours we flew, trying to find a hole in the soup so we could let down over enemy territory. We finally turned around, dropped our bombs in the Channel to keep from having to land with them, and returned to home base.

That night, Blick laughed as he told me Rimmerman was impressed and a little frightened to see the tip of my wing practically sitting in his lap all the way down the runway. The colonel's supercharger had malfunctioned, preventing him from getting full power out of his engine.

"Rimmerman wondered if you would have flown right into the trees and crash-landed with him if that was necessary to hold formation," Blick said with a grin.

My tight formation flying with the colonel, almost into the trees, chalked up another point in favor of the former instructors: it showed we were able to fly the airplane in adverse situations.

The weather was lousy over Britain and the Continent on June 18, 1944, and the Germans were taking advantage of it. With the soup keeping our fighter pilots on the ground, the Jerries were pushing men and supplies to the front lines. Our ground troops were in a rough spot without the protection we could give them under normal circumstances. I felt nervous and restless, waiting for the weather to change.

We finally got a break in the weather in England, but it was still socked in over the Continent. The bombers could use radar to hit German industrial targets once they were aloft, so we were scheduled to fly another bomber escort mission.

It proved to be another milkrun. It was too easy. On our return to base, Blickenstaff assembled our pilots in the ready room and proceeded to chew us out about sloppy formation flying on the mission even if we hadn't met EA. "Dammit, I want you characters to tighten up your formation. We've got to cut out this business of having stragglers all over the sky. By God, when we come back over the Channel, I want this squadron 'dressed up' and flying as a unit. Let's show the rest of the group we are proud of our squadron and proud of our formations."

One of the younger pilots couldn't see his point. "What difference does it make whether we fly good formation or not? The important thing is to get back home without getting our asses shot off," he retorted.

Blick blew his top. "It makes a helluva difference," he exploded. "Enemy aircraft are reluctant to attack a sharp-looking outfit. Furthermore, tight formation in the overcast helps prevent the squadron from getting separated. You guys who have been here awhile had better shape up if you want to become flight and element leaders. The way to get chosen for the job is to fly tight formation, stick with the squadron when the shooting starts, be ready and willing to join in the battle, know where you are at all times, and know the direction to get home when the fracas is over. If you guys don't snap out of it, I'll be pushing some of these former instructors up ahead of you, and you'll be flying on their wings, instead of the other way around."

There, he had said it for the first time. It gave us all something to think about.

The younger pilots had already sensed there might be some competition. In addition to the prestige and self-satisfaction, flight leaders were entitled to the rank of captain, and every one of us was interested in being promoted.

Some pilots grumbled. Blickenstaff proceeded to set them straight. "Let me make it clear. I don't care if you've been here so long you're down to your last five missions. If you lag behind in formation and don't shape up, I'll have you flying tail-end Charlie."

On a mission, the last ship in a squadron was known as "tail-end Charlie." The flyer rated this position because he was the worst pilot or the goof-off, which really meant he needed more protection than anyone. But ironically tail-end Charlie was usually the most vulnerable and the first to be attacked by enemy aircraft.

Most of the time, our squadron's tail-end Charlie was one of our older and more experienced pilots. He had some pull at Eighth Air Force Headquarters and had been with the group several months before I arrived. He was never around when things got rough. He regularly turned around and came home when the weather over enemy territory was bad, and if the flak got heavy he streaked for home base. I figured he would have been kicked out of the squadron long before if not for his rank—he was a captain—and some good connections at headquarters. Sometimes I felt sorry for him, because he was practically an outcast, on the ground or in the air.

But I had my own problems. My fanny was now so sore the pain was excruciating the moment I sat down on the hard raft. Evidently I had bruised a bone. The solution was to lay off flying until my butt healed, of course, but by now I had a mania about reaching that three hundred hours of combat time—the end of my tour, and a transfer back to the States where I would be with Harriett and our Little Princess.

The next day I saw I had been left off the flight schedule for the first time in a week. But I persuaded Blick to let me trade places with one of the pilots who was complaining about having to fly day in and day out.

I learned we were going to attack a German airdrome and try to knock out their planes on the ground. The Luftwaffe had run short of pilots, airplanes, and supplies. As a result, they did not put their planes into the air until they had a clear advantage. If they weren't going to get into the air, then we were going to go after them on the ground.

Strafing an enemy airdrome was by far the most dangerous of all combat missions. The bases were well protected by antiaircraft guns of all sizes. No other target took such a toll of pilots and aircraft. The manuever involved setting up a gunnery pattern above the field. Pilots would trail one another, make a pass, circle, and come back again. There was no hiding from the enemy ground gunners below; at low altitude we were easy targets. The Germans knew our procedure and threw everything they had at us.

As usual, at the morning briefing I felt sick. When I learned what we would be facing, I became terrified. I never made it to the latrine with so little margin.

I was to fly wingman for "Little Joe" Furness. He would be leading our flight of four. "Little Joe" was an affectionate and fitting name for this popular pilot. He was so short that he had to stretch hard to meet the Air Corps height requirements. He was slight of build and mild of manner. This was to be his final mission, one way or another. It would complete his combat tour.

Blickenstaff scheduled us to fly top cover. We were to stay above the pilots who would strafe the airplanes on the ground and protect the squadron from a surprise attack from the sky. He picked Little Joe's flight to fly top cover because it was customary to give the safest job to the guy on his last mission. "It plays hob with group morale to get a pilot shot down flying his last mission," Blick said.

Little Joe called Ted "Kid" Novak, Russell Barker, Jackson, and me together for our own private briefing. I could see he felt a little embarrassed. "As you guys know, this is my last mission. Don't be surprised if I don't get down into it if the going gets real rough. When you get to your last mission you can't help being extra cautious."

We understood how he felt and didn't blame him for taking it easy. We didn't really expect much trouble flying top cover.

We took off a little before dawn. When we reached our target area it was still not fully light because of the cloudy weather.

Colonel Rimmerman called on the radio: "Jonah here. Target ahead, men. Keep your eyes open and make every pass count. We'll go straight in and try to take them by surprise. You guys who are last to go down, watch for the flak gunners. If you can find them, forget about the aircraft and strafe hell out of the flak positions. If we can neutralize the flak, we can have things our way. Good luck."

A German Heinkel-111 had just landed and was taxiing across the field. He speeded up when he saw us. In a flash Rimmerman and Rafferty, his wingman, were on him, raking the plane with their machine guns. As they passed over, the Jerry ship was burning hotly.

Our pilots dove on the airdrome, dropped their bombs, and strafed the planes on the ground. Then the German gunners went into action. In seconds the sky was filled with white puffs of smoke; the deadly 20-millimeter shells exploded around our planes. But the P-47s were finding the flak batteries. In two or three minutes, columns of smoke began to rise from the ground. Two of them represented Thunderbolts that crashed after being hit; the pilots had been too low to bail out.

Little Joe's flight circled in safety four thousand feet above the battle. Watching for enemy aircraft, we had a grandstand seat.

"Jonah here. Come on, men. Let's get out of here! We've had enough for one day," Rimmerman called.

As the group pulled away from the airdrome, I spotted several enemy aircraft hidden in a nearby clump of trees. "Seldom Red Two here," I called. "There are three or four undamaged 109s just beyond that clearing, south of the field, at three o'clock. How about us going down after them, Little Joe?"

"Hold your position, Bledsoe. Stay on my wing," he replied.

At that Novak piped up. "Hey, Little Joe, how about me and

my wingman going down and shooting up those 109s? I see them, too. You and Bledsoe could cover us."

"Forget it, Kid. Hold your position," Little Joe ordered. But after thinking it over for a few seconds, Little Joe was back on the radio. "Seldom Red Leader here. Jonah, our flight is going down and take a crack at some 109s. Okay, you guys. Let's go! Cover my tail, Bledsoe."

I was right on Little Joe's tail as he peeled off toward the deck. My finger curled around the trigger that would fire those eight guns. I felt tense and excited. I still hadn't got used to the thrill of the kick of my guns and the smoke pouring back over my wings as I blazed away.

Little Joe and I fired at the enemy aircraft parked among the trees. It wasn't until we passed directly over the top of them that we realized they were not airplanes but decoys. The flak gunners were concentrating on us as we skirted around the trees.

"Kid, don't come down. You and Jackson pull away. This looks like a trap," Little Joe called. "Come on, Bledsoe, stay low and get out of here. Stay on my tail, Bledsoe. Keep me covered!"

We stayed low until we were well out of the range of the gunners. We got home without any difficulty and without a scratch on our ships. Little Joe had made it.

The rest of the group had not been quite so lucky. Fourteen enemy aircraft had been destroyed and the German airbase was no longer usable, but we had lost two pilots and a number of aircraft were badly damaged.

When I parked the Little Princess I had trouble climbing out of the cockpit. Once I was out it was painful to straighten up. I moved so slowly my worried ground crew thought I had been shot. "Are you okay, Lieutenant?" Swanson asked.

"Yeah, I'm okay, Swanson," I said wearily, "but that life raft is killing me. My butt is so sore I can hardly move."

Getting shot couldn't hurt any more than this. But there was no way I would stop flying even temporarily. I was too eager to roll up combat time. I persuaded Blick to schedule me for the next day's escort job.

I was flying on first Lieutenant Don Markson's wing as we headed out and hit the cloudy overcast. The Kid's element was right behind me, trying to stick with the flight in the thick, dark clouds. Markson was flying on instruments while we flew formation on his wing.

I thought Markson was going too slow, but I was too close to him to take a chance and glance at my own instruments. It felt as if we would stall out at any moment if he didn't pick up airspeed.

Watch it, Markson, pick it up, pick it up.

Suddenly Novak screamed, "Markson, I've lost you, I fell out of formation. I think I'm in a spin!"

I was holding back pressure on my stick in order to stay in position behind Markson. The nose of my ship felt in an upward position to me, threatening to flip the ship over on its back. It was possible to have the feeling of climbing while going straight and level.

Could be vertigo, so hang on to Markson!

Suddenly Markson fell out of sight and I was unable to hold position on his wing. My controls were mushy, not responding; I went into a stall. One quick glance at my instrument panel and I saw what had happened.

Markson had become totally confused. He simply did not know how to fly on instruments. He had gone into a stall and ended up on his back. Right now, he was probably in a split *S*, racing full speed for the ground.

If he doesn't have enough room to level out between overcast and ground, he'll crash for sure.

I could imagine him slamming down out of the clouds in a vertical dive, trying desperately to pull out but unable to, and an instant later crashing into the ground.

My days of instrument instructing at Luke Field were paying off yet again. I ignored the spinning compass and gyro, centered my needle and ball, got my airspeed and direction under control, and was soon heading upstairs to climb out of the overcast.

Kid and his wingman were nowhere in sight when I pulled up into the bright sunlight. I saw a flight of Thunderbolts a couple of miles away and flew full throttle to catch them. I stayed with them for the rest of the mission. It turned out to be another milkrun.

When I returned to base I thought I was seeing a ghost. Markson looked embarrassed. "I got mixed up on my instruments and just went haywire," he said. "I got over on my back and sucked back on the stick. That put me in a split S and without knowing it I was in one hell of a dive when I broke through the overcast. The ground was coming up at me like crazy. I never thought I could pull out in time. I just barely made it. I was so shook up I decided to abort and come on home rather than try and fly through that overcast again. I'm still feeling jittery."

There wasn't much I could say. I did promise myself that it was the last time I would rely on one of the younger pilots to get me through the clouds. I remembered General Woodbury: he didn't want some junior birdman "augering him into the ground," he'd said, and if I became his aide he would do the flying. From now one, like the general, I was going to rely on myself instead of a junior birdman when it came to flying instruments in bad weather.

I found Novak a little later. He too had been unable to find the rest of the squadron and had also aborted. So had his wingman. He cussed Markson for causing him to fall out of the overcast when he could no longer hold position.

It had been a fiasco. We were lucky not to have lost a couple of pilots to the weather, along with airplanes we couldn't spare.

A few days later Markson was killed when he spun in near our home base. He became another statistic, his name added to the list of pilots who crashed as a result of bad weather and lack of proper instrument flight training.

Next day I was late arriving in the pilots' ready room. When I got there I could tell something was in the air. Instead of the usual horseplay, I saw the younger pilots huddled together at the flight board, which listed the position each pilot was to fly on the next mission.

I had been greeted by suddenly hushed tones and hard stares when I came in. A look at the board told me why. With only a few days combat time, I was scheduled to fly as an element leader in Captain John Rose's flight. Most of the younger pilots were still flying as wingmen even though they had been with the squadron for months.

Kid Novak didn't try to hide his reaction. "I'll be goddamned if I'll fly some instructor's wing," he snorted. On the way to briefing other young pilots made the same feeling known.

"Bombers are going to Berlin again today. We're going to stay with them to the maximum of our endurance," the briefing officer said. "Intelligence reports we might get some action from the Luftwaffe on this one, so keep your flights together and stick with the bombers. If we get bounced by fighters, give 'em hell, but don't chase them down to the deck. Our job is to protect the Big Friends."

Blick took me aside. "The brass is skeptical about my pushing you instructors ahead of the other pilots in lead positions. Don't let me down. Some of these guys will just be waiting for you to screw up. Be sure and keep your element with the flight."

An element consisted of two ships. An element leader had a wingman and a better chance to look around. He also had some independence of operation, as long as he got the okay from the flight leader.

Blick was wise enough not to assign one of the younger pilots as my wingman. He selected Lieutenant James Ruscitto, who had been an instructor at a Texas training school. Ruscitto had heard Novak's remarks. He told me, "Hell, Bledsoe, I'd rather fly your wing any day than one of those kids. Let's stick tight and show them how it's supposed to be done."

We rendezvoused on schedule with a thousand B-24

Liberators and B-17 Flying Fortress bombers. The bombers flew strung out in a long line, and it would have been extremely difficult for our fighter ships to protect them had the Germans struck in force; they would have scored heavily. But for another day Jerry chose to remain on the ground, so it was another milkrun for us. Not so for our Big Friends. The flak had been well concentrated over the target and the bombers had suffered severe damage.

As we crossed the Channel, I signaled to Ruscitto to close up on my wing. Rose's wingman was straggling, but when he saw me pull up next to him with Ruscitto stuck close to me, he closed in on Rose's wing. We were in tight formation when we came over home base. It looked good, so Rose buzzed the field to show us off before landing.

My crew chief was waiting for me at the parking strip. "The buzz bombs are giving the Limeys more trouble, Lieutenant," he said. "I got that reliable rumor from the third stool in the latrine. Anyway, there's another mission scheduled just as soon as we can get the ships serviced. I hear it's to look for buzz-bomb sites. By the way, Marv, that was sure a nice-looking formation."

I checked the flight board in the ready room but the schedule hadn't been set up yet. When I found Blick and told him I'd like to fly the next mission, he said, "You'll probably have to fly it whether you want to or not. We're shorthanded. I sure wish those replacements would arrive." He went on, "Hey, that was some nice formation when Rose's flight came over the field. I hope we can get some of these other guys to dress up formation."

"They'll come around," I said. "I noticed that Rose's wingman closed up when Ruscitto and I tacked onto his wing. When we got on the ground he told me he felt good about it."

Crew Chief Jackson was right about the next mission. Rafferty flew my wing as the group spent two nervewracking hours cruising at three thousand feet over the Pas de Calais area on the French coast, looking for buzz-bomb sites.

The coast bristled with antiaircraft guns and we made good

targets, but the ground gunners held their fire, not wanting to give away their locations. Except for a few bursts of heavy flak that missed, we were left alone.

As we neared home base, I couldn't get the number-two man in our flight to close up on the leader's wing, so we couldn't duplicate the last mission's landing. But I signaled Rafferty to move in closer, and then I broke away from the sloppy flight and dove on the field. Rafferty was grinning crazily, his wing tucked in next to mine, as we roared down the runway a yard off the ground. At the halfway mark, I pulled up in a steep climbing turn, keeping back pressure on the stick and maintaining steady rudder pressure to tighten the turn. White misty streamers were coming off the end of our wingtips as we held our tight turn to get into position for landing. Our landing gears locked into place just before we hit the runway. We landed in unison, Rafferty sticking tight. It was a glorious feeling.

I was pleased with everything that night as I wrote Harriett about my promotion to element leader. It had been a good day. I was setting some kind of a record for hours spent in combat in such a short period. More important, I had logged nine additional hours of combat time.

CHAPTER 9

Flak Alley

The thrill of combat was getting into my blood. Frightened as I still was, I remained eager to try my hand at air-to-air combat with the German 109s now that I had a little experience. It was then June 22, 1944, and I had learned a lot in the thirteen days since Dewey Newhart and I had gotten bounced by the large group of enemy 109s. I was really waiting and hoping for another encounter where we would not be outnumbered. I knew it was a heck of a way for a family man to feel. I told myself to take it easy. Enjoying combat could be my undoing.

I didn't really understand why I yearned to pit my flying ability against the enemy's. I didn't hate the German pilots or people. We had German prisoners of war at Luke Field and they didn't seem any different than other human beings. (I was then totally unaware of the German concentration camps.) I did have an intense hatred for the flak gunners who caused so many casualties in our group, but that was a very personal matter. Yet the danger of putting my life on the line, day after day, was exciting and fascinating, like playing Russian roulette.

The bombers were still pouring it on Berlin. We were to escort again. "Rimmerman is leading the group on today's mission," Blick said. "He asked me to assign you to fly as his wingman. No need to impress upon you his thing about the wingman sticking with him. I'm counting on you."

Just before takeoff, Colonel Rimmerman found me in our ready room. "By God, Bledsoe, I hope we have better luck getting off the ground than we did the other day. I almost augered us both in. If that ever happens again, you break away. You did some damn good formation flying to stick with me, but no need for both of us to knock those trees down at the end of the runway."

I told him the truth about that day, that I had thought maybe he was testing me, and I was about to take off on my own when we became airborne. I hadn't been about to plow into those trees with him.

Rimmerman listened and just grinned. He was a regular guy.

In a few moments we were in our ships on the runway, and Rimmerman gave me the high sign to pour on the coal. We were on our way. I put my wing up to his. We became airborne like a single ship.

We flew into the overcast with my prop churning close to Rimmerman's wing. I was still in that position when we broke out into the bright sunshine above the clouds. He had ordered me to stay close. I was determined to follow those orders to the letter and be almost at arm's length whenever he turned around to check my position.

When we passed over the enemy coastline, all hell broke loose. The antiaircraft gunners held their fire until we were directly overhead, then the sky grew black from bursting flak. I could feel the concussion and the "whoom-whoom" of the shells exploding all around me. I could see the red flashes that came just before the black puffs.

Rimmerman took violent evasive action. He did a wingover and peeled off for the deck. I was right on his tail. The Jerry gunners concentrated on him as the leader of our group, and the flak was exploding right behind him because they weren't leading him enough. Once again I seemed to be catching the brunt of it. I could feel my ship lurch each time it hit. The next minute seemed like a year.

When we got back on course and beyond the range of the coastal guns, Rimmerman leveled out and looked around. I was still in position on his wing. He gave me a thumbs-up salute. My ship was responding to the controls okay, but I thought it was time to check it out.

"Jonah, White Two here. I caught a lot of flak. How about looking me over?" I called as I pulled up above Rimmerman. He slid in and around me, checking my airplane at close range. "You've got several good-sized holes, Bledsoe, but I can't see any serious damage. Does she fly okay?"

"Yeah, everything seems okay, Jonah. If I have any problems I'll head for the barn." I got back in formation

An hour later we made our rendezvous with the Big Friends. They had dropped their bombs and were on the way home in good shape. Evidently the flak over the target had taken it easy. The P-51s that had escorted them on the way in were still in position and would help get them home.

Rimmerman kept looking around and I could tell he was getting restless. Finally he called over the radio: "Jonah here. Jockey Leader, you take over the group and stick with the bombers. I'm going to take a section of eight and see what we can find to shoot up on the deck. With the P-51s helping out on the bombers, I think we can spare a couple of flights. But regardless of what you hear us talking about, you guys stay with the bombers. Seldom Red Leader, bring your flight along with mine. The rest of Seldom stay with Jockey and the Big Friends. Any questions?"

"Jockey Leader here, Jonah. No questions. Just wish we were going along. Good luck."

Rimmerman gave me the signal to follow him down.

Our eight ships plummeted from high altitude to head for the overcast below. The wind whistled and pulled contrails off our wingtips as we streaked down through the thin moist air. I felt like a knight of old, charging out to look for dragons to slay. My ears never gave me any problem, then or on any other flight. Doc explained it was similar to Tuttle's eczema not itching on a combat mission.

Rimmerman leveled out on top of the overcast at six thousand feet. He was having trouble finding a hole in the soup where we could drop through the clouds. We didn't know where we were or how close to the ground the overcast would be. It was too dangerous to let down blindly. We were going to have to find a hole if we wanted to get to the deck.

We finally ran across a thin spot in the clouds and caught a glimpse of the ground below. "Jonah here," Rimmerman called. "My flight of four will go down through this shit and see what happens. Red Flight, you stay above the overcast and don't come down unless I call you. If I do call, get down here in a hurry! We might catch the Germans napping, or it could be the other way around. Stay off the radio unless you have something to say. All set? Let's go, Bledsoe." Rimmerman dove through the thin hole in the clouds and I squeezed in even closer to make sure I'd be right on his tail.

The instant we broke through the overcast, Rimmerman spotted a train a couple of miles away. He charged down on it with me in pursuit. He was too eager and made a poor pass, putting only a few bullets in the locomotive.

It was the first time I had ever shot at a train and it really had me excited. The train was traveling at top speed and I thought I should lead the engine a little. I estimated the distance and squeezed the trigger, and was disappointed to see my bullets kicking up the dirt in front of the engine. I had led it too much. I tried to lead a burst of bullets into the engine by kicking rudder but only got in a few hits. A little steam came spewing out as I passed over.

The Chief came in right behind me and blew hell out of the locomotive. The train skidded to a stop with the engine pouring geysers of steam high into the air.

We made a circle back over the train, but it was full of civilian passengers and we didn't shoot. People jumped off the train even before it came to a halt. They ran into the fields, diving onto the ground and flattening out to hide from our expected bullets. Even though we saw soldiers in uniform mixed in with the women and children, we held our fire.

As we completed our circle, I spotted two other trains a short distance away. The white smoke from their puffing engines had given them away. I called, "Jonah, White Two here. Trains at three o'clock."

"Okay, Bledsoe. I see them. Keep your eyes peeled for EA."

In the excitement I had forgotten all about enemy aircraft. I remembered when Dewey Newhart and I got bounced by the 109s as we were strafing targets on the ground. I swore under my breath for being so careless.

"Seldom Red Leader here, Jonah. We're still circling. How about us coming down to join the party?" The flight above the overcast was getting eager to get in on the shooting.

"Stay up there another minute or two, Red Flight, till we know what's going on down here. I'll call you later," Rimmerman replied.

When we got within range of the two trains we found they were going in opposite directions. The engines were only a hundred yards or so apart as we made our pass. Rimmerman was shooting at the train on the left. I eased out of formation to shoot up the other one.

This time I corrected my mistake of leading the engine. I zeroed in to aim at the nose of the huge locomotive as it raced down the railroad track. I squeezed the trigger and the Little Princess bucked as her machine guns went into action.

Hurrah!

The stream of bullets struck the engine. Smoke and steam billowed into the sky as I pressed the attack to make sure the locomotive would be destroyed. Just as I passed over the train, it blew up. The smoke momentarily blinded me and I could feel the surge of my ship as the explosion knocked me into the air. I learned a lesson. Hereafter, I would shoot and skirt around the engine.

Rimmerman had destroyed his train and made a turn to circle back over the wreckage. I cut him off and was back in position on his wing without ever losing sight of him. Chief and his wingman strafed the freight cars, setting them on fire.

"Nice going, Seldom," Rimmerman called. "There's another train dead ahead. Let's get it. Stick together and keep your eyes open for EA. This party could get rough!"

"Hey, Jonah. This is Red Flight again! We're getting eager. How about joining you?"

"Okay, Red Flight. Come on through that hole in the overcast. The clouds are about a thousand feet above the ground so they shouldn't give you any problem. We're on a course of two hundred degrees, flying directly above railroad tracks. You ought to be able to pick us up in a minute or so," Rimmerman answered.

By this time we were on the other train. Rimmerman hit it first and I finished it off. We raked it with gunfire.

As I pulled up I spotted yet another train. "Locomotive at ten o'clock on that little siding," I called.

"Okay, Bledsoe, go get it," Rimmerman responded.

I kicked rudder and an instant later was pouncing on the parked train. Once more the steam and smoke poured skyward as my bullets tore into the locomotive.

I was back in formation and Rimmerman was after another locomotive backing up toward the railroad siding. Then the sky suddenly fell in on us!

Unknowingly, we had worked our way to the ouskirts of a city. Flak of all descriptions came up from all directions —tracer bullets from machine guns, tiny white puffs of exploding 20-millimeters and large black blossoms from the heavy guns. Flak was flying everywhere. The flak gunners who were not shooting directly at us were laying up a barrage of steel over our heads. In every direction the wall of bullets and shrapnel had us hemmed in. We seemed to be trapped.

"Jonah here," Rimmerman yelled excitedly. "Everybody out! Jesus Christ, we're right in the middle of the Ruhr Valley. You guys get the hell out of here the best you can. Red Flight, don't come down. Go back, Red Flight. Come on, Seldom, let's get out of here!"

We made a tight turn on the deck and headed away from the industrial section ahead. Rimmerman was going like a bat out of hell, so low to the ground that the trees and bushes swayed back and forth as he passed over them. I poured the water injection to my ship to get maximum emergency power and stay with Rimmerman.

The sky was full of death for miles around. It was impossible to dodge the flak. Our only escape route seemed to be through the overcast. The thousand feet to the comparative safety of the clouds was going to be like a thousand miles. As soon as we headed upstairs every gunner in the area would be after us.

I stayed on Rimmerman's tail, my throttle wide open, calling on every ounce of power I could drain from the 2,000-horsepower engine. Rimmerman twisted and turned as he made for the overcast. I could see where the flak was hitting his ship. At the same time I could feel the Little Princess shudder at the impact of exploding shells. My heart was beating wildly in my throat as we leaped into the clouds.

I had been able to pull up on Rimmerman's wing and stuck with him as he made his way through the overcast. I was still able to feel and hear the concussion of exploding flak in the darkness of the clouds. Rimmerman and I were alone. Although we were out of sight of the flak gunners below, we were not out of range. We continued to climb and take evasive action. The flak was still bursting in our direction, controlled by radar.

Above the clouds, the flak was even more intense. The higher we climbed, the better opportunity the long-range heavy guns had to work on us. Our only consolation was that we had finally escaped the deadly aim of the light stuff, the scourge of all fighter pilots.

Just as we thought we were getting away, a large burst of flak exploded between us. Those gunners seemed to have us zeroed in. Holes suddenly appeared in my left wing. Rimmerman peeled off on a wingover in a twisting dive. I yanked my stick over and wheeled after him. We were diving at more than five hundred miles an hour, but still we barely managed to keep one jump ahead of the flak.

Rimmerman and I kept zooming, diving, twisting, and turning, trying to get away. The black smoke pods of exploding flak kept bursting all around us.

For a moment when the flak became extremely heavy I lost Rimmerman. "Are you okay, Bledsoe?" Rimmerman called almost immediately. "How badly have you been hit?"

"I'm okay, Jonah. A couple of good-sized holes in my left wing that I can see. I've been hit at least a dozen times, but this baby is still flying. I've got you in sight and will cut you off in a second. I'm still trying to shake these damn flak gunners."

The Little Princess must look like a sieve. Thank God, she's still flying right and responding. Good baby.

A minute later we were in the clear. The flak had disappeared. We were over Holland and it wouldn't be long until we'd make the English Channel. Chief and his wingman had joined our formation and Red Flight was in sight.

Rimmerman was right. We had let down in the Ruhr Valley. The first day I reported to the squadron, I had been told about the Ruhr Valley. It was usually called "Flak Alley" or the "Valley of Death," and it was to be avoided under any circumstances. More flak guns were concentrated in the Ruhr than in any other area in the war zone. No wonder we had found so many trains in such a short time! We had invaded the heart of Hitler's industrial empire.

We had all come out of Flak Alley alive. Miraculously.

"Bledsoe, here. I see two trains at five o'clock, Jonah," I called as I scanned the ground some fifteen thousand feet below.

"I thought you were all shot up, Bledsoe," Rimmerman answered.

"I'm okay, Jonah. How about me making a quick pass and knocking out those two trains?"

"Hell, Bledsoe, we're almost to the Channel."

"I know, Jonah. But it'll only take a couple of minutes. They sure look tempting," I pleaded.

"Okay, but make it snappy. Make your pass and let it go at that. Don't fool around down there. We haven't much gas. Red Leader, you and your wingman cover Bledsoe. The rest throttle back and we'll wait for them. Go ahead, Bledsoe, if you feel you have to."

It felt great to do a wingover and streak for the deck to pounce on the trains. The first one I spotted was pulling into a station. It was a good spot for flak gunners to be waiting, so I changed course a little to make my pass out of the sun. I blazed away and the locomotive blew up in a cloud of smoke. I turned to go after the other train, but Red Flight beat me to it and left it in shambles.

I kept low to the ground, barely skimming houses and treetops while making a circle back to a clear spot where I wanted to start my climb to rejoin Rimmerman. Then I spotted another train. I reversed my turn, climbed five hundred feet to get diving room, and came in for a pass. As I held the trigger down, I could see the bullets hitting the engine. But where was the steam? It wasn't until I passed over that I realized it was an electric train. It caught fire, but I missed the great satisfaction of seeing the steam spout into the sky.

"This is Jonah. You guys get up here. We can't stay here all day."

A couple of minutes later we were all back in formation and on our way to England.

Our small force of fighter planes had really done damage. I

had personally destroyed four locomotives and had helped destroy two others. I felt elated.

I parked the Little Princess. My ground crew immediately saw the holes in the ship and the black powder marks around my guns and on my wings. They couldn't wait for me to tell them about the mission.

"I could hug you guys for the way this ship performed," I said. "Tommy, you've really got these guns harmonized and sighted in perfectly." Tommy, my armorer, was an expert; he had shown me that. He was just nineteen.

The Little Princess was shot full of holes and not seriously damaged, but it would take the rest of the day and all night to get her ready for tomorrow's battle. The crew went right to work.

CHAPTER 10

Down We Dive

When I came into the pilot's ready room, Blickenstaff was talking to a fellow I had not seen before. He motioned for me to come over.

"Marv, this is Park. He has just got back from leave and is going to take up as a flight leader again. Parker, I'd like you to meet Bledsoe, an old roommate of mine through flying school. Bledsoe likes shooting up those German trains, so you'd better get busy or he'll take your train-busting record away from you."

First Lieutenant Henry Parker glared at me. He ignored my outstretched hand. "Shooting trains is kid stuff," he said. "I'm going to concentrate on getting EA. I've only got a few more missions to go but I'm going to knock at least ten Huns out of the air." He turned and strode out of the room. I was taken aback.

Blick laughed, "Don't pay any attention to Parker. He's a real character, but you'll get used to his popping off. He's had a thing against instructors ever since he left flying school. He puts all instructors in the same category. His theory is, 'Once a goddamn instructor, always a goddamn instructor.'"

Parker was good-looking, twenty-two, lanky, with blond hair. But his personality was not "good looking." To hear him tell it, he was the world's greatest flyer. He bragged a lot about what he was going to do when he ran up against the Luftwaffe. He also spouted off constantly about flight instructors. The younger pilots in the squadron rallied around him.

I came across him in the ready room later that day. He was holding court.

"All instructors are good for is to give cadets and enlisted men a rough time of it," he said. "Back in flying school I had to tell the instructor who was giving me a check ride to go to hell if he didn't like the way I was flying. This goddamn instructor was trying to tell me what to do and I could fly rings around him! If I can just get some of those 109s to come up and fight, I'll get my ten EA in short order. Hell, I can fly better than all those bastards put together." So Parker could fly better than anybody—according to Parker.

I didn't like Parker and I told Doc. "What's wrong with that guy? He sounds like a real jerk. I don't see how he can be an effective flight leader."

"Parker suffers from diarrhea of the mouth," Doc replied. "Funny thing, I'm told that in the air he's totally different. Blick says he knows how to fly, makes a good flight leader, and does well under pressure. But it sure is easy to get sick of that popping off. On the ground he really is a jerk!"

Colonel Glenn Duncan, our group CO, would lead the mission of June 23, 1944, with Seldom Squadron. Blickenstaff assigned me to fly as Duncan's element leader, with Rafferty as my wingman.

The stories about Duncan were becoming legend. He was a real hot rock, one of the leading Aces in the ETO. I had never flown in his flight before and was anxious to see him in action.

Duncan briefed us for the mission.

"Intelligence got a tip from the French underground about a chateau where some of the Luftwaffe brass is billeted. We're going to bomb the place from low altitude and see if we can eliminate some of those guys."

Our ships would carry "Duncan Cocktails" on each wing. These were large tanks holding a mixture of oil and high-test gasoline, with a fuse that would ignite them on impact.

"We've been told the Jerries have some planes hidden in the nearby woods. We'll burn 'em out if we can't strafe them. Let's try and get the guys in the chateau on our first pass. If we give them time to get set, they'll run for the cellar where we can't get to them."

We took off. As usual we maintained radio silence to the target. Duncan signaled to me to move out a little and indicated the chateau was dead ahead. We would make our pass without further ado.

Duncan and his wingman peeled off, heading for the target. Rafferty and I were in trail position. Duncan blasted away, pouring lead into the big house, with the rest of us following his example. We dropped our bombs as we passed over the chateau and flames spread throughout the area.

After our pass, I saw men in uniform scrambling out of doors and windows. The bombs had missed their mark. We raked the building with machine guns, but it was doubtful that our strafing did much damage.

Now it was the turn of the German ground gunners. We were drawing heavy and accurate flak. "Jonah here," Duncan called as we regrouped at two thousand feet. "I'm afraid we botched the job. I'm going down and take some pictures." He didn't say anything about Rafferty and me waiting for him, so I followed him down with Raf right behind me. As soon as the chateau came within range I started firing to discourage the gunners on the ground.

The flak came up furiously. Instinctively I tried to make

myself smaller in the cockpit to hide from the enemy bullets. As usual, fear hit me in a wave when I felt the flak tearing into the Little Princess.

Duncan swooped over the target area, taking his pictures as the ground gunners let us have it. We had really stirred up an angry nest. Flak was everywhere. It must have been an important headquarters to rate this many antiaircraft guns.

"Jonah here. Let's get the hell out. We might as well have stayed home for all the good we did. We really screwed up on this job, good and proper. Couldn't even find those EA in the woods, damn it!"

So far, we had been lucky: the group was still intact. But the radio was jammed with pilots reporting damage sustained by their ships. I was listening intently when I heard: "Parker here. My engine caught a direct hit. It's missing badly. I don't know if I can maintain flying speed. I'm heading for the emergency strip on the beachhead. Good luck, you guys."

By God, the report about Parker settling down to business once he was in the air was correct. His voice was calm and he sounded cool and collected. This certainly did not sound like the guy with the loud mouth.

"Parker again. I'm losing power and altitude. Looks as if I may have to set my ship down in a field somewhere. I'll keep heading for the beachhead but doubt if I can make it."

"Jonah here, Parker. Keep on course for the strip. If you can hang on for just a few minutes you can make it. In case you have to make a forced landing, my flight will cover you until you can get away from your ship. The rest of you guys go on home. My flight will stick with Parker," Duncan ordered. Then he asked each of us for a damage report.

"Seldom White four here," Rafferty called. "I've got some big holes in my ship but she's flying okay. I'll stick with the flight, Jonah." Like Rafferty's, my ship was full of holes but my engine wasn't missing a beat.

Our flight of four led the way for Parker, trying to give him protection so he could skirt around the flak. When the ground gunners shot at us, Parker was able to ease his plane out of range. The Little Princess seemed to draw lead like a magnet, and I winced as I felt more steel rip into the ship. I saw the emergency strip on the beachhead. It made me remember the Jockey Squadron pilot who had crashed in flames on this same runway a few days before.

Good luck, Parker, I hope you make it okay.

Parker made a perfect landing.

"Thanks for the escort, you guys," he called over his radio. Cool. "I'll see you as soon as I can get a ride back to the base."

Incredible.

"Okay, boys, let's close it up and go home," Duncan called. I eased my ship in next to his wingman and signaled him to move in closer to Duncan. Rafferty snuggled up next to me. Duncan nodded approvingly at our tight formation. When we got home we did a buzz job over the base, peeled off in a tight turn, and came in for landings in perfect order. It was a nice show.

When I pulled into the parking revetment, my crew shook their heads at the holes in our Little Princess. Another all-night job! The poor plane had been patched up so much already that she looked like one of the old battle-weary ships. Well—I guess she was.

That night we celebrated Blick's twenty-fourth birthday. Doc broke out a couple of bottles of booze. "Good excuse to get a load on," Doc said. He and Blick proceeded to get high. Blick was also celebrating the fact that with a few more missions he would complete his tour of duty and since he had volunteered for another combat tour he was to be given a 30-day leave to go back to the States. I quit after my third drink. The next day I intended to log more combat time, and I didn't need a hangover.

The topic of conversation at breakfast on the morning of June 24, 1944, was the buzz bombs that had been blasting London lately. A buzz bomb, as we called the guided missiles, carried a full load of high explosives that could demolish several buildings. It was Hitler's brand-new secret weapon, and just then it threatened to blow London off the map.

Some pilots had just returned from London and described the terrible damage the pilotless projectiles had inflicted. One told of a single bomb that had demolished one half of a city block, killing a score of civilians. This was all being kept secret—no hint of the real damage was seen in the newspapers or heard on the radio. The English government played down the seriousness of the situation in order to mislead the Germans and to prevent deterioration of home-front morale. But the British were not fooling the Germans. They weren't fooling the people either, hundreds of thousands of whom were living in the Underground to escape the rain of death from the sky. They were "muddling through," they said; the courage of the British civilians was phenomenal.

Later that day, Blick told me he was going to schedule me as a flight leader on my next mission. We both wondered about the reaction of the younger pilots. When he placed my nametag in a flight leader's position on the board, it brought the expected grumbles.

"Shit, Bledsoe doesn't have a third of the combat time some of us have. Now, he's leading a flight and we'll be flying on his wing," Novak bitched.

Blickenstaff ignored the moans and groans. "You'll just have to show them, Marv," he said to me. "I haven't the slightest doubt, so to hell with their bitching. Come on, let's go to the briefing."

Rimmerman looked grim as he stood there on the briefing platform. "We're going to see what we can do today about finding the location of the buzz-bomb launching pads," he said. The announcement brought murmurings of displeasure. We knew this meant flying low and slow around the heavily fortified French coastal area. "We'll get our asses shot off for sure," one pilot moaned.

"Okay, settle down," Rimmerman declared. "Orders are orders. Let's do our best and get it over with. If we can locate those launching pads, the heavy bombers can go after them. Then maybe we can get back to our own work again." He sounded as irritated as anyone else.

"Why don't they send the RAF?" the pilot next to me complained. We seldom saw RAF fighters. "Goddamnit, all they ever talk about is the Air Battle of Britain. They keep telling us they can't go on missions with us because their aircraft don't have the range. What's their excuse now? The French coast is only thirty miles away. It's a cinch they've got range enough to get that far."

"Haven't you heard? This is America's war now," someone else said.

Fighter pilots often raked the British over the coals. Most Americans liked the English, but they resented the attitude of some who suggested that the British had done enough and now we should take over the war. They said we should have entered the war much sooner than we did. It wasn't unusual to hear Limeys complaining about Yanks, "overpaid, oversexed and over 'ere." If we had to be "over 'ere," they added, at least we could fight more and shut up about it.

We let off a lot of steam before we headed out to our ships and a mission that we did not like.

The target area was just a hop, skip, and a jump from our Suffolk base. It seemed odd to start letting down seconds after making landfall. Because of the German guns, we usually avoided the area as if it were quarantined. Today we were going to cruise around. The heavy flak that greeted us at the outset seemed to be a prelude to much worse.

"Jonah here," Rimmerman called. "This flak is too thick to let down here. We'll go in a little deeper, make our letdown, and then come back toward the coastline. That way Jerry might not think we're going to work this area over. Keep your eyes open, men. This may be it!"

"Your're right there, chappie," someone chimed in.

We were near several large towns, so the flak could be horrendous. When we started our letdown, goose pimples ran up and down my back. We leveled off at three thousand feet

Left to right: Captain William "Willie" Price, "Doc," and Major Wayne "Blick" Blickenstaff standing before Willie's P-51 Mustang, "Janie."

Captain Joseph "Doc" Canipelli, our popular flight surgeon who had a yen to fly with the combat pilots. At the outset of the war he volunteered for the Army Air Corps but qualified doctors were in such great demand the Army opted to make him a flight surgeon instead of a pilot. "Doc" is pictured here in the front seat of the Advanced Trainer, an AT-6, which he was taught to fly by the author during a lull in the fighting as a result of bad weather over the Continent.

"There I was . . . ," Denny "The Kid" Novak is explaining with the use of his hands as he relates to members of his crew what had taken place on the mission. Novak was hooked on flying and would rather be in the cockpit of a plane than eat. "We all have to die some day," he told fellow pilots, "and what better way to die than to 'get it' while flying a P-47 Thunderbolt during a combat mission?" He meant every word of it. The popular nineteen year old "kid" was killed August 4, 1944 by enemy fighters during a combat mission over Germany. Novak had reported to the 350th squadron as a flight officer on May 20th and was promoted to Second Lieutenant on July 14, 1944.

Pilots of the 350th Fighter Squadron pose at their home base in England prior to D-Day, June 6, 1944. It was one of their last group pictures as the fighting that ensued took its deathly toll. (U.S. Air Force photo)

Colonel Glenn Duncan, Group Commander, briefs 353rd pilots about the forthcoming mission. Standing by the blackboard is Lieutenant Colonel Ben Rimmerman. Duncan, one of the leading aces of the 8th Air Force with over nineteen victories, was shot down while strafing an airdrome in Germany on July 27, 1944. He was picked up by the Underground and remained with them for several weeks, fighting Germans and destroying German facilities before returning to his home base. Rimmerman, who took charge of the group until Duncan returned, was killed May 1, 1945 while riding as a passenger in an airplane piloted by Captain Bret Thompson, also of the 353rd fighter group.

The author, Captain Marvin Bledsoe, in the cockpit of the beloved Thunderbolt.

This drawing by Blickenstaff hung in the pilots ready room as a warning against flying down on the deck to face the murderous flak guns. After D-Day it became routine for the high altitude Thunderbolts to be fighting the German military machine from tree-top level.

Left: First Lieutenant Swift T. "Ben" Benjamin reflects the youth of most of the combat fighter pilots. Ben became an Ace with over seven victories credited to his nerve and skill. *Right*: Flight Officer John Phelan, assigned to the squadron on May 4, 1944 and killed in action on June 12, 1944. He was one of the six out of eleven 350th pilots shot down by an outnumbering group of German ME-109s who attacked when they were shooting up targets on the ground.

Left: Captain William D. Smith, one of the former instructors reporting to the 350th Fighter Squadron on June 8, 1944. Smith was killed while strafing a German airdrome on August 29, 1944. *Right*: Second Lieutenant George W. McInis reported for duty on July 27, 1944 and was killed on a strafing mission some two weeks later on August 13, 1944.

Left: Second Lieutenant Carl A. Larsen, assigned to the squadron on August 20, 1944 and who was subsequently shot down, became a prisoner of war, and returned to the base after the surrender of the Germans. *Right*: First Lieutenant Alger Aal, flying as the author's wingman, was killed when pilots of the 350th Fighter Squadron attacked a German airdrome. Before being shot down by flak gunners that ringed the field, Aal was credited with destroying two of the sixteen German aircraft that were knocked out of action.

Left: Lieutenant Richard "Dick" Bedford, one of the six out of eleven 350th pilots to be shot down by the Luftwaffe on June 12, 1944. He fared better than the other five as he was returned home after being taken a prisoner of war. *Right*: Lieutenant Marvin "Olie" Albertson, killed in a midair collision over England while returning from a combat mission during bad weather on October 7, 1944. He was only minutes away from his home base. The fate of the other pilot is unknown.

Captain "Willie" Price, 350th fighter squadron, 353rd fighter group and his North American P-51 Mustang, "Janie". These long range planes took the place of the group's beloved P-47 Thunderbolts. (U.S. Air Force photo)

Left: First Lieutenant Don Markson was killed at his home base in Raydon, England on June 28, 1944 when he returned from a combat mission. He became another statistic when he crashed as a result of bad weather and lack of proper instrument flight training. *Right*: Second Lieutenant Milton H. Graham was killed in action strafing an enemy airdrome—the most dangerous mission in the war for fighter pilots.

 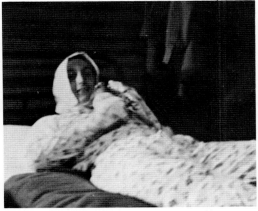

Left: First Lieutenant Robert "Lout" Hart, who, upon completing his first combat tour escorting "big friends" on bombing missions volunteered for a second tour. Returning from a leave in the States on August 2, 1944, Hart was distressed to learn the escort missions were now few and far between and the squadron was "down on the deck" fighting the Germans at tree-top level and within range of deadly flak guns. Hart was killed a week after his return when an ammunition truck he had strafed exploded, blowing him out of the sky before he could evade the concussion and flying debris. *Right*: The author in his "bunny suit," which covered feet, hands, and head in an attempt to keep warm while sleeping in the damp English weather that made the Nissen huts feel as cold as icebergs. Kidded unmercifully by his fellow pilots when he first donned his "bunny suit" because of the long ears his wife had playfully attached, it worked so well he became the envy of the squadron and pilots later argued over who would inherit it when he left.

Duffy's Tavern and the base theater are favorite hang-outs for personnel of the 353rd fighter group at their base in Raydon, England. In the weeks following the D-Day invasion of Hitler's fortified Europe there was not much time to enjoy either facility. (U.S. Air Force photo)

The bombs and rocket launchers under each wing and the external belly tank to increase its range bely the fact that this P-47 Thunderbolt was designed as a high altitude fighter plane. This plane will soon be over Germany on a low level flying mission "down on the deck." (U.S. Air Force photo)

This flaming B-24 Consolidated Liberator Bomber is the lone survivor from its squadron that hit an industrial target in Austria. German fighters attacked the bombers with vengeance. Five of the German fighters were destroyed. The flame and smoke of the B-24 fades into the clouds over enemy held territory. (U.S. Air Force photo)

A message to Hitler is being written on this 500 pound "baby" by Sergeant Thomas Zettervall, 22, of Portland, Oregon. (U.S. Air Force photo)

"Bombs away!" calls the lead bombardier of this group of Flying Fortresses. At his signal the B-17s drop their loads in unison. This is the 92nd bomb group in action on September 29, 1944 as their rain of destruction drops from the sky. (U.S. Air Force photo)

A flight of 353rd fighter pilots buzz over their home base at Raydon, England in preparation for a landing after a successful combat mission. (U.S. Air Force photo)

Bursts of deadly flak explode around this formation of B-17 Flying Fortresses during a bombing run over Kassel, Germany. The flak appears as innocent puffs of smoke, but each burst showers approximately 1400 jagged pieces of metal at any plane nearby. (U.S. Air Force photo)

This P-47 Fighter-Bomber has added some "frags" to go along with the rest of the load. Not shown is a 500 pound bomb under each wing. After dropping the bombs, the pilot of this Thunderbolt will spend a couple of hours on the deck shooting up targets of opportunity. (U.S. Air Force photo)

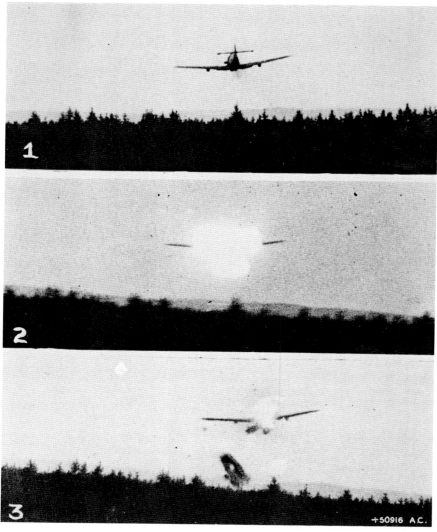

A Nazi Messerschmitt 109 loses this dog fight with an American fighter: (1) the German pilot heads for the deck to escape; (2) direct hits are shown by the gun camera of the victor; and (3) the ME 109 begins to disintegrate. What is not shown is that parts from the enemy plane lodged in the wings of the American fighter. (U.S. Air Force photo)

Opposite page: A camera is activated with the firing of the eight .5-caliber machine guns on the P-47 Thunderbolt. Pictured here is a German JU-88 being shot down. This twin engine aircraft was one of Hitler's best. The camera catches the American pilot closing in for the kill. Hits were made on the right engine and seconds later the plane crashed into the ground. (U.S. Air Force photo)

This 350th fighter pilot has a birds-eye view of a locomotive spewing steam and smoke after a pass by a flight of Thunderbolts led by Colonel Ben Rimmerman. The German supply train will be immobile until a new engine can arrive under the cover of darkness. (U.S. Air Force photo)

This locomotive did not get far before a fighter pilot brought it to a halt. This engine may have been on its way to replace one that had been destroyed while moving a supply train because it appears that a lone car is attached. It was not unusual for several locomotives to be destroyed before the Germans could get a supply train moving again. (U.S. Air Force photo)

Death plunge of an American B-17 on a bombing run over Merseburg, Germany. One engine has been wrenched off and a propeller can be seen flying into space. The crew is still inside this flying coffin. The target for the day was a synthetic oil plant and the plane in the upper right corner has just called out "bombs away!" (U.S. Air Force photo)

A wing man follows his leader who has just destroyed an enemy aircraft at a German airdrome. The Thunderbolt pilot is right on top of the deck in an effort to avoid the flak gunners protecting the field. (U.S. Air Force photo)

This German "buzz bomb" is seen on its deadly mission over the Picadilly section of London, England. The robot flying bombs caused great destruction in this historic city. Contrary to Hitler's prediction the robots would bring the British to their knees, the "buzz bombs" strengthened civilians resolve to resist the Nazi aggression. (U.S. Air Force photo)

353rd personnel examine this Thunderbolt that made an emergency landing near their base at Raydon, England. (U.S. Air Force photo)

and fanned out wide; there was no point to keeping bunched up and giving the ground gunners a field day. I was extremely nervous as I waited for another burst of flak. I couldn't shake an ominous feeling that this was my day to get shot down.

Where is it? Why don't they start shooting?

We cruised for an hour or so, but the German gunners didn't pay much attention to us.

"Jerry doesn't want to give away his position," Rimmerman called. "I'll bet those launching sites are near. They know if we find them the heavy bombers will be calling. We aren't doing good here. We might as well go home."

I sighed with relief. When it came time to land I was still nervous. There was no buzzing the field this day. I kept a close watch on the planes behind me against the threat of being rammed. I made it home safe one more time.

The next day, heavy rain kept everyone on the ground. By 10 A.M., we knew no mission was possible. I marveled at the sudden change in the pilots as they relaxed. It was as though we had been given a 24-hour reprieve from execution. Pilots with visible cases of nerves let go and acted their age.

Captain James Merchant, a former instructor, had been complaining for days about flying on the wing of young second lieutenants; in fact, he seemed to complain about anything and everything, a good example of combat colic. But the rain seemed to do something for him. He joined in the horseplay as if he didn't have a care. Not having to go out and face antiaircraft fire made a different character out of him.

Even the brass and older men were in a holiday mood. It was as though there was something to celebrate. In a way, there was. Since I had arrived at Raydon, each day, each mission, seemed rougher than the one before. A day off really was a day of reprieve. We had lost so many men, I had forgotten the names of those who had been killed in my first days of combat. Only two weeks had elapsed, but I couldn't even remember the faces of the flight leaders who had been knocked down on my second mission.

I fell to wondering, as I did constantly, if and when I'd ever get to see my beloved Harriett again. I felt a million miles away from her and our baby. I missed them so.

Late in the afternoon the tension began to build again and all of us sooner or later went to the ready room. There was no need to report in, but it was as though a magnet drew us there to see the schedule for the next mission

On July 1, 1944, the mission was to Evreux, sixty miles west of Paris. Our orders were brief: "Shoot any goddamn thing that moves."

Blick would be going on his thirty-day furlough soon and Major Douglas Winfield from group headquarters would take over the squadron until Blick returned for his second tour of duty.

Winfield reported early to get acquainted with our operation while Blick was still around to help out. Winfield was leading the mission and just after dawn we arrived over the target area. Someone spotted a lone ME-109 leap into a cloud, and our whole squadron converged on him. The poor guy was darting from one cloud to the next when Winfield got in a good burst and blew the 109 into a hundred pieces. It was Winfield's fifth victory, making him an Ace.

I was sure the pilot had been killed, but suddenly a parachute appeared. He had bailed out before his ship exploded. I flew close by him and could see the terrified look on his face. He was obviously afraid I would shoot him. He was startled when I gave him a wave. He grinned weakly and waved back. It was a strange world.

Some two hours later, when we were getting ready to head for home base, I saw an enemy aircraft diving out of the clouds. "Seldom Red Leader here," I called on the radio. "My flight's going after a single 109. He's heading for the deck at ten o'clock. Okay, you guys, let's go after him!"

I peeled off from ten thousand feet, hot on the 109's tail. He was a long way ahead of me, about to make a landing at a German airstrip. I was hitting four hundred miles an hour as I neared the field. The 109 had made it to the ground and was taxiing, trying desperately to reach a group of trees at the end of the strip.

I was too low and going too fast to get a good shot. My bullets kicked up dust behind and to one side of the aircraft. I applied a little rudder guiding my bullets by sight, and raked the 109 from stem to stern. It swerved out of control and burst into flames. I felt pleased with myself, but at the same time felt a surge of compassion for the pilot who probably would not come out of that burning airplane alive.

I quickly forgot about him when a string of 20-millimeter shells burst over my cockpit. I was about a hundred feet from the ground, but I rammed the stick forward to get lower and out of sight of the ground gunners. I had learned from past missions that if I was low enough, the ground gunners could only see me for a second or two, not long enough to aim and shoot.

"Stay low, Red Flight. Get down on the deck!" I warned the guys coming in behind me. "I'm going up this little valley. I'll make a steep spiral to get away from the flak. Join up at three thousand feet." The rest of my flight had followed me down but had momentarily split up in the flak-infested sky.

"This is Rafferty, Marv. You really clobbered that bastard. I shot up another one that was making a wheels-up landing on the other side of the field. I've caught a helluva lot of flak but seem to be doing okay. I'll join up in a minute."

"This is Winfield. The rest of the squadron is five thousand feet above you, Bledsoe. We'll circle so you can catch up, then we'll all go home together. That was a good job you guys did down there, but it's time to head for home."

I took stock on my way upstairs. I had felt the shells hitting the Little Princess and could see holes in my right wing. That was the only damage visible from the cockpit. She had kept right on purring as I eluded the flak gunners. So far so good.

At the sight of the Little Princess, my ground crew shook their heads in despair. I hadn't seen one hole about the size of a basketball, three feet behind the cockpit. The crew was in for another all-night repair session, if what could be seen was all there was.

Tommy seemed especially excited. "By God, Marvin, you just made me twenty bucks! I bet one of the guys in the next crew that if anyone in the squadron fired his guns, you would come back with yours smoking. It'll be a pleasure to clean them."

I told all of them about shooting up the Messerschmitt. I always tried to keep them informed and give them an idea of what combat was like so they would know how much I depended on them to get me home.

That night Doc got drunk and confided in me that he was having serious trouble with one of the pilots, First Lieutenant Ray Carson. I felt partly responsible. He was one of the instructors I had recommended to Blick when he had asked me to pick out some good fliers for the squadron. Rafferty had been my first choice, Ray a close second.

After Ray had flown his third mission, he refused to go on any others. He said an old back injury made it impossible for him to stay strapped to the cockpit for more than an hour at a time. Yet, as an instructor at Luke Field he had logged fifteen hundred hours of flying time without complaining of a bad back. On two of the three missions, he headed back to home base the instant the flak appeared. Both times he claimed he had developed mechanical problems but they had cleared up by the time he landed. The one mission he did stick through was a milkrun.

Ray wanted Doc to recommend his release from flying duty that involved combat. As flight surgeon, Doc had the authority to do this, but he refused. Ray then went over Doc's head and demanded a physical examination at Wing Headquarters hospital. Later, we learned they could find nothing wrong with his back. He was grounded for refusing to participate in combat flying. He was given the choice of flying combat or being stripped of his coveted silver wings. He chose the latter rather than face those flak guns.

"Maybe Ray was lucky at that," Doc remarked. "Anything is better than getting killed. Worse than that, he might have gotten someone else killed by not being there when he was needed. Or he might have been court-martialed and faced a firing squad for desertion in the time of war. But, to hell with him," Doc said as he poured another drink, "I've got my own problems."

Doc's problems turned out to be processing a half-dozen replacements. This always meant extra paper work, which he complained about, but we welcomed the new pilots with open arms.

The replacements had been out of flying school only a short time, but in England they had gone through several weeks of combat training. This really helped. They were ready—at least readier than they had been just out of flying school in the States—and desperately needed. No time would be lost in putting them to work with the rest of us.

The flight board indicated an open spot on the next mission. Blick said I could fly it if I could find a ship; the Little Princess was out of action—that damage had been worse than we expected. I found a spare Thunderbolt.

That day Merchant was flying my wing. When we came in sight of the flak over the French coast, he turned tail and headed for home base. This hurt because I already knew what the younger pilots would say: "Standard procedure for chickenshit instructors."

On this mission we were to find targets of opportunity. It didn't take long for us to get into action. We shot up trucks and cars that looked like they were trying to get men and matériel to the front lines. (We learned later that we had killed a number of French Maquis and destroyed several of their vehicles. It was unfortunate but it could not be helped. From the air, we could not distinguish between Nazis and Allies.)

We were getting ready to pull out and go home when off in the distance we sighted a dozen enemy aircraft. At the sight of those 109s my heart bounced clear up in my mouth. One of the younger pilots was flying as my wingman. I gave him a hand signal to close out and called "Come on, Burke, let's go after those 109s at eleven o'clock."

"I can't, Bledsoe. I'm short of gas. Let's turn back."

"Are you sure? You should have plenty of gas. We can catch those guys if we hurry." I pushed my throttle forward.

I was overtaking the Jerries and they were breaking for the overcast. Once they made the safety of the clouds, we would probably lose them.

"This is Burke. I'm going to peel off and head for home. I'm almost out of gas."

"Suit yourself, Burke. I think you've got plenty of gas to take on these guys." I thought of the rumor that Burke was on the verge of a breakdown—too many rough missions. "I'm still going to try to put a burst into the tail-end ship."

I watched Burke pull out for home. An instant later Rafferty pulled up alongside me. "Go get 'em, Marv. I'm with you. My wingman and I will stick it out. Maybe we can be in range before they make it into the overcast."

We were a thousand yards away as the 109s approached the cloud bank. It was too far for accurate shooting. I took aim and emptied my guns anyway. Some Jerry pilots who got nicked a couple of times would go over the side. Unlike our pilots, they were over home territory; bail out today, fly tomorrow.

The 109s disappeared into the overcast. I couldn't tell whether I even came close. Even if we had enough gas to look for them, I was out of ammunition. "Okay, let's go home. Chalk up a big fat zero," I said to Rafferty.

When we got back to Raydon, Rafferty made it a point to check the gas left in Burke's plane. "Shit, Burke, you landed with an hour's worth of gas," he told him in disgust. Burke didn't say anything and just walked away.

That night Blick told Rafferty and me privately that he wanted us to work with the replacements. "It won't be long now," Blick said, "until most of the other pilots are through with their tours. That'll leave the squadron with you former instructors, the replacements, and a few old flight leaders who'll be getting back from leave."

In the next few days, Rafferty and I took the replacements on training flights over the English countryside. We introduced them to some hairy rat races in the clouds and to buzzing at tree-top level. We taught them to fly tight formation, and we just generally put them through their paces.

We celebrated July 4th with our own brand of fireworks, a strafing mission; "targets of opportunity" again. I was leading a section of eight Thunderbolts with First Lieutenant Robert F. Unangst as element leader in my lead flight of four.

Unangst was a twenty-one-year-old pilot with two hundred hours of combat time. He was peeved at having to follow me as flight leader because I had been in combat for less than a month and he had been here for a year. It didn't seem to make any difference to him that I had more than ten times as much flight experience.

After we had been over the target area only a short time my flight had destroyed three locomotives and shot up a convoy of tanks and trucks. Unangst suddenly pulled out of formation, taking his wingman, to strafe a column of trucks hidden in a nearby woods. After a couple of passes, he had the trucks burning fiercely. "Hey, Unangst," I called, "that is some beautiful shooting. Nice going, you guys."

Evidently he had expected me to chew him out for breaking away. He came on the radio with "Thanks, Marv, you didn't do so bad yourself. Looks as if we've done a lot of good this morning!" Then I knew we would never have a problem again with him.

It was turning out to be a productive mission. I had shot up two locomotives and a score of trucks by myself and the other boys had done their share of destruction.

We were looking for more targets when I heard a terror-stricken scream on the radio.

"My God—109s, 109s! Break! For God's sake, break! There's a 109 on your tail!" Without hesitation I straight-armed my throttle for maximum power, kicked rudder violently, and horsed back on my stick to get away from the 109. Every man in the squadron followed suit. Each thought he was about to get shot down by a 109. There was nothing there.

"It got him! The 109 got him! Oh my God, I told him to break and now he's on fire and going down," the same panic-stricken voice called hysterically. It was impossible to tell who had called or who had a 109 on their tail.

"Jonah here. Who called out that 109?" There was no response. Duncan got back on the radio. His voice stayed calm. "Who ever called out the 109, take it easy. Give us your position. We can't help if we don't know who you are and where you are. Now, come in and identify yourself."

"Jonah, this is Jockey Red Three. My wingman kept lagging behind and two 109s sneaked out of the clouds and shot him down. It was terrible. He was a new man on his first mission. Jesus, I warned him about lagging behind. Now he's gone." The voice was trembling.

We looked around for the two German fighters but couldn't find them. When we got back to Raydon, Colonel Duncan lectured the entire group on radio procedure. "You have to identify yourself so the rest of the group will know who the hell you are and where the hell you are.

"For Christ's sake, calm down before you come on the radio. When I heard that 'Break, there's a 109 on your tail,' I did a snap roll trying to get away. I thought sure someone was lined up behind me. It scared the living daylights out of me and I imagine it scared everyone else who heard 'there's a 109 on your tail.' With the proper identification on the radio we might have been able to box in those two Jerry pilots."

The look on everyone's face was serious. We had all learned an important lesson in a sad way, that day.

It was announced later that my flight had done more damage to enemy transportation on this mission than any other flight in the group. I felt a glow of satisfaction. My locomotive score was rising.

The debriefing came to a quick halt with the announcement of mail call, the most important aspect of our day-to-day life. The pilots of the Eighth Air Force were lucky compared to most other men in the military. We got mail almost as regularly as the people in the States. Harriett never let a day go by without writing about events at home and about our Little Princess. I could hardly believe it when she told me the baby I had left in a bassinet was now standing by herself and trying to walk.

I was seldom dry-eyed at the first reading of Harriett's letters. I filed them away in my footlocker and saved them for the days when I had time to start from the beginning and read them all over again.

Every man would read parts of his letters to anyone who would listen. I'd have to wait patiently while Doc and Rafferty gave all the news about their kids, who I'd never met and probably never would. Then I would make them hear all about my own Princess, who they would probably never meet either.

But next morning letters went into the duffel. It was to be another escort mission; fifteen hundred bombers were scheduled to destroy industrial plants deep inside Germany.

"This will be at least a five-hour mission, so we're going to have to sweat out our last drop of gas," stated Duncan at the briefing. "We've been ordered to put as many ships in the air as we can on this one. Let me emphasize that I don't want any of you guys aborting without cause. There've been too many pilots returning to home base lately. Any guy who turns back today had better have a good reason."

When I arrived at the parking revetment, I found Jackson working on the belly tank, bleary-eyed and grouchy from another night of drinking. He said the tank was okay. For the past week I knew he had been pushing most of the work off on Swanson, and I was just about fed up with Jackson's nonsense.

We always drained the belly tank first and then jettisoned it, so shortly after takeoff I flipped the switch that activated the tank. My engine quit. Momentarily I fell out of formation. I switched back to wing tanks, got back in formation, and a moment later tried my belly tank again. Again it failed. For the next hour I kept trying. No soap.

This was a hell of a thing to happen after Duncan's lecture about aborting, but there was nothing left for me to do but turn tail for home.

When I got back to base Jackson was not around. He had gone into town, Swanson reported. A short time later, I learned that Jackson had gotten drunk at a nearby pub, got on his bicycle, and run over an English pedestrian. He was put in the guard house, awaiting court-martial. I asked to have Swanson promoted to crew chief of the Little Princess. I needed someone I could depend on every day without a moment's doubt.

CHAPTER 11

The Kid

July 10, 1944—I was starting my second month with the 350th Fighter Squadron. I found it hard to believe I had been in combat only four weeks! I had seen so much action and faced death so often it seemed as if I had been here a lifetime.

I was scheduled to stay on the ground so I joined Doc to watch the group take off. When our pilots returned hours later, they reported that Colonel Glenn Duncan had been shot down. The news made front pages in England and the United States, and Axis Sally gloated over the radio. Often Axis Sally broadcast accurate information about our losses before we returned to Raydon; at least this time we learned the bad news first from Americans. Duncan was a popular CO, a regular guy and a first-rate fighter pilot. Tears were in Rafferty's eyes as he told me what had happened.

Duncan spotted an airdrome in Germany and took his flight down on the deck to shoot up parked enemy aircraft.

During their strafing spree a 20-millimeter shell blew an oil line off Duncan's engine. He knew his minutes in the air were numbered.

"This is Jonah, boys," Duncan called over his radio. "Looks like this is it for me. My engine's shot up and the oil pressure is gone. This baby won't fly much longer. I'm going to try to get as far away from this airdrome as I can and land in an open spot somewhere while I still have power. I sure hate to have to stop flying and fighting with you guys. You're a great bunch." Duncan's voice was as calm as if he was on the telephone saying he would be late for lunch, Rafferty said.

"Land on the road, Jonah, and I'll pick you up," Kid Novak, his wingman pleaded. "I can land on the road behind you and we'll fly out of this place together. The rest of the flight can cover for us."

"Thanks, fella, but I doubt if we could get away with it. No need for both of us to be left over here," Duncan responded. "I'll be okay. It may take a long time, but I'll be showing up back at our base one of these days. Rimmerman, you'll be taking over the group while I'm gone. Take good care of it for me in my absence."

Duncan's Thunderbolt kept flying for several minutes without oil pressure. The rest of the pilots hovered around, trying to protect him from flak or enemy aircraft.

"Jonah again. Look at this P-47 fly. What a beautiful ship. No oil pressure and still she keeps plugging away. My engine is starting to miss, though, so I don't have much flying time left. I'm going to make a letdown into the clearing straight ahead. You boys cover me. As soon as I land, I'll run for the forest."

As he made his approach into the open field, the entire group circled with guns ready. "Shoot any son-of-a-bitch you see on the ground," Rimmerman called on the radio. "We've got to give him time to get to the forest. If a bush so much as wiggles in the wind, strafe it up one side and down the other!"

Everyone in the group knew there would be hell to pay if

the Germans ever caught Duncan. Our group had given them so much trouble we were sure they would take it out on Duncan. They would have traded an entire Luftwaffe squadron to take him prisoner. He was one of the great leaders in the Eighth Air Force and a top Ace.

"Duncan made a perfect wheels-up landing," Rafferty told me. "The moment his ship came to a halt, he worked furiously to free himself from his safety belt, crash straps, and parachute harness. The Thunderbolts above were ready for blood. It would have been a rough place for any Jerries to have put in an appearance."

Duncan jumped out on the wing of his ship and waved at his buddies circling above. As a final gesture, he reached into the cockpit of his dead ship, picked up his radio mike, and said, "Good luck, fellas. Give 'em hell for me. Remember, I'm coming back!"

Our pilots continued to patrol the area until Duncan made it into the woods. He waved once more and then disappeared into a dense thicket. His flight shot up his ship, watched it burn, and sadly headed for home base.

Duncan was one of the most aggressive pilots in the war. He had twenty-four enemy aircraft to his credit. Yet the flak got him as easily as if he were a green replacement on his first mission. His loss was a tremendous blow to our group.

Although losing Duncan was felt deeply by every man in our group, it didn't slow things down for a second. Before the engines of our planes had cooled off, we were primed to fly another mission escorting bombers over France, a milk run. Colonel Ben Rimmerman took up where Duncan left off.

Blick pushed me up to be Blue Flight Leader, with eight ships under my command. Rafferty would be leading my second flight. It marked his first mission as a flight leader and brought the same sort of grumbling among the younger pilots that had been directed at me when I led my first flight.

Novak was scheduled to fly as my wingman and didn't like it. To him I was still a goddamn instructor, and he hated instructors and flying school personnel. He swore that if his advanced training instructor ever showed up in England, he would personally see to it that the bastard never got home alive. Novak, at a bare nineteen, was the youngest pilot in the group. He was eager to fly, anxious to fight the enemy, and a good-hearted youngster. I was fond of him and figured he'd soon get over his antagonism.

I was not only fond of Novak. I also had great admiration for him, because he was the only one in the group who would rather fly than eat. When he wasn't out on a mission, Kid would manage to find a spare ship somewhere, and go out and buzz the countryside or rat-race by himself in the clouds. If a spare ship wasn't available, he would offer to test fly one of the repaired planes on the flight line.

Despite all the hours he spent in the air, he was a scatter-brained pilot if there ever was one. Novak made more mistakes in flying than all the other pilots put together; he made so many pilot errors it was almost a wonder that he was still alive. I couldn't understand why he hadn't washed out in flying school. Evidently his eagerness to fly caused his instructors to give him the benefit of what must have been many doubts.

Blick had tried to use Novak as an element leader, but Kid made so many mistakes that he had to be put back to flying wing position; that was where he belonged. He had one great ability: he could always be counted on to stick out the mission no matter what happened. Antiaircraft fire never got so thick that he would desert his leader. Still, I considered him a menace. He was just too bad a pilot. The formation was never so tight that he wasn't trying to move in closer, but the danger was that he would screw up and ram his leader. He had to be watched to keep him from being to close and ramming the plane ahead on landing.

Guts? The Kid had enough for all of us. Triggerhappy? He'd give his arm for a chance to fire his guns at the enemy.

The future? He wasn't counting on one. The war was his whole life. Everybody had to die sometime, and what better way to go than on a combat mission? That was Novak's philosophy.

Duncan was not our only loss. The past couple of days had taken a heavy toll of the pilots living in our hut. Two nights earlier, eight men had been sleeping there. Now, after two quick strafing missions, there were four empty bunks. There were some very nervous pilots in those bunks that were occupied. They were attempting to relax their taut nerves and ease their fears as well as trying to get over the pain of losing their buddies.

Because the weather was so terrible on July 11, 1944, eleven hundred bombers were scheduled to penetrate Germany and make a bomb run by radar. Rimmerman would lead the group on this mission. The Big Birds would be at thirty thousand feet, dropping bombs through the overcast. We doubted if they would do much good, for although the newspapers played up the fine results of radar bombing, we had had too many firsthand views of missed targets. The land outside the big cities was pockmarked with bombs aimed at factories by radar. When we got down on the deck we could see how badly they had damaged the farmers' fields. But more tragically, radar bombing took a heavy toll of civilian lives when the bombs fell in residential districts.

On this mission other fighters, P-51 Mustangs, would escort the bombers into the target area. But they would not have enough fuel to escort them home, and we were scheduled to rendezvous with our Big Friends when the P-51s left them. Our job was to act as withdrawal support.

When we met the bombers that day, one look told the story: German flak and fighters had made them pay dearly for this mission. Individual ships were scattered all over the sky, limping home. Only a few flights bore even a semblance of a military formation.

"Jonah here," Rimmerman called. "Looks as if we're going to have our work cut out for us. Round these guys up the best you can, and head them for home base."

Our fighter planes kept buzzing back and forth, trying to protect the crippled bombers and herd them in the direction of England. It was almost like trying to round up cattle in a storm. Many of the bomber pilots seemed to have no sense of direction. If we didn't keep them on course, they would run out of gas before they ever made it to England. We finally got the main bunch to the English Channel, then turned back into enemy territory to look for stragglers.

"Jonah here. Okay, you guys. Break up into individual flights. Spread out. We've got a lot of territory to cover. These poor guys are scattered all over hell."

He had no more than spoken when I spied a lone B-17 about ten thousand feet below. The crew was shooting distress flares to attract attention.

"Bledsoe here. Taking my flight down to help a fort at two o'clock low. Let's go, Seldom Blue," I called as I peeled off to intercept the bomber below. When we got within range, I threw my belly and wing up in the air so the B-17 could recognize us as friendly fighters; those bomber gunners were quick on the trigger.

I circled the crippled ship and noted the "R-Robert" insignia on its tail. The bomber looked almost shot to pieces. I switched over to C channel on my radio so I could contact the pilot. "Hello, Big Friend. Hello, R for Robert," I called. This is Seldom Blue Leader circling you with a flight of Thunderbolts. Can you read me, Robert?"

"Hello, Seldom Leader. Yeah, I can read you, boy. Thank God you're here! We're all shot up, fella. Can you stay with us for a while? We just can't make it alone. Stick with us, will you?" The voice on the radio was trembling.

"We sure hate to see you in such bad shape, Robert. Don't worry about us. We'll stick with you as long as our gas holds out. How is it inside?" I inquired.

"My navigator and radioman have been killed and one of

the other boys has been seriously wounded. He's bleeding badly and we can't seem to stop it. I've only got two engines. I can barely keep this bird in the air. I'm not sure of my bearing home. Can you give me a heading?"

"Change course twenty degrees left for the quickest way off the Continent," I replied. "I'll send a ship upstairs. We'll get an exact bearing if we can reach the controller in London. Stand by. I'm going to change frequency."

"You're going to stay with us, aren't you, Little Friend? Christ, but we need all the help we can get," the bomber pilot pleaded.

"Take it easy, buddy. We'll stay with you. I'll be back on the radio as soon as I can get that compass heading."

I switched back to our fighter frequency. "Chief, these boys are in bad shape. The navigator is dead and they need a bearing home. Take your wingman and climb to twenty-five thousand feet. See if you can contact the controller. We don't care where he sends us. Just get the most direct compass bearing to England."

The Chief started his climb. In a few minutes I could hear him calling London. "Hello, Larkspur. Hello, Larkspur. This is Seldom. Hello, Larkspur, this is Seldom. We have a damaged bomber that needs a bearing to England. Give us a bearing on the shortest possible route to England. Come in, Larkspur."

I could faintly hear the air controller in London and was surprised we had been able to pick him up so quickly. "Hello, Seldom. This is Larkspur. This is Larkspur here, Seldom. Give me a long count, Seldom. I can barely hear you. Go ahead with the long count, Seldom."

I kept my fingers crossed as Chief followed instructions. "Hello, Larkspur. This is Seldom again. Give me a quick route home, Larkspur. Give us a direct bearing to England. Do you have our position, Larkspur? Do you read me now? Did you get the message for a direct bearing home? It's yours now, Larkspur. Over."

I could picture the controller in England trying to pick us

up on his radar. Once he got a fix he could give us the right compass heading. When the controller gave his reply, I thanked God for radio. "Steer two, six, zero, Seldom. Repeat. Steer two, six, zero. Two, six, zero is your bearing, Seldom. Acknowledge. Over." The controller's voice was crisp and precise as he delivered the message; he knew radio contact might be broken at any instant.

"Seldom here, Larkspur. Read you five by five. Steer two, six, zero. Wilco. Thanks, Larkspur. Seldom out," Chief acknowledged. "Hey, Bledsoe, this is Chief. Tell our Big Friend to steer two, six, zero. Do you read me, Bledsoe?"

"Loud and clear, Chief. Will check in with you later," I responded.

I went back to C channel.

"Hello, R for Robert. Seldom Leader here. You are thirty degrees off course. Steer two, six, zero, Two, six, zero, Robert. Did you get that, Robert?" The bomber had been nearly fifty degrees off course before we intercepted it and would have never made it to the Channel.

"This is Robert, Seldom. Got the bearing. Steering two, six, zero. Hey, we just had a report from our group leader about a big bunch of bandits in the area. Stick with us, Little Friend. My crew asked me to make sure you stay with us. For God's sake, stay with us. We're in no shape to face enemy fighters," the bomber pilot pleaded frantically.

"We are going to stay right with you, Robert. Don't worry about the bandits. Just get that ship headed home. You'll make it. We'll make sure you're not bothered by bandits," I replied. I wish I had felt as confident as I sounded. A lump rose in my throat.

The crew of the bomber were busy throwing out everything they could tear loose inside the big ship to lighten their load. Guns, ammunition, boxes, clothing went over the side. They dismantled the lower gun turret and it, too, was soon hurtling toward the ground.

"Okay, Seldom," I called. "Lean back on your mixture. We

are going to have to sweat out our gas on this one. Make every move count. We don't want to waste a single drop of gas."

The bomber was doing a little better now, flying about 150 miles an hour and holding altitude.

Because of the heavy overcast we couldn't see the ground. The enemy gunners had radar, so it was impossible to avoid the flak when we passed over the German cities below.

"Okay, Seldom," I called to the flight, "let's stay out in front of Robert. If the Jerries shoot at us, it will give our Big Friend a chance to skirt around the flak." It was a little hard on our nerves as we were throttled way back in order not to run away from the slow-moving bomber, but it seemed to be working out okay.

It was time to call Larkspur for a new position report. We were so low on gas, we couldn't afford to get off course for a single minute. Larkspur indicated we weren't making much progress. We had encountered a terrific head wind and were gaining a bare eighty miles an hour of ground speed. It meant touch and go with our dwindling fuel supply. I called Robert to change altitude in the hope of avoiding the head winds and told the flight to lean out the fuel mixture still further.

"Hey, Bledsoe!" Novak suddenly yelled. "There's another Fortress at ten o'clock below us. It's smoking and losing altitude and heading back toward Germany."

"I've got him in sight, Kid. You and Chief go down and take a look and see if you can turn him around. But don't go down into the overcast. With bandits and no gas we could all be in trouble."

Jerry gunners had riddled every inch of the Fortress. Two engines were out and it was too damaged to maintain flying speed. Their radio wasn't functioning and we couldn't contact them. The Kid and Chief circled a couple of times and the pilot of the B-17 gave them a dismal wave, indicating they were helpless and were going to ride her down. We assumed there were injured crew members on board who couldn't bail out, and that the pilot was not going to abandon them.

It was sad to watch the crippled ship disappear into the overcast. Those clouds might go right down to the deck and the bomber crew might crash into the ground. It was going to be a rough ride for them.

R for Robert was barely maintaining flying speed. I cautioned the pilot about conserving his fuel. He came back with: "We've got plenty of gas. Our only worry is whether or not yours will hold out. We sure don't want you guys leaving us out here alone."

Ever so slowly we pressed forward, making our way toward the English Channel. I broke silence again to encourage our Big Friend. "Hello, Robert. How're you doing? We'll be hitting the coast soon. Hang in there. We're going to make it okay."

"We're in a little better shape since we jettisoned everything we could get loose. My two engines are strong. We've stopped the tail gunner's bleeding so that's good news. We're all worried about those damned bandits though, so stick with us, Little Friend." He sounded more confident.

We had been with the damaged Fortress for nearly an hour when I sighted a group of bogies at twelve o'clock high. I alerted the flight. R for Robert saw them at about the same time.

"There's the bandits, Seldom," the pilot called. "Fighters at twelve o'clock. See them? Do you see them? EA at twelve o'clock high. Stay with us, Seldom, stay with us!"

"Take it easy, Robert. We're going to be sitting right here beside you until you get home. I think those are P-51s. But we'll be ready for them, whoever they are!" I sounded a lot more optimistic than I felt.

The bogies above us started maneuvering for combat. There were six of them. They were trying to get between us and the sun, which would put them in position for an attack. I knew that once they were ready they'd have the jump on us. Their leader peeled off and they were headed for us like a bolt out of the blue.

"Hold your position, Seldom," I called. "They may be 51s but don't count on it. When they get closer I'll give the signal and we'll turn into them. If they're bandits don't get sucked away from Robert. Let them make their pass but stay with Robert," I ordered.

I shuddered to think what the next few seconds might bring. We were too low on gas for a dog fight. If they were EA, within the next minute somebody was going to be killed. But we were going to protect our bomber.

We turned to meet the bogies head on. An instant later, with a sigh of relief, I recognized the characteristics of the P-51 Mustang. I switched my radio over to fighter frequency. "Seldom to the flight of 51s. What's the idea, you guys? Why the pass!"

"Hi there, Seldom. We thought your flight might be FW-190s playing cat-and-mouse with our Big Friend there. Sorry we upset you. Looks as if that bomber really caught the flak. Can we help?"

"You sure can help," I replied. "We're sweating out our gas. We're almost running on fumes. Can you stay with Robert while we take off for home?"

"Sorry, fella. We've been out here a long time ourselves. We were headed home when we saw you guys. We can't stretch our gas anymore. We can stay with you a minute or two, but that's about it. We heard there were bandits in this area. That's why we started to jump you guys."

"Okay, thanks anyway. We've had the bandit report too but haven't seen any sign of EA. I think we can stay with our Big Friend to landfall out."

The Mustangs stayed with us for several minutes, then dipped their wings in farewell and took off for home. The pilot of the bomber called me again to make sure we were going to stay with him. A little later we could make out a break in the cloud cover below and ahead of us. The weather front seemed to bank up along the coastline of the Continent. For once, England and the Channel were clear. I recognized the coast of Holland. Just then my fuel warning light came on, indicating I had no more than fifteen minutes of flying time left. We were still a long way from home and the water in the Channel below looked cold and menacing.

"Hello, Robert," I called. "Looks as if we've made it out okay. We can't stretch our gas any longer. We have to break off now and head for home. Are you going to land at the first base you come to or try to make it home?"

"My gang wants to land at home. We know where we are now. Our gas supply is okay and it'll only take us a couple of minutes longer to reach home base instead of an English field. How about you? Can you make it okay?"

"I'm not sure how the rest of the flight is fixed for gas, but I can make it. We're sure glad to see you got out as well as you did, Robert. Good luck to all of you!"

When the bomber pilot got back on the radio his voice cracked and quavered with emotion. What he said sent a tingle up my spine. "Before you go, Seldom, my crew says to tell you we all love you guys. We mean it! We owe you plenty. How about meeting you fellows somewhere? We'll throw you the biggest damned party this country ever saw. We've got cause for celebrating. How about it? Let's try and get together."

"Thanks, Robert. Thanks a lot. You don't owe us a thing. We're based at Raydon. My name's Bledsoe. Bring your gang over to our place and the party will be on us. It's been a pleasure. Good luck. We'll see you later." I dipped my wing in salute to our gallant Big Friend.

Heading for home base, I felt like a lioness who had saved her cub. If the EA had found us, they would have had a battle on their hands to get at Robert. Every man in the flight was ready to fight to the death to protect "our bomber."

When we came within sight of our field we made a straight-in approach, no attempt to tighten up formation or buzz the field. We were all sweating out that last ounce of gasoline. We'd been in the air nearly six hours. It had been very close.

As I landed I kept an eye on my rear view mirror. Kid
Novak was behind me, and for me this mission wouldn't be
over until I got on the ground and out of his way. He was
coming in hot, forgetting to let his flaps down. I pulled off the
runway into the dirt, and shook my fist at him as he rolled past
me. He would have rammed me for sure if I hadn't gotten off
the runway.

I ran out of gas just as I was parking my ship.

The day's mission gave me more personal satisfaction than
any of my strafing flights. I had a soft spot—we all did—for
the bomber boys who were forced to face that wall of flak
target without being able to deviate from course to protect
themselves.

By July 13, 1944, in only five weeks' time, I had rolled up so
many combat hours I was near the halfway mark of my
300-hour tour. Blickenstaff was after me to slow down. His
furlough had been delayed and he wanted me to spread my
tour out over the next six months. "I don't want you finishing
up your tour so fast. We'll need you more in the squadron in
the future than we do now, so relax." Doc concurred and gave
me a choice: take a few days off or he would send me to the
"flak home" for a week.

I used the time to visit an English friend stationed at an RAF
base nearby. I had met André Fer at Luke Field, where he had
been sent as a flight instructor on a lend-lease arrangement
between the two countries. He had a pass for the weekend and
invited me to spend a few days at his parents' home. Before
leaving Raydon, I got some things at the PX and made a trip to
the mess hall, where I loaded up with canned goods and fresh
fruit.

I was surprised to find his parents financially well off. They
lived in an imposing two-story house surrounded by rose
gardens. The spacious grounds included a first-class tennis
court. André's father had been a manufacturer and dis-
tributor of photographic equipment. With the German invasion of France and the outbreak of hostilities, the English

government converted his factory to make airplane parts for the British Mosquito bomber.

After the formality of introductions, I gave Mrs. Fer the box of fresh oranges, canned fruit, cooking oil, soap, candy, sugar, and meats. Tears welled in her eyes as she contemplated items she had not seen in years. Mr. Fer seemed just as overwhelmed with the gifts. I had not realized how hard things were for the English.

I spent most of the first day at their house relaxing in a large easy chair and listening to Bing Crosby records. It had been many weeks since I had sat in an easy chair. What a relief to my sore bottom! But the romantic music made me terribly homesick for Harriett and our baby daughter.

The next day a neighbor invited all of us to a rabbit hunt on a nearby farm. The group numbered about fifteen. When the Fer family introduced me as a Thunderbolt pilot, I was warmly received. They honored me by selecting me to be one of two men who would use shotguns in the hunt. The others were armed with clubs. The strategy was to surround a wheatfield that was in the process of being mowed, moving in closer as the size of the standing crop diminished. If a rabbit broke out of the field and escaped from the inside ring of the people with clubs, it was the job of the shooters to bring the rabbit down with the shotgun.

This was not a sporting affair. The hunt was serious business. It meant meat on the table, a rare commodity for English civilians in those days. A miss by the shooter would bring on the wrath of the crowd; not only had he caused someone to miss a rabbit dinner, he had also wasted a precious shotgun shell.

I could feel the pressure mount when the other shooter missed two rabbits in a row. Luckily all four of my shots were good.

The hunt ended with eighteen rabbits bagged. I had expected to give my four rabbits to the Fer family, but instead they were all laid at the feet of the property owner. I didn't understand this turn of events at all.

"Custom, old boy," André explained. "The rabbits belong to the owner of the land. He will dole them out according to need." The Fers were given one rabbit in my honor.

André and his family did everything possible to make my stay pleasant and restful, but I found it impossible to relax. I listened tensely to the first sound of airplanes overhead. After three days I decided to cut my leave short since André had returned to duty.

On my return to the base, I learned that the group had lost several pilots as the result of a couple of rough strafing missions and a big dog fight with the Luftwaffe. A replacement had been killed when his ship crashed on the edge of the field, the second time this month a replacement had been killed right at the base. The new pilots—inexperienced—had tried to peel off too tightly and had stalled into the ground while trying to follow the more experienced pilots in a rat-race landing pattern.

Those few days off, along with a couple of days of heavy rain that kept us grounded when I first got back, made it seem a long time since I had been in combat. With the shortage of pilots, Blick didn't object to putting me on the schedule as soon as it was possible. At the briefing I learned it would be a strafing mission. This meant we'd be down on the deck and those ground gunners would be lying in wait for us! The latrine called again.

I was to lead the second section of Seldom Squadron. The Little Princess was still out of commission, waiting for parts, so I would fly a spare ship that had just come out of the shop. When I tested the controls, I felt that something about the plane was not right. After checking and rechecking everything I could think of, I couldn't discover anything wrong with it. I began to think I was getting my own case of combat colic.

We were busy dodging the flak over the enemy coastline when my radio went dead. I tinkered with it but couldn't get it to work. Then I felt the ship slow down. I was losing power. I fell back, behind the rest of the group. Since I couldn't communicate with them because of the defective radio, the seven pilots following me proceeded to throttle back, figuring I had spotted something and was getting ready to make a let-down. They didn't know I was looking around for a level spot to make an emergency landing should my engine fail completely.

Moments later, my radio suddenly came back on and once again I had full power. I checked every electrical switch in the cockpit. Everything seemed to be functioning properly. My sixth sense told me to turn around and go home while I had the chance, but I was anxious to log more combat time.

An hour later, we were in the target area. I made a pass at a locomotive racing down the railroad track. I tried to ignore the flak bursting all around me as I lined myself up for the kill. The picture of my bullets tearing through the locomotive was in my mind. I squeezed the trigger. Instead of pouring a burst of bullets out, my guns malfunctioned, my radio went dead, and I lost power again. The mechanism connected to my guns had overloaded an already faulty electrical system.

I was down on the deck with just enough power to maintain level flight! I used the speed from my dive on the train to gain a little altitude, managing to level off at four hundred feet.

I was in a bad spot. I was several hundred miles from my home base, over enemy territory, and unable to maneuver away from the heavy flak coming my way.

Damn fool, you should have gone home when you lost power the first time.

I salvoed my bombs and my belly tank to lighten my load and decided to head for the emergency strip on the beachhead.

I gave hand signals to my element leader and my wingman indicating radio trouble and that I was heading out. I made them understand my wingman was to escort me home while the rest of the section was to stick with Jonah.

I spent the next ten minutes fighting to hold the ship in the air. I skirted around areas where I thought flak guns might be located. I prayed the Luftwaffe was on the ground today and not in the skies looking for trouble; if bandits showed up now I'd be a sitting duck.

Suddenly my radio was working and once again I had full power! What was going on? I advanced my throttle and had climbed to about five thousand feet when I heard the boys from my section talking. They were attacking a large convoy of enemy trucks and tanks.

I told myself to forget it, to get about 25,000 feet of sky under me and get home before this bird conked out again. But I was high enough to check things over without danger. If everything worked, I could get in on the shooting. If it didn't, I was also high enough to make it home.

I squeezed the trigger and my guns worked perfectly. I tried twice more and felt the ship buck as my guns fired. *Do it again.* I squeezed off another short burst.

I turned my radio off and on. It seemed to be working okay. "Seldom Blue Leader here. Can you read me, Blue Two?" I called to my wingman.

"Loud and clear, Blue Leader. What's up?" Davis responded.

"Just a little electrical problem. It's okay now. Let's join the rest of the squadron."

We could see the smoke rising from where our guys were shooting up the enemy convoy. On the way to the area, I spotted a train speeding for a tunnel. I zeroed in and left it a twisted mass of rubble. I found another locomotive on the other side of the tunnel. I lined up for my pass, squeezed the trigger—and my guns failed to fire.

My stupidity in not going home at the first power failure could now keep me from ever getting home at all.

Waving to my wingman, I turned around and headed for the emergency strip on the beachhead. Fifteen minutes later I was just holding my own, limping out of enemy territory with reduced power.

Then I saw a large truck and trailer escorted by German

mechanized units. They were trying to keep out of the sight of roving American pilots by using a back road. A huge cannon was mounted on the trailer, the largest gun I had ever seen. It was camouflaged with large tree limbs that blended in with the other trees on the country road.

Destroying that mammoth gun could be a prize kill.

I'd give a month's pay to have the Little Princess right now. Come on, Davis, get that gun!

Davis hadn't seen the convoy and couldn't understand my hand signals when I tried to indicate he should attack the truck pulling the massive cannon. This was only his second mission and he couldn't be expected to understand. I decided I'd make a pass at the truck, and maybe Davis would get the message and blast them.

I gave him more hand signals to indicate he was to follow me and strafe a target below. He shook his head to show he didn't understand, but I could see him get ready to follow me down. He was right behind me when I made my gunnery pass. The trucks were loaded with enemy soldiers who jumped off the vehicles and hugged the ground when they saw us coming.

I passed over the huge gun and to my dismay saw that Davis was not firing his guns. I pulled up and made the best turn I could with the little power I had in my engine. I made a few more hand signals at Davis and went down on the cannon again. Davis was right behind me. When he failed to fire a second time, even when the Germans shot at us, I decided to forget it and make my way to the beachhead.

As I was contemplating a landing at the emergency strip my electrical system began functioning properly, and once again I had plenty of power. This time I wasn't taking any chances. I headed upstairs and climbed until I reached fifteen thousand feet. Now I had plenty of altitude to get over the English Channel.

After we had landed at home base, I asked Davis why he hadn't shot at the convoy. He blushed in embarrassment.

"I didn't know what you wanted me to do. I didn't realize

your guns weren't working. Did you see those Germans shooting at us the second time we went over them? I can kick myself for not letting them have it."

I checked with the crew chief of the ship I had flown and was not surprised to learn it was Novak who had given it a test flight. He said Kid had mentioned some kind of electrical malfunction but hadn't considered it serious enough to be reported.

When I saw Novak in the ready room I was ready to chew him out. He had been flying in the second flight of my section as Rafferty's wingman. During debriefing he was still so excited about shooting up the enemy convoy. I didn't have a chance to get a word in. Davis mentioned passing up a chance to destroy the big cannon and Novak went out of his way to speak to me. "I sure wish I'd been along, Bledsoe. I'd given those Heinies a dose of lead poisoning. You wouldn't have had to make hand signals to me. Hell, I'd have given them a burst for both of us."

I couldn't chew out somebody who was talking like that. "I wish you'd been along too, Kid," I said. "That was the biggest cannon you ever laid eyes on." I had to say something to him about what had happened. "By the way, you test flew that ship I had. Did you have any problems with the electrical system?"

"Yeah. Funny thing," Novak said innocently, "for an instant the radio went out and then I lost power. Since everything started working okay again, I didn't think it was very important. Maybe I should have written it up in the Form Five, huh?"

I nodded. "I always make it a point to report any kind of problem or strange incident, just to keep the record straight," I said, trying not to sound like an instructor chewing out a student. "Write it down, is my motto. It also puts the next guy on notice."

"Not a bad idea. I'll make it a point from now on," Novak said.

"Yeah, Kid—please do that."

We awoke the next morning to learn the weather was expected to be so bad over the Continent that we might not fly over enemy territory for several days. Doc approached me and asked like an excited schoolboy if I would take him up in the Piper Cub and let him do the flying. Blick and a couple of other pilots had given him some flight instruction in the small aircraft. He wanted to get in some more practice, if I'd take time to ride with him.

"All you have to do is go along for the ride. I'll do the flying," Doc kidded. "The weather around the base is good enough to fly the Cub." He was so eager, I couldn't turn him down even though I wanted to spend more time in the sack.

Doc was at the controls as we taxied out to the runway. He appeared to know what he was doing as we lined up for takeoff, so I decided to let him go all the way. "Go ahead and take off, Doc. You're the pilot of this outfit."

"Hey, wait a minute, I've never taken off by myself before. I've followed through on the controls, but I never actually took off on my own."

"You can do it."

"Well, okay, but be ready to help if need be," Doc said as he started rolling down the runway. The little Cub was easy to fly and I knew it would take off from the ground almost by itself. All Doc had to do was keep it straight and give it some throttle. When it got going fast enough it would leap off the ground and we'd be airborne. Doc fairly glowed as we climbed away from the field.

We flew around the countryside for about an hour before we decided to call it a day. When we neared the field, Doc yelled over the roar of the engine: "I've never tried a landing before, Marv. How about letting me take her in and you follow through on the controls?"

"Forget it, Doc. I'm not following through on any controls. I'm just along for the ride, remember? It's up to you to get this bird down on the ground, unless you want to stay up here forever. You're doing okay. Just cut your throttle, glide down to the runway, hold it about five feet off the ground, and it'll land itself. All you have to do is keep it straight and not level off too high. There's nothing to it, so get going."

Doc made a good approach and landed without using much of our long runway. I reached over and pushed the throttle forward. "What the hell are you doing?" Doc demanded.

"Just giving us enough power to take off again. That was such a lousy landing I want you to practice a few more," I replied—instructor to student. Doc grinned and made his way around the field to come in for another landing. We repeated it a half-dozen times.

Doc really wanted to fly by himself. We both knew I could step out of the airplane and he could solo. We also knew it was strictly against regulations. If some eager-beaver saw us and reported Doc at the controls of a military aircraft, even a little Piper Cub, we both could be court-martialed.

On the ground, I congratulated him on his flying. "But why not fly the AT-6, Doc?" The advanced trainer was kept on the base as a utility plane. "You'd get a lot more fun out of flying that than you would the Cub. It has all the flying characteristics of a fighter plane."

"God, I'd really like a chance to fly that," Doc replied excitedly. "Blick let me handle the controls once when we were on a cross-country, but I was in the back seat and couldn't see where I was going. Nobody around here knows how to fly it from the back seat, so I guess I'm out of luck."

I understood what he was talking about. In the rear seat of the AT-6 the forward visibility was nil. Very few pilots, other than instructors, could fly the airplane from the back seat, much less check out a novice like Doc, who'd be flying from the front seat.

"Wake up, Doc. Don't you remember what Novak has been saying? I'm a goddamn instructor. I've logged a thousand hours flying the AT-6 from the back seat. Let's go. I've had worse students than you try to spin me in."

Doc was as pleased as a kid. As we taxied toward the runway, he waved at everyone in sight. Ground crews and some of the pilots on hand looked in awe when they saw him sitting in the front seat and in control of the airplane.

Doc was a natural pilot. Within minutes, he had the feel of the new ship and was having the time of his life. I had him shoot a few landings and never touched the controls. All I had to do was give him instructions over the intercom. The pleasure he got from flying this hot ship more than paid for my loss of sack time.

That night, sitting in our Nissen hut, Doc was still talking about his day's experience with the AT-6. Parker came in for a visit and Doc went out of his way to brag about it taking "a goddamn instructor like Bledsoe" to be able to fly the plane from the back seat. He knew he was needling Parker as he kept praising instructors.

Parker had downed a couple of shots of Scotch and was feeling the effects. "Bledsoe can't fly any better than the worst junior birdman," he brayed. "If I ever get him into the air with me, I'll auger him into the deck!"

I couldn't figure the guy out. I'd never done anything to draw such resentment. Was he trying to pick a fight? It was so childish I decided to use ridicule instead of getting involved in a needless brawl.

"Parker, I'm too scared to be in the same sky with a hot shot like you. I'll hide on the ground every time I see you take off. I'd sure hate to have you auger me into the ground."

This brought snickers of amusement from some of the other pilots. Parker got the drift. Not being sure what to do next, he started muttering more silly threats.

"Knock it off and go to bed, Parker," Rafferty snapped. "You're making a fool of yourself."

Even Kid Novak got into the act. I was surprised to hear him come to my defense. "Bledsoe's not like a lot of those instructors in flying school, Park."

That was too much for Parker. "I'm not going to let this son-of-a-bitch make fun of me and get away with it. He can't talk to me like that," he fumed.

I could put up with Parker's nonsense, but it made me see red to have the joker swear at me. I sprang off my bunk and started toward him. Doc and Rafferty grabbed me before I could get to him.

"Parker, shut your mouth and get out of here before we let Bledsoe loose. He'll knock your teeth down your throat," Doc hollered, wheeling Parker outside the door while Rafferty sat on me. Doc was mad. "The damn fool. The goddamned fool. Won't he ever wise up?"

Doc's reaction cooled me off. "Forget it, Doc," I said. "He's just not grown up yet. The guy is a juvenile. Let's consider the source and let it go at that. It's not worth worrying about."

Kid Novak explained that Parker especially did not like me because he thought Blickenstaff favored me since we were roommates in flying school. Parker couldn't wait for Willie Price to get back from the States and take over as operations officer when Blick went on leave. Park claimed Price would have me flying tail-end Charlie. The Kid laughed at the thought.

A few days later, Rafferty and I were selected to represent the squadron on a London radio program to be broadcast live to the States. Harriett would be notified in advance so she could listen. Hearing my voice was one sure way of letting her know I was still okay. By the time any of my letters reached her in California, there was always the possibility that I might not still be alive.

I was to tell about the importance of being properly briefed before going out on a mission. Though we had been warned to stick to the script, I couldn't keep myself from blurting out, "And if my beautiful wife Harriett is listening, I want her to know I always take the straightest and quickest way home from the target." Everybody smiled; nobody said a word to me about it.

It was our first visit to London, so Rafferty and I decided to look around after the broadcast.

As we made our way back to the hotel, we passed through Picadilly Circus, the theater and restaurant center of London.

I don't know where they got the name, but they were right about it being a circus. The sidewalk was wall-to-wall people. American soldiers were milling about everywhere. So were hundreds of prostitutes.

I had heard something about this from one of our "groundpounders." He was always bragging about his sexual exploits—if you could call them that—with the London whores. With a wife and kids at home, his grimy tales didn't make him very popular.

I had found it hard to believe some of his stories, but now I was seeing it first hand. If anything, he had understated things.

Rafferty and I made our way through the mass of people. Army MPs tried to keep the crowd moving, but it took several minutes to negotiate a single block. In that time we were continually propositioned by streetwalkers. " 'Ow about going 'ome with me, Yank? Only eight pounds for the evening," was their usual approach.

Many soldiers were grabbing any female within reach, and it wasn't one-sided. Three girls walked toward us, looking for customers. Quick as a cobra, one of them flicked out her hand and grabbed the front of my pants, playfully trying to open them. I almost jumped six feet. She laughed at my discomfiture and made a remark about "the goddamn Yanks and their zips."

It was late afternoon, night was falling fast. The prostitutes and soldiers didn't take long to pair up and depart the scene. As the crowd thinned out the remaining girls became bolder. They were openly inviting one and all to have a "quickie" in the nearest doorway.

Rafferty and I shook our heads in disbelief. As we walked along the street, we could see the forms of men and women, half-standing, half-lying, in almost every storefront doorway along the way. Others were copulating while standing, uncaring about being observed.

We were propositioned by teenagers and by weary-looking women in their forties. The younger girls used the pitch that they had never done this before but needed money for some emergency. The older women were blunt. "Don't waste your money on those young bitches, Yank. I've been in this business a long time and really know how to show you a good time. I've got some angles you'll really enjoy, Yank, and I'll give you back your money if you ain't satisfied!"

Later, when we returned to our base, I tried—and failed —to describe the scene to one of the fellows who had never been to London. He would have to go to Picadilly Circus and see for himself.

CHAPTER 12

Esprit de Corps

Another fighter mission was scheduled on July 31, 1944. Again it would be targets of opportunity. The ceiling was down on the deck when we took off but we broke through the overcast at 2,500 feet with the entire squadron still in formation. Wonder of wonders! We were doing much better as a unit since the younger pilots had started taking pride in their flying. They seemed to have given up all thought of taking the job of flight leader away from former instructors. Our latest replacements caught the new spirit right away. They were eager to learn and looked to the instructors for guidance. That attitude made everyone try to improve his flying ability. The squadron had come a long way in the past couple of weeks.

I never got over the strangeness of taking off in miserable weather, skimming along the ground, climbing into the solid overcast, and then breaking through the clouds above only minutes later to find the sun shining brightly. It wasn't unusual to return to home base sunburned, especially from a bomber escort mission when we flew for hours above the clouds in the bright sunlight.

Major Douglas Winfield was leading the group with Seldom Squadron. I was leading his second section with Novak on my wing. The layer of clouds spread over the Continent as far as the eye could see. The overcast was so thick it was impossible to find our assigned target area, so Winfield decided to take the group down through the first hole he could find.

The moment we broke under the cloud cover, I spotted the telltale sign of a locomotive. I could see a small spiral of gray smoke making its way up through the sea of haze that covered the ground.

"Seldom Red Leader here, Jonah. Got a target at one o'clock. Let's get that train, Red Flight," I called over the radio. I peeled off from the rest of the group with the other boys in Red Flight trailing behind me. The engineer in the locomotive saw us coming. He and his fireman bailed out of the cab and tumbled into the field alongside the track. I delayed my pass long enough for them to get in the clear and then came in for the kill.

The engineer wasn't the only one on the train who saw us coming. The Germans had placed flak gunners on the train and they were throwing 20-millimeter shells at us as fast as their guns could shoot.

"Kid, those Jerry gunners are on a flatcar in the center of the train. See if you can pick them off while I knock out the engine." I dove in and brought a cloud of steam from the hot locomotive racing down the track without benefit of engineer or fireman.

Novak was right on my tail and poured another burst of bullets in for good measure. He was too intent on helping shoot up the locomotive to pay any attention to the flak gunners. The steam was rolling high into the sky and the destroyed engine was grinding to a halt by the time we made our circle.

The Jerry gunners were still pumping away at us with their guns but fortunately weren't doing any damage. My flight had made a successful pass on the target without any of our planes being hit.

I made a turn to the right and came bearing down with my guns blazing away at the flatcar where the enemy gunners were positioned. They fired a long burst at me, then gave it up as too risky and dove headfirst off the flatcar. I could see them hiding alongside another car so I gave Novak the word.

"Yippee!" the Kid yelled over the radio as he fired at the spot where the gunners were hiding. His yell brought a grin to my face. I knew he was having a good time. The rest of the flight and I worked the train over. We all hoped a few stray bullets might find their way into the Jerries' hiding place. We bore a personal grudge against all flak gunners.

I searched the area for more locomotives with no success. I did see a long string of oil cars parked on a small track siding. They looked innocent, right out there in broad daylight with no attempt at camouflage. Undoubtedly they were empty, I thought, but we might as well knock them off.

"Bledsoe here. Let's go down on these oil cars straight ahead of us. I'll take the one on the left end, Kid, you take the next one, and the rest of the flight pick the next ones in line. We'll pick them off on a one-for-one basis, going right down the line. Keep an eye out for EA. We don't want any surprises down here.

I checked my tail and looked around to make sure no enemy aircraft were lurking in the area to pounce on us while we were strafing. I made my pass, gave the end car a short burst, and almost jumped out of the cockpit in surprise when it exploded, sending smoke and blue-white flame soaring into the sky. The cars were full! As the rest of the boys passed over, I looked back to see we had four precious oil cars in flames.

"Nice shooting, Red Flight. Keep your spacing and we'll take care of those other cars. Watch your tails for bandits!" I warned. This was no time to forget about the Luftwaffe.

"Oh, happy day," Novak sang out as he blew up his second oil tanker. "Hitler's going to give somebody hell for this little party."

The Kid was right. Gasoline and oil were the Nazi's most precious commodities. In a few minutes we had reduced the long string of oil cars to rubble. Heavy black smoke was pouring a thousand feet into the overcast above.

"Hey, who shot up the oil tankers?" Winfield queried.

"Seldom Red Flight, Jonah," I replied.

"You guys seem to be having yourselves a time. Any more need working over? We haven't found much to shoot at," Winfield said.

"No help needed here, Jonah. That's the end of the oil tankers," I responded, proud of what our flight had accomplished so quickly.

We continued our quest for more targets of opportunity. The radio came to life with chatter. Jockey Squadron had found an enemy airdrome and had gone down to knock out some parked German aircraft. They were running into trouble and we could hear them yelling over the radio.

"Flak! Flak! Somebody get those goddamn flak gunners!" an excited pilot called,

"Jesus Christ, did you see that guy plow into the ground? Who was it?"

"That was my wingman, Candy," came the reply. "He went straight in. Those dirty bastards must have killed him in the air. He made no attempt to pull out."

"Hey, I just found a couple of ME-109s parked under those trees. Somebody help me shoot them up!"

"Blue Three here. I just caught a direct hit in my engine. Oil's getting all over me. I've got to get out of here," an element leader cried.

"Come on, let's blow this firetrap! Hit the deck, you guys, hit the deck. Those flak guns are going to nail us," another yelled.

"Help! This is Blue Four. My ship's shot to hell. I need help!

Somebody escort me home. I'm pulling out."

Jockey Squadron had run into a hot spot that made hitting our targets seem like childs play.

"Jonah here. Everybody out. Come on, show's over, we're pulling out," Winfield called.

I started to join Winfield when Novak suddenly pulled off my wing, streaking for the ground. He started making quick passes at a steam shovel and truck that were doing some work in a field below. "What's going on, Kid?" I called.

"It looks to me like these guys are building an airstrip for the goddamn Germans and besides, one of them took a shot at me," he replied.

The operator of the steam shovel jumped from his machine and took out across the field, running as fast as his legs would carry him. A burst from Novak's guns knocked him high into the air. "You'll never shoot anyone again!" Novak called.

"This is Jonah. Pull out, you guys," Winfield said as he passed overhead.

A moment later the Kid was back on the radio again. "Hey, Bledsoe, this is Novak. I see two more locomotives about ten miles away. Let's get 'em."

"Okay, Kid. Go after them. We'll be right behind you. Come on, Red Flight," I called.

"This is Jonah again. Bledsoe: get your flight home. I've had a report the oranges are sour as hell and are expected to get worse. Forget about those trains," Winfield ordered.

"Okay, Jonah. We'll join up with you in a few minutes. Novak's hot on the trail of those two trains and we'll have the job done in no time at all." I knew it would be all right to get in these few last licks. Flight leaders usually ran their own show when out looking for targets of opportunity.

Novak dove on one of the trains and hit it dead center, but the engine was cold and brought no steam. I clobbered the other locomotive, then discovered some water tanks that looked for sure as if they were strategic watering points for the trains in the area.

"Bledsoe here, Red Flight. Let's shoot up those water tanks at one o'clock. That could cause another headache for old Adolf."

"Goddamn it, Bledsoe. You get your flight out of there! That's an order," Winfield said.

"Roger, Jonah. We'll be right with you."

I was flying about fifty feet off the ground and started firing at one of the water tanks. At the bullets' first impact water started spewing out of the holes. I held my finger on the trigger and the tank disintegrated. Both tanks completely disappeared as we pressed our attack. Those eight 50-caliber machine guns we carried really packed a wallop.

My last burst emptied the right bank of guns and caused the ship to be pulled off course a little while my left bank was still firing. The bullets riddled the small railroad station and the station building seemed to jump up and down as my bullets hit home. I hoped no one was inside. I didn't want to kill any civilians.

I was getting ready to pull out and join the rest of the squadron when I saw an automobile tearing down a dirt road a short distance off to our left. Targets seemed to be appearing out of nowhere. I wobbled my wings to catch Novak's attention. When he pulled up alongside I signaled toward the speeding car.

The men in the car saw us coming. They jumped out, turning end over end as they rolled along the ground. The car swerved out into the field and came to a stop, undamaged. I don't know why, but instinct told me we shouldn't shoot the men or the car. "Hold your fire, Red Flight," I yelled.

It must have been mental telepathy. Instead of hitting the brush as the enemy invariably did, the men picked themselves off the road and started waving their caps. French Maquis. I brought the flight back over them, waving my wings in salute. The Kid, like a damn fool, did a slow roll not ten feet over their heads. That really got the Frenchmen excited and they kept waving at us till we were out of sight.

'Jonah here. What are you talking about, Bledsoe? What's that French Maquis crap? For the last time, you get your fanny headed for home. Larkspur reports the weather is closing in fast!" Winfield sounded mad. I'd probably get a little chewing out when we got back to home base. But I hadn't been able to resist the temptation.

"Roger, Jonah. Red Flight joining up now. Okay, boys, close it up," I called, signaling them to tack onto my wing and pour on the throttle so we could catch up with Winfield.

Jockey Squadron was having difficulty as a result of the shooting spree over the enemy airdrome. "I've got gas and oil all over me. What'll I do?" cried one pilot.

"Which way to the beachhead? I'm never going to get this ship home. I've got to make an emergency landing. Somebody lead me to the beachhead!" another begged.

One after another, the Jockey pilots reported battle damage. That pilot whose ship was spewing fuel was near panic. "Help me, somebody! I'll never make it home. My ship is covered with oil and it's liable to catch fire. My instruments are all shot up. I can't read them. For Christ's sake, somebody help me!"

Jonah kept repeating instructions to him on the course to the beachhead, pleading with the pilot to keep his head. But the poor guy was panic-stricken.

"For God's sake, shut up. We can't help you!" someone blurted. "You're on your own, just like the rest of us!"

I felt sorry for the battered pilot, but he wasn't the only one in trouble. His monopoly of the radio was jeopardizing other pilots. It was getting late, we were all low on gasoline, and we needed to organize our withdrawal. It was not time to tie up the radio. None of us could crawl into that cockpit with him or pull him to safety. The only way we could help him was to work our way to the beachhead and protect him from flak and enemy aircraft.

The worst danger in tying up the radio lay in being bounced by EA. The Jerries could sneak up on us and shoot down two or three of our pilots before anyone could sound the warning. Cluttering up the radio could cause someone else's death.

"Jonah here. The beachhead is just a few miles away. The rest of you guys go on home. How you making out, Jockey?" Winfield asked.

"I don't know, Jonah. I'm soaked to the skin with oil. Jesus, but I hope my ship doesn't catch fire." He seemed more in control of himself.

Larkspur was reporting from England. "Oranges are getting sour. To all pilots, oranges are getting sour." His emphasis made us realize we were going to be bucking really bad weather. As we turned toward England we saw the weather front looming up like a brick wall.

"Close it up, boys, and hang on tight!" a flight leader called to his straggling flyers.

I got a fix on my position from Larkspur and signaled for my flight to tighten up formation. I was going to start my letdown early to make sure we'd be over the Channel when we broke underneath the clouds. I didn't relish letting down over the ground and running into a building or a barrage balloon.

The forbidding weather seemed to drift into the cockpit and place parts of the clouds between me and my instrument panel, making it difficult for me to read the dials. It was a case of combat nerves again, and I had trouble concentrating on my weather flying. I relaxed a little when I heard Jonah congratulate the oil-soaked pilot on a safe landing at the beachhead.

Thank God, he made it.

I took a glance over my right shoulder and could barely make out the outline of Novak's wing tucked in next to mine. It was sobering to realize there were two other ships behind Novak. They were flying off my instruments, yet I couldn't see them myself. Nor could they see me. Each of them had to hang onto the guy in front and hope the leader would get safely through the weather front.

At the 200-foot mark, I flattened out and started praying

for a break in the overcast. I continued my letdown, ever so slowly. We were getting too close to the ground, or to the water, to breathe easily. My altimeter showed one hundred feet and I was still on the way down, with the other guys hanging on tight. An instant later, the clouds thinned and I could see the choppy water of the English Channel.

The fog and haze obliterated everything but the heavy overcast above and the churning sea below. Visibility was only a few hundred feet. The clouds merged with the water; it was the worst weather I had ever encountered.

Even so, the Kid had a grin on his face as we leveled out over the water. The other two pilots gave hand signals to indicate everything was okay with them. A thrill of pride swept over me when they gave me reassuring looks that seemed to say: "Lead the way. We count on you to get us home."

We raced across the Channel in formation, with the tail-end ship a bare twenty feet above the water. Even then, the overcast was so low that it seemed the top of my canopy was in the clouds.

Our fuel supply was diminishing rapidly. My only choice was to aim for the English coast, quickly orient my position, and hope we could find home base without a moment's delay. It was useless to try to get a radio position fix; I could hear a dozen pilots calling Larkspur trying to find out where they were. The group would probably be scattered all over England before the mission was completed.

As the coastline came in sight, I checked my map. I guessed we were about forty miles south of course. I made a slow turn to make sure the boys could maneuver with me and headed north. Our base was located in a Y between the rivers Stour and Orwell. I was looking for the confluence of the rivers at Harwich.

A few minutes passed and I hit the inlet like a homing pigeon. But now we had to sweat out the barrage balloons the British often put up over Ipswich. The steel cables that anchored the balloons were as much of a danger to us as anything we could have expected from the enemy.

In this foul weather it would be impossible to see the cables until it was too late. They could shear our wings off like giant razor blades. But anticipating low-flying friendly aircraft in the area, the balloons had been pulled down and the cables were no problem.

I headed inland, estimating it would take about three minutes to get to the field. We had to hedgehop, sliding and skirting obstacles on the ground, but the only alternative was the overcast.

My guess on the time was off, but only by fifteen seconds. My calculation as to direction had been perfect. Now if I could just make the turn and get into landing position without losing sight of the field in this lousy weather, we'd by okay.

"This stuff is too thick to make any kind of a pattern," I called to the flight. "Watch your positions and we'll peel off to the right and come straight in for a landing. Keep close to the field."

Ground crews were lighting flares to help the returning pilots find the runway through the soup. Just as I got into position and was settling down for my final approach, another flight broke through the fog right in front of me. My wheels and flaps were down, making it difficult to do much maneuvering to get out of their way. I chopped my throttle and pushed forward on the stick, letting them pass overhead. I could see the startled look on the leader's face when he realized how close we were. A midair collision fifty feet off the ground would have been sure death for both of us.

Seconds later I was touching down on the runway, keeping a watchful eye on Kid Novak who was right behind me and landing a little long. He'd ram me for sure if I didn't get out of the way. I poured on the throttle and kicked my ship out into the grassy area on the side of the runway. None too soon. Novak came sailing by, his brakes smoking as he tried to stop before he ran out of runway.

I was relieved to see my flight on the ground. As we taxied into the parking area, I could hear Winfield on the radio, "Jonah here. Land anywhere you can set down. This stuff is too thick to fool around in. This is Jonah, men. Get on the ground at first opportunity. Land at any base you find." I could see several of our planes dart over the field, attempt to turn around to come in for a landing, only to lose sight of the runway and become totally lost in the pea soup. Most of our pilots would have to land at other fields, wait for the fog to lift, and then come home.

As I saw and heard the planes floundering in the weather, flown by pilots not able to instrument fly with any confidence, I remembered my old boss at Luke Field telling me to pass students whether they were proficient or not. I wished he were up there on the wing of one of those students.

In the ready room, it was confirmed that the oil-spattered Jockey pilot had landed okay at the emergency strip on the beachhead. Another Jockey pilot was not so lucky. His engine quit over the Channel and he had to bail out into the freezing water. The weather was so bad the other pilots in his flight couldn't look for him. They didn't even know if his chute opened. All they saw or heard was, "My engine just quit. I'm going over the side!" It would be all over for him if he wasn't picked up immediately by the rescue boats.

Jockey Squadron claimed three ME-109s, but had lost three men. One man for each enemy ship was too high a price. If the mission had been rough for us, it had been a disaster for Jockey.

Novak was so excited he didn't cool off for hours. "Man, did we give that Hitler hell! Best goddamn mission I've been on. Old Bledsoe had us shooting up everything in sight. Most fun I've ever had!" The Kid sounded drunk with excitement.

Rafferty teased Novak about Bledsoe being "a goddamned instructor," throwing the Kid's own words back at him. Novak brushed the barbs off like lint, and proceeded to defend me!

"He didn't want to be an instructor. He wasn't like those other chickenshit guys. You said so yourself, Rafferty. I'm sorry I ever included either of you with the no-good bastards. You're both good guys. But I still hate those other S.O.B.s."

I went to bed feeling rewarded that Kid Novak was at long last happy to be my wingman. Doc and Blick were also pleased. It was the beginning of the end of the civil war between the younger pilots and the former instructors.

The bad weather hung on and was predicted to be so lousy we were ordered to stand down for a couple of days of rest. This became an excuse for some of the guys to throw a base party. They planned to truck in a hundred girls. From the rumors flying around I gathered it was going to be a real orgy.

Rafferty and a couple of other married men from his hut joined Doc and me for a stag party of our own. We gathered in our Nissen hut with a supply of "combat rations" and reminisced about home and loved ones. After three stiff drinks, I could feel my nerves relax. The booze and the warmth of the pot-bellied stove made us all forget how soon we would again face death in the sky.

By midnight, we were ready for something to eat and decided to head for the officer's club where a large buffet had been laid on. As we stepped outside our room, we heard female voices from the hut next door. We opened the door a crack to look inside, and in the semidarkness saw a naked girl leave the bed of one man and climb into the bed of another.

"Come on in, there's room for all," the nude girl giggled when she saw us. "Sure, and there's plenty of ass to go around," another laughed as she raised her head up out of a bed.

"By God, if they come in they'll have to wait their turns," her bed partner yelled. I recognized the voice—one of the groundpounders, a married man with two kids at home.

"Don't forget your VD lectures!" I yelled as we retreated; it was the best comment I could think of after those drinks.

Some loud laughs and vulgar comments followed us out the door.

We left the road and took a shortcut through a barley field to the club. Along the way, we came across several "love nests" in the barley occupied by our guys and the English whores. They didn't even look up.

Entering the club was like coming into a skid-row poolroom, flophouse and saloon combined. The air reeked of smoke as usual—doors and windows were always closed to conform with blackout orders—and also of spilled beer, whiskey, cheap perfume, and sweaty bodies.

There must have been fifty men from our outfit and even more women, and they were real tough-looking females; no ladies here. They all seemed jammed together in a moist heap. There wasn't a sober soul in the place. (Of course, neither were we.)

"Jesus, Doc, I've never laid eyes on anything like this," Rafferty said. "I can't see the attraction. These women are real dogs."

"If you think this looks bad, wait a while," Doc replied. "This orgy will go on all night and most of tomorrow, or I'll miss my guess."

We were backing for the door when a woman threw her arms around Rafferty and suggested they find an empty bed so she could do her patriotic duty. Rafferty flinched. "Get the hell away from me! I'm not interested."

Once we were outside, the experience at the club had sobered us up just enough to take the glow off our own get-together, so we agreed our party was over and it was time to get some sleep. I went to bed.

Two hours later, I was awakened by voices and sounds of activity across the aisle from my bunk. The girls from the hut next door had worked their way into our hut. One of them came up to me, offering to "serve her country." I declined. Somebody else shouted, "Hey, for Christ's sake. Turn off the noise. I'm trying to get some sleep. I don't mind you making a whorehouse out of the place, but be quiet about it!"

On our way to the mess hall the next morning, Rafferty reported the same thing had gone on in his hut. "It was one big nightmare. These two naked bitches crawled from one bed to another. It was so dark they had to feel their way around the hut. Half the guys turned them down and I'm damned if I can understand the guys that took them on. They couldn't even see them."

"Maybe that's why," I said.

At one breakfast table, we found three bleary-eyed girls taking advantage of the free food. They were plastered with makeup, stank of stale perfume, and looked grotesque. "How would you like to wake up sober and find something like that in bed with you?" Doc asked. "There're going to be a lot of sad guys around here today, fighting a hangover and seeing how these chippies look in broad daylight."

One girl was straddling a bench, her dress pulled up over her thighs. Her legs were dirty, and she was totally unconcerned about exposing herself.

"That's enough to make me puke," Rafferty exclaimed. "Let's get out of here." Doc and I agreed.

I was surprised that the CO would countenance such a wild affair. He must have thought it was a good way for the guys to let off steam. Personally, I would rather have faced the flak than those broads.

"If you think we had a wild party, you ought to attend one of the bashes they throw at the bomber bases," one of the old hands remarked later. "Flight crews can go for several days before it's time to fly a mission, so some of their parties last a whole week."

At about the time the hangovers ended so had the bad weather. Within a matter of hours those same guys were out of one saddle and into another, headed for a dive-bombing mission in France. Winfield was leading the group with our squadron and I was heading his second section again.

We cruised around our assigned area for a couple of hours

with no action. Second Lieutenant Harold Pasley spoke up: "Red Flight, let's drop our babies on those old boxcars in that siding at two o'clock. I can't find anything else."

We made a slight circle as Pasley's flight peeled off toward the boxcars and hit. Suddenly there was a tremendous blast. The whole sky lit up for miles around.

"Jesus Christ! Did you see that? I damn near got blown to bits," Pasley said.

"Looked as if the whole cockeyed world blew up. I wonder what we hit?" his wingman chimed in. "There's not even a splinter left down there."

"Jonah, here," Winfield called. "You hit the jackpot. Those boxcars were filled with ammunition. Nice going, but join up now. It's time to go home. Okay, everybody out, we're heading for the barn."

As we closed up, it seemed to me that Winfield was heading in the wrong direction. He was pointed at Le Havre, a major port, which bristled with antiaircraft guns. He leveled off at a thousand feet, with the rest of the group bunched up behind him. This would make us a peachy target for the flak gunners. I was already sweating out that first burst.

"Come on, man. Let's get some altitude. We're going to get our fannies shot off stooging along like this," a voice blurted over the radio. I recognized it as Chief's. He was almost through with his tour and his nerves were strung out tight.

"Jonah here. Who's squawking?" Winfield asked angrily.

Chief didn't identify himself but came right back on the radio. "We'd better get some sky under us, Jonah. These lousy Germans will shoot our ass off at this altitude!" Chief had the whole outfit nervous by now. My wingman closed in next to me and gave a hand signal indicating he, too, would like a little more altitude.

Winfield blew his stack. "Stay off this radio unless you've got something to report. I'm leading this group, not you, and you better not forget it." The firm confidence of his voice quieted everybody down.

In a few minutes we were in sight of the coastline. My God, I thought, we really were heading right toward Le Havre.

It was a ticklish situation. Winfield had chewed the Chief out for suggesting we get more altitude, and now I wanted him to get away from Le Havre. The last time I was in the area, in addition to the flak I had seen a dozen barrage balloons deployed around the fortifications. I wasn't sure how he would react, but I had to speak up.

"Bledsoe here, Jonah. Watch out for barrage balloons ahead. I saw a bunch of them here the other day. I'd suggest we skirt the area. The Jerries have a lot of guns around that harbor."

"Thanks, Marv," Winfield responded. "I'll keep my eyes open." His voice was casual and friendly. Thank God, he changed course to skirt around to the side of Le Havre. The weather had gotten very hazy and the German ground gunners may have thought we were "friendlies." Not a shot was fired.

Although Winfield had been in the ETO for a long time, much of his work had been connected with administration. He was a good pilot, eager and willing to learn, but was a little short on combat time to be leading the squadron.

It had been a mistake to keep us cruising at a thousand feet over enemy territory but luckily we were able to avoid the flak without incident. His second mistake was made when he headed toward Le Havre, not only because of the intense concentration of flak guns in that area but also because it was the long way to get to home base and we were short of fuel.

I liked Winfield but knew today's errors would cause some of the other pilots to be skeptical of his leadership ability.

The 353rd Fighter Group flew three missions on August 3, 1944. I got to fly the second one. The buzz bombs were still smashing London and the politicans were yelling: "Why doesn't somebody do something?" We were the "somebody." We were ordered to muster all fighters to escort a group of

B-25 twin-engined medium bombers into enemy territory where the missiles were thought to be launched. It was to be a very short mission. The buzz bombs came from the French coast just a few miles across the Channel.
bombs came from the French coast just a few miles across the Channel.

Most of the pilots were out on our group's first mission when the orders came to fly with the B-25s. We managed to put two aircraft in the air from our squadron, and joined with some Jockey Squadron pilots and a group of P-51s to make our rendezvous.

I was flying Rimmerman's ship, which had just been equipped with a new secret gun sight supposed to make shooting EA as easy as knocking down duckpins. Second Lieutenant William P. Knowling, one of the new boys, was on my wing. When we rendezvoused with the B-25s, Jockey had picked up some extra pilots, so Knowling and I weren't needed. "You can take your wingman and go home, Bledsoe," Jockey Leader called.

"Okay, Jockey, but first we'll have a look-see on our own," I replied. We lagged behind the B-25s and watched as they dropped their bombs and then took off for home in high gear. They missed the target. The bombs fell harmlessly into an open field.

"Jockey Leader here. Let's head for the base."

"Jockey, this is Bledsoe. We're a ways behind you, so go on home without us. We'll see you later." I wanted to stick around and log more combat time. That 300-hour mark kept getting closer. And so did Harriett!

Since this was a pick-up group of pilots, I was not bound to follow Jockey Leader's order to pull out. If one of our squadron leaders was in Jockey's position we would be out looking for targets of opportunity to keep the mission from being a total bust. I knew staying to fight the enemy was not going to get me in trouble with the brass, regardless of Jockey's admonition to head for home base.

We were in the Calais area, about twenty miles inland, when

I spotted a train making its way toward a good-sized town. I wobbled my wings at Knowling as a signal to follow and came charging down on the train. My bullets missed by at least a 150 feet. The new gun sight on the colonel's ship was completely out of focus. I kicked rudder and tried to lead a stream of bullets into the train's engine. It took Knowling to do the job. He made a nice pass. Steam shot into the air as the train ground to a screeching halt.

"Nice shooting, Knowling. Here's another one right ahead of us."

"Jeez, she really blew up, didn't she!" Knowling sounded happy. It was his first train.

"This is Jockey Leader. Where are you, Seldom? I thought you were on your way home." He had evidently been surprised to hear Knowling and me talking.

"Bledsoe here, Jockey. We were just looking around and found a locomotive to shoot up. We'll be on our way in a minute or two."

I started my pass on the other train. The engineer saw me coming. He jammed on the brakes and dived out of the cab like an old hand who had done this many times before. I tried to make allowances for the defective gun sight but missed the engine by several yards. I had to guide my bullets into the engine. I brought a little steam, but again it took Knowling to finish off the train.

"Attaboy, Knowling. Now let's get that truck over there by the bridge at two o'clock." We had let down in a hot spot with targets all around us. I cussed that new gun sight. I'd just have to shoot by feel.

We caught a large canvas-covered truck racing down the highway. I started firing and saw my bullets hit the pavement behind the truck. I held the trigger down, eased the stick back a little, and led a stream of death up through the back of the truck and into the driver's compartment. The German vehicle careened off the highway, struck a tree, and burst into flames. Knowling gave it a short burst for good measure.

"There's another big truck. It's coming out of the little town on your left, Bledsoe," Knowling called.

"Okay, he's all yours," I replied. "Go after him. You're doing some good shooting."

"Seldom, this is Jockey. What are you guys doing on the deck? Get out of there and head for home. Nobody told you to go off on your own."

"Take it easy, Jockey. We'll pull out soon. We've lined up a couple more targets," I responded.

Just as Knowling was making a pass on the truck, a military staff car came racing up the highway, unaware that enemy aircraft were in the area. It was one of those Mercedes touring cars with the canvas top, the sort that generals rode in. When the passengers recognized the Thunderbolt and saw the flashes from my guns, they opened the doors of the car, dove into the ditch along the road, and rooted their noses in the soft ground as their car bounced out into the field. I shot up the car while Knowling clobbered the big truck.

We were finding so many targets because our fighter planes hadn't dared come down on the deck in this heavily protected area along the coast. We were there only by accident, because some politician had hollered for somebody to do something about those buzz bombs.

We had destroyed three trains and had shot up several military vehicles in just a few minutes; we were just getting started. I found another locomotive and a convoy of German trucks. "Here we go again, Knowling. Another train and some trucks ahead. Let's get 'em."

We were making our pass at the next train and I was shooting up the locomotive when Knowling screamed, "Flak! Bledsoe! I've been hit!" The Jerry flak gunners had found us. The sky around us became a solid mass of white and black puffs from exploding 20-millimeter shells, and then the heavy flak guns got the range.

It was the thickest concentration of flak I had yet encountered. I could feel the colonel's ship lurch. The gunners must have held their fire till we were really close and then let us have it full force.

"Hit the deck, Knowling! Get down. Get down on the deck!" I yelled as I threw my ship over on a wing and went screaming toward the ground. If we got low enough, the gunners would lose sight of us until we passed close to their position. Then it would be too late for them to do much shooting before we were out of sight again. At least, that's what I hoped.

When I leveled out, I was as close to the ground as I could get without hitting something. Knowling was trailing behind me but was still a couple of hundred feet in the air and drawing fire from the flak guns. "Get lower, Knowling. Get right down on the deck where they can't see you," I warned.

It was really time to go home. I cursed myself for pressing my luck and for putting Knowling in such a tight spot.

I kept on the deck for a minute or so and headed inland. The idea was to get away from the coastline. I wanted to get clear, gain some altitude, and then cross land toward the Channel at fifteen or twenty thousand feet. At that altitude, we had a better chance of getting away from the flak.

As we headed back into enemy territory, I spotted a large wooded area. Chances were that there would be no flak guns there so I started our climb. "Knowling, let's try to get some altitude here by climbing in a spiral. If the flak gunners get the range, hit the deck as fast as you can and we'll try again in some other spot."

"Hello, Seldom Leader, this is Larkspur. This is Larkspur, Seldom. Give me a report on your position. Over."

"Seldom here, Larkspur. Right now, we're in a hell of a position. We're close to the coast and trying to get out. I'll call you later, Larkspur."

We were so close to the English Channel that when the air controller in London picked us up on radar he found it hard to believe friendly aircraft were in this area. He probably figured his radar reflected German planes. To make sure we were not EA, he wanted us to report our position.

Larkspur had evidently heard Jockey calling me Seldom Leader and wanted to know my position. If our location did not check out with the aircraft shown on their radar, they would have a pretty good idea they had picked up EA. The flak gunners were on Knowling and me again and we had all we could handle. When we hit a thousand feet they really cut loose. They had just been waiting to see where we would appear next.

"Come on, Knowling. Head for the deck," I called as I peeled off toward the ground in a vertical dive. I knew for certain I had been hit by this last barrage in two more places on my right wing just a few feet from the cockpit. But in spite of the damage, that beautiful Thunderbolt was giving me a great performance.

Stay with me, baby.

I was down on the tree tops and the flak was bursting over my head. Knowling was still hovering a couple of hundred feet above the ground and the flak was getting closer to him by the second. "Get down, Knowling. Get down lower. You'll get your ass shot off sitting up there!" I yelled over the radio. The words were no more than out of my mouth when his ship lurched violently from the impact of a solid hit.

I cursed under my breath. "Get on the deck, Knowling. For God's sake, get lower. Get right down on top of the trees!"

"I can't. I've been hit, Bledsoe. I've been hit bad!"

"Can you control your ship? Is she flying okay?" I asked.

"Yeah, she's flying okay, but I've been hit bad," Knowling answered.

I felt the blood rise to my face, I was so mad at Knowling for not getting down where it was safer. "Knowling, that airplane will fly just as well ten feet off the ground as it will a hundred. You better get that ship down on the ground, or you're going to get blasted out of the sky. You're too good a target at that altitude. Now, get down lower!" I ordered.

I may as well have been talking to myself. He was still hanging up there in the sky, a hundred feet or more off the ground. Every German in the country seemed to be shooting at him. Luckily they were shooting too high and behind him as we raced across the countryside. I continued to curse myself for getting us into this predicament, and I cursed the regulations in the States that prohibited students from learning how to buzz the ground.

In flying school Knowling had been one of those good students who followed regulations and had never gone below five hundred feet. That's what he had been told to do and he had done it exactly according to the poop sheet. Well, we'd both be lucky if his so-called poop-sheet training didn't kill him. Flying low was the only thing that was going to save Knowling's skin.

We got out of the guns' range and tried to gain altitude again so we could cross over the coast and go home. Again flak stopped us cold and we had to get back on the deck. It seemed as if the flak gunners were trying to force us back into enemy territory and drive us into a trap.

The best plan would have been to stay low to the ground and fly deep into France before we surfaced again. But that was out of the question. Knowling's gas supply was rapidly diminishing because of his damaged ship. There was only one possible solution. Stay on the deck and streak across the coastline at fifteen feet instead of fifteen thousand feet. I hoped this strategy would outwit the flak gunners and we could sneak out alive. I had to bank everything on surprise.

Well, this is it, brother!

"We're going out the hard way, Knowling. We're going out on the deck. Get down low and stay with me. We'll hit that Channel at tree-top level."

Knowling responded by dropping down to about fifty feet. But he still wasn't low enough to satisfy me. "Lower, Knowles. Your fanny is still sticking up there in the sky," I called, but he refused to get lower to the ground.

When we made our reverse turn to head back toward the Channel we came over a large hospital. I stayed so low I was passing between the buildings and could look up at the top floors. I could see people scurrying around and looking astonished as we roared by.

While streaking around the hospital, I caught a quick glimpse of a huge concrete revetment, which was a part of the hospital complex. In front of the revetment was a scorched-looking runway that trailed off in the direction of London. The runway was pointed right at the heart of England.

I had stumbled on the buzz-bomb launching site! By accident I had spotted what the Allies had been seeking for weeks.

I called Larkspur, hoping they could receive me at low altitude.

"Hello, Larkspur. This is Seldom Leader. Larkspur, this is Seldom Leader, giving you a position report. Take a fix on us, Larkspur. It looks as if we are in the buzz-bomb launching area. There's a missile site right next to a big hospital. I'll check in with you later. Do you read me, Larkspur?"

"Loud and clear, Seldom. This is Larkspur. We've got a fix on your position. Thank you, Seldom. Larkspur out."

In a few moments the Channel would be in view. "Pour on everything, Knowling. Let's really roll out of here at full speed. Get lower, Knowling. You're still too high!"

I remembered hearing about another pilot coming out on the deck. His greatest danger had been when he hit the beach, where there were no trees or buildings. The Germans had a clear tail-end shot at him as he raced out over the English Channel. They even used their heavier guns, causing large geysers of water to loom up in front of him. Running into a wall of water would have killed him instantly. His ship did catch some of the spray and he almost lost control and crashed into the Channel. He made it out okay, even if he did get the hell shot out of his ship.

If he made it, maybe we can too.

Knowling had finally gotten the message. At last he was down on the deck. He was still higher than he ought to be but lower than before, and he was only drawing a scattering of shots.

Electric wires loomed up in front of me. I debated whether

to bounce up over them quickly and give the gunners a momentary target, or to fly right through them. I was sure the Thunderbolt could wipe out the wires and still keep going. At the last instant, when the wires were almost at my nose, I jerked back on the stick and then jammed it forward. My plane literally hurtled over the wires and was right back on top of the ground again before the gunners knew what had happened.

As the Channel came into view, I could see the gun positions on the beach. The coastline looked like one long column of guns and fortifications. There was no choice. We had to fly right over them.

I made up my mind to fly so low that if a gunner so much as stuck his head up to take aim, I was going to cut it off with my propeller. I was so low I could see my prop wash kicking up sand on the beach below me. I stayed down and roared out over the surf lapping up on the beach.

The instant I hit the Channel, bullets sprayed the water ahead of me. Those Germans were going to make it rough.

"Stay with me, Lord. This might be the end."

I really started flying that Thunderbolt. Those damn Germans were trying to kill me.

I pulled my ship over on the left wing and almost cartwheeled away from the barrage of lead hitting the water in front of me. The belly of my plane was all but scraping the waves.

Within seconds, I had escaped the bullets and was headed out to sea. Soon it would be on to England and home base. I was safe. I looked back to see how Knowling was making out. Thank God, there he was. He was charging out over the beach firing his guns as he came. I realized then that it was his bullets I had been ducking. He was firing his guns to discourage the flak gunners on the ground from shooting at him, but he had nearly shot me down!

I pulled up to gain a little altitude, slowed down, and wobbled my wings to signal Knowling to catch up. He was in a sweat, and I didn't blame him. I could see a hole near his cockpit big enough to crawl through. It was only about three feet from his back. I shuddered at how close he had come to getting killed.

A feeling of relief and exhilaration passed over me. We had caught the Jerries with their pants down and would live to tell about it. I took off my oxygen mask and grinned at Knowling as he pulled up on my wing to get into formation. He gave me a thumbs-up salute to let me know everything was okay, then grinned back as if to say, "We're a couple of lucky fools, aren't we?"

Larkspur called again, asking our position. "Seldom here, Larkspur," I answered. "We are over the Channel and glad to be seeing Jolly Old England again."

"Roger, Seldom. What is your mission?" The air controller couldn't figure us out. There was nothing on their records to indicate that a couple of stray fighter ships should be coming out on the deck from one of the hottest spots in enemy territory.

"No particular mission, Larkspur. We were just out for a ride," I replied. I felt heady with excitement.

It was great to buzz the field and come in for a landing. Our battle-scarred ships brought shouts from the guys on the ground. They waved at us as we taxied to our parking area.

Knowling confessed later that it was the first time he had ever flown close to the ground. He said it had scared him silly.

I reported finding the buzz-bomb launching site. It was easy to locate on the map because of the hospital zone. I felt a glow of satisfaction as the intelligence officer had me stand by while he passed the word along to higher headquarters. It was a hot potato. Headquarters would have to figure out a way to destroy the launching site without killing the sick and wounded in the hospital.

I went into the ready room, where I found Blickenstaff. He told me about the first mission. It did not have a happy ending like ours.

It was a bomber escort job, led by Winfield, a strike deep

inside German territory. The bombers were again unloading on Hamburg. Novak was flying on Blick's wing. Over the target the bombers were attacked by a heavy concentration of ME-109s and the battle was on.

After an initial dog fight, aircraft was scattered all over the sky. Blick and the Kid found themselves all alone, facing six enemy fighters. They turned into the Jerries and were met by a head-on barrage of 20-millimeter shells. The first blast hit the Kid's belly tank and his ship caught fire in midair.

"Bail out, Kid! Bail out!" Blick screamed over the radio.

It was no use. The smoke from the Kid's burning ship trailed down to the ground. The P-47 blew up as it hit. Only a burned spot on the German countryside marked Novak's final landing.

As Blick described how Novak went down in flames, I fought back tears. Just a few days before, the Kid had asked Blick to schedule him as my permanent wingman. It was as if I had lost part of my own flesh and blood. Through the rest of my tour the loss of the Kid haunted me. Whenever I flew near Hamburg, I thought of his statement: "I'd rather die in combat than be transferred back to the States while the war's still going on. What better way to die than in a combat flight?" Well, he'd gotten his wish.

But EA hadn't killed him. His death came as the result of his own error. It was a cardinal rule to salvo your belly tank at the first sign of enemy aircraft. In the heat of battle, Novak had forgotten something just once too often.

During the flight, Winfield destroyed two 109s and damaged two others. He had been caught in the middle of a nest of enemy and claimed he could have shot down a half-dozen if he'd had someone to cover his tail. "I'd be on a 109, shooting at it, when I'd see tracer bullets coming past my own ship. I'd look around, and there'd be three or four Jerries running those tracer bullets right up my ass. I'd have to break away to save my skin," he grumbled. "I didn't know what the hell had happened to my wingman."

Winfield had failed to break fast enough during one encounter and his ship got filled with lead. He was hit so hard, he went into a spin at twenty thousand feet. "When I came out of the spin," he said, "I was at least ten thousand feet lower than when I started. But I fell right behind the tail of another 109. All I had to do was squeeze the trigger to blow him to kingdom come."

Marvin "Olie" Albertson had been flying on Winfield's wing. He had his own story to tell. "Winfield was after this guy and I was covering him, but I had to break off when two 109s lined up on my tail. I turned away from Winfield and they followed me. We got into a dog fight and I was starting to get in position on the number two man. He did a half-roll, peeled off, and raced for the overcast below. I tried to follow him but lost him in the haze. Then I saw another 109 by himself, a few hundred feet above me, so I went into a climb. I came up underneath this guy and got a good burst into his belly. That 109 went down in a trail of smoke and plowed into the ground."

Second Lieutenant Tom Creekmur, a replacement, said he got on the tail of a 109 that dove for the ground with throttle wide open. "He was going like greased lightning and I was right behind him. Suddenly, he tried to pull out of the dive and his damn wing came off. It was weird, watching his plane come apart like that."

Merchant became separated from the rest of the squadron when he tangled with another 109. "We went from twenty thousand feet down to the deck, then from the ground back up to twenty thousand feet. A second later, we were headed for the deck again. I was chasing this Kraut for a full ten minutes when he managed to get on my tail and started chasing me. We went round and round. I got back on his tail when he rolled for the deck and was heading home. He must have thought he had lost me in the haze because he slowed down and leveled out. That's when I let him have it!"

About a hundred ME-109s had jumped the bombers and tangled with our forty-eight Thunderbolts. Our pilots kept the enemy aircraft off the bombers and came home to claim sixteen confirmed victories and a dozen or more 109s probably destroyed.

The Hun's score for the day was a number of damaged Thunderbolts, and one nineteen-year-old Kid.

Minutes after Blickenstaff told me about the first mission and the loss of Novak, the group had saddled up and was ready to roll again. There was to be no letup.

The main target of this next mission was an airdrome that one of the pilots had spotted on the earlier flight. He had seen a number of enemy aircraft dispersed among the trees. Approval had been obtained from wing headquarters to go after the EA parked on the ground, and now the group was going back to work it over. It was a volunteer mission.

Strafing an airdrome was the most dangerous flying job in the war; nothing else took such a toll on pilots and their aircraft. I wasn't disappointed to find that the flight schedule had been assigned during my absence and that I was to sit this one out.

All in all, it had been one full day of action. The group had rung up an impressive record: forty-one enemy aircraft destroyed on two missions, in addition to the damage Knowling and I did on our little foray.

When I hit the sack I was worn to a frazzle, but I couldn't sleep. It was impossible to shut the day's events from my mind. I mourned the loss of Novak. Then I thought about how the squadron was shaping up, and I finally fell asleep feeling pride at being a part of such an outfit. I would be content to stay here, if only I didn't miss Harriett and my Little Princess so much.

CHAPTER 13

"What Field Is This?"

The famous veterans of our squadron—Willie Price, Robert Hart, and Carl Mueller—returned after their leaves in the States, back to start a second combat tour. Their return paved the way for Blick to get ready for his leave.

The prospect of quick promotion was one of the attractions to another tour. The thrill of combat and the association with other combat pilots was another. Price, Hart, and Mueller had been flight leaders when they left and, with their experience, would resume their leadership roles. They were mildly surprised to learn that former instructors had been used as replacements during their absence. They took the news in stride and were not prejudiced against us as some of the younger pilots had been when we first arrived.

Parker had cooled off and had kept his mouth shut after our last run-in, but now, with Willie Price taking over as operations officer, Parker was once again running true to form. He spread the word: "Boy, oh boy! Watch Bledsoe get sent back to flying tail-end Charlie when Willie takes over. Things will be a lot different around here now that our old flight leaders are back."

It struck me as ludicrous to find myself involved in a petty entanglement with Parker. We had much more important things to do—such as getting on with the war and trying to stay alive from day to day. I couldn't understand why he was conducting this personal war against me and why he seemed to dislike me so much. Doc said it was just simple jealousy. "You've stolen some of his thunder," Doc said, "and he can't stand the competition."

Mueller was 26, from the midwest, and of stocky build. He was the quiet one of the three veteran flight leaders. When he heard about the daily strafing missions and how we had lost so many pilots to ground fire, he had second thoughts about his signing up for another tour. He had been accustomed to bomber escort missions on his first go-around. At that time it was taboo to go down on the deck. The bomber escort missions had been milkruns, except when the Luftwaffe attacked in strength. Mueller didn't like the idea of being down on the deck where the Nazis could throw everything and anything at you—and usually did.

Willie Price was a different sort, wiry, twenty-three years old. When I first heard him speak I knew he had to be from Chicago's South Side; I recognized that Windy City taxidriver lingo. And it was obvious from the very beginning that he had even less regard for military discipline and petty regulations than I did. Much to Parker's surprise and dismay, Willie and I hit it off from our first meeting.

Robert Hart was a lanky 24-year-old Texan who was dismayed to discover that fighters were now getting down on the deck to do battle with the German military machine. He had been taught such tactics were suicidal but now he was told such missions were routine. I was to see him only a couple of times before he became a victim of the flak.

Price, Hart, and Mueller were still sleeping after their arrival when I took off on the morning flight. Our job was to escort bombers into an area where the Luftwaffe was expected to be out in full force. So far the only dog fight I had been involved in was on that second mission a century ago in June. I was more experienced now. I found myself itching to get on with it.

Winfield was leading the group and once again I was in charge of his second section. We were scouting the area when I spotted a flight of bogies ten thousand feet below us.

"Seldom Blue Leader here," I called. "Half a dozen bogies at four o'clock low. I'm going down and take a look. Come on, Blue Flight!" I peeled off and maneuvered my flight into position where we could attack from out of the sun.

"Jonah here, Marv. Where are the bogies?" That was Winfield, anxious to join the fray.

"The bogies are at eight thousand feet at four o'clock from you, Jonah. You can spot them in that group of scattered clouds," I replied. We had picked up some speed and were in hot pursuit.

I was almost in range but still unable to make a positive identification. They could be P-51 Mustangs, but it would be unusual for a lone flight to be cruising along at this altitude. I moved in closer and curled my finger around the trigger. A second later, the bogies made a turn and I recognized their distinctive features. They were P-51s. It had been a perfect bounce; they were blinded by the sun and hadn't seen us. The slightest pressure of my trigger finger just then would have sent a burst of lead toward their tail-end Charlie.

"Seldom Blue Leader. Hold your fire. The bogies are friendlies," I called to my flight.

When the P-51s finally saw us they scattered like birds in a storm. They thought we were bandits. I turned and hung my ship up on a wing to let them get a good look at our Thunderbolts. It was then that I saw Winfield's flight racing through the clouds, hot on the trail of an elusive ship. "Jonah, the bogies are P-51s. They are friendlies. Hold your fire," I called frantically.

"P-51s hell! I just shot down an ME-109," Winfield responded excitedly.

I had my doubts. The flight we scattered was P-51 Mustangs. There could be no mistake about that. I had gotten close enough to get a wave of acknowledgment from their flight leader.

If Winfield had knocked down a friendly fighter it wasn't the first case of mistaken identity. It had happened before and would no doubt happen again. It was a normal reaction in the heat of combat to shoot first and wonder later.

It was easy to recognize the difference between enemy and friendly aircraft in the flying-school classroom. But in the air, in combat, the matter of recognition wasn't that cut and dried, and there was never any time for reconsideration. Maybe Winfield had shot down a P-51 and maybe he had shot down an ME-109. That was how the war went.

Winfield's wingman told me privately, "I could see it as plain as day. We got on the tails of a couple of those guys and I was sure they were 109s from the way they were acting. Winfield came charging in and poured a long burst into the ship. After he shot up the bogie, we made a turn and then I thought for sure it was a P-51. The poor guy's ship started coming apart, then blew up into a thousand pieces. I never did see the pilot bail out. I looked around for a parachute but didn't see one. But what the hell. No need for me to disagree with Winfield. What good would it do? If he thinks he shot down an enemy fighter I'm willing to leave it at that."

Price had taken over as operations officer and had me scheduled to fly as squadron leader on August 6, 1944. I was thrilled at the opportunity to have the entire squadron under my command. Rafferty, Ruscitto, and Smith were leading the flights.

We were to escort bombers over Germany. We rendezvoused with our Big Friends right on time. Our fighter group was running into very little action but the bombers were taking a beating over the target. The ground gunners had set up a pattern of flak at the point where the bombers were to drop their bombs. In order to make a good pass on the target, it was necessary for our Big Friends to fly into that waiting wall of death. Not a bomber hesitated. By God, the song was right—"Nothing can stop the Army Air Corps."

As the bombers hit the wall of flak, I could see the planes bounce around like straws in a windstorm. One of the B-17s dropped its bombs, peeled off to the left, fell over on a wing as though the pilot might have been killed, and then blew up. I could see the fragments of ship and men dot the sky, then fall slowly to the ground.

Another B-17 exploded, still carrying a full bomb load. There was a terrific flash, a puff of smoke, and it was gone. I looked to see if part of the crew could have escaped. There wasn't so much as a splinter; the airplane had completely disintegrated before my eyes. Nothing was left but a trailing wisp of smoke carried along by the breeze.

Dozens of other bombers were badly damaged, but we escorted them and kept them safe from attack as they limped home.

The Luftwaffe chose to stay on the ground. What had been a tough and fateful mission for the bomber pilots was a milkrun for us.

After crossing the Channel, I rocked my wings and signaled everyone in the squadron to close up so we could fly over the base in close formation. It looked beautiful. I felt proud to be leading them. I took the squadron in about twenty feet off the runway to buzz the field. As we roared over the heads of the men on the ground, I could see Doc waving and jumping up and down. I could almost hear him shouting: "What'd I tell you! What'd I tell you! I knew we could make a real honest-to-God fighter squadron!"

We must have looked even better than I thought. Colonel Rimmerman passed the word along that the rest of the group ought to make an effort to fly formation "like the pilots in Seldom Squadron."

On August 8, 1944, Hart and First Lieutenant Thomas C. Creekmur were killed. Creek was one of greenest replacements. Muller had taken him out on a training flight; they had started feeling frisky and Mueller did a couple of slow rolls on the deck. Creekmur evidently got excited, tightened up too much on his controls, and hit the ground upside down. It was probably his first acrobatic maneuver on the deck and he couldn't handle it. He was killed instantly. It was a particularly rotten break because Creek's wife was expecting a baby within the next few days.

Acrobatics and buzzing were overlooked—as long as no casualties occurred; everyone expected that Mueller would have to answer to the brass for what had happened. The responsibility for Creek's death had to fall on his shoulders; he was the experienced one. Mueller's chances for promotion went out the window that day.

Hart failed to return from the first mission of his second tour of duty. He was reported as killed in action almost before he had time to unpack.

A few days after Hart's and Creek's deaths, we were told at briefing that we were bound for the Pas de Calais area to hit the buzz bombs again. I wondered if the mission had anything to do with that buzz-bomb site I had spotted next to the hospital.

The buzz bombs were highest priority, but if we could not find the site we were to destroy trains and locomotives in the area. Headquarters figured that if bombs could not neutralize the launch pads, at least we could stop delivery by destroying the rail transportation facilities. It made sense, but Knowling and I had barely made it out alive the other time. The thought of facing the coastal antiaircraft guns again scared me plenty. I figured I would be pushing my luck to go in twice.

During briefing, I could feel myself breaking out in sweat as chills ran up and down my spine. For the first time, I was forced to make the dash for the latrine before a briefing ended.

I wasn't ashamed about being scared. Just before a dangerous mission the latrine was always full of nervous pilots. We were all scared.

Swanson and the ground crew had the Little Princess patched up and flying again. When I broke the news that we were headed back for the same spot where I had gotten Colonel Rimmerman's ship all shot up, Swanson shook his head. "This baby is really getting battle scarred, Lieutenant," he said. "It's a good thing we're not having any mechanical trouble. We wouldn't have time to work on it with the schedule you're flying. It seems like I spend all my waking hours patching up this baby."

Swanson wasn't complaining, he hastened to say. "Cripes, I'd rather spend the rest of my life patching up holes than be in the cockpit for even one of those missions when the flak starts popping." He meant every word of it.

The weather was working against us today and we had to make our letdown many miles inland. Knowling was flying my wing and I knew he was as glad as I that the foul weather had forced us away from the coastline. We were not looking forward to seeing the Calais area again. There were no complaints from us when orders came to disregard plans to let down in the buzz-bomb area. We were turned loose to look for targets of opportunity, my favorite type of mission.

We finally found a hole in the clouds and were able to let down in the soup. When we broke through the overcast, visibility was only about a quarter of a mile, but I spotted an enemy aircraft hidden among some trees.

"Seldom Leader here. There's a 109 behind those trees at three o'clock. Keep your eyes open. We might have found something. Looks as if the Jerries might be using this field," I called. "Watch for EA in the air. Keep your tails covered."

I dove down on the 109 and gave it a good burst. It jumped back and forth as I raked it but it didn't burst into flames as I expected. It was evidently out of fuel.

We found more parked ships dispersed among the trees.

It looked as if we'd discovered a good spot to spend the morning.

On my next pass, I salvoed my belly tank and splattered the parking area with high-test gasoline that burst into flames. The rest of the flight followed suit.

As we went to work on the aircraft, the ground gunners went to work on us. One of them in particular was shooting away for all he was worth with a pair of 20-millimeter guns. White puffs were bursting directly in our path.

On my next pass, I could feel the Little Princess tremble as a direct hit found the front of the plane. This time I caught sight of the gun position that was causing us so much trouble. It was well camouflaged, located at the end of a small barn. From there the guns could cover three sides of the airstrip.

"Bledsoe here. I've spotted the 20-millimeters. Don't follow me on this next pass. You guys go ahead on the parked ships. I'll see if I can silence the guns."

As I pulled up from shooting another parked ME-109, I wheeled to the right instead of making the circle to the left with the rest of the flight. A second or two later, I was bearing down on the gun position. For the first time since my combat flying started, I was in a position to fight a battle to the finish with enemy ground gunners. I relished it.

I saw the guns swing around and start blasting in my direction. They left the other guys alone.

I had already begun firing, but in my haste I had scattered my shots and evidently I hadn't done much damage. As I passed over the ground, gunners swung their guns around and hit the Little Princess time and again. I hugged the ground and tried to get out of the line of fire.

Wait till this next pass, you bastards!

I kept going straight ahead for a few moments, attempting to get away from the stream of bursting white puffs that followed me. As soon as I was out of range I kicked the ship around and pulled up next to the overcast to get more altitude and zoom down. This time, I was going to make a steep dive and not stop shooting until they were done for.

I was ready for them and they were ready for me. As they

blasted away, one shell caught the leading edge of my wing not more than six feet away from the cockpit.

I started my dive with guns blazing. The job could be done properly only one way: center the needle and ball on my instruments and keep in a straight line to insure accurate shooting. There was no time to take evasive action. I had to let them have a good crack at me in order to get off a good burst of my own.

My bullets kicked up the dirt directly in front of their gun position. I yelled triumphantly. The volley was so concentrated it completely hid the gun position from view as my bullets tore at them. I held my finger down on the trigger and kept firing away.

I was so intent on killing every gunner in the flak nest as I pressed the attack that I almost mushed into the ground. I broke into a sweat and eased back on the stick, trying to keep the ship from plowing into the ground beside the gun position. I held my breath. My heart was fluttering as I passed over the flak nest and got the ship under control. It had been close.

The gun position was silent. When I returned to check it, I saw the torn bodies of three Nazi gunners, laying half in and half out of their hidden flak nest. I felt no regrets. Kill or be killed was the name of the game. I went back to helping shoot up the half a dozen aircraft the Germans had parked on this auxiliary field.

As a result of continual attack by our bombers, the Luftwaffe was abandoning most of its large airdromes. Individual squadrons were scattered, operating from dirt fields adjacent to wooded areas where they could hide their planes on the ground. Each such field was protected by these flak nests.

When we returned to base, I was the envy of the squadron. The real ambition of every fighter pilot in the group was to find a flak nest and be able to give it his undivided attention as I had done.

We lost Grady on the mission. The report was brief— Second Lieutenant Milton Grady, killed in action.

The Little Princess had to have a second new engine cover and she needed considerable patching. What a beating that ship was taking! Yet she still flew like a million bucks. I wouldn't have traded her for any other airplane ever built. I vowed that if I was lucky enough to get home alive I was going to tell the workers at Republic Aircraft so. They had built a great fighter plane!

Headquarters was pleased with the day's results. A score of locomotives and trucks had been destroyed, in addition to the six EA on the ground. Our intelligence officer reported, "The Jerries may have been using that field to make surprise attacks on our guys. They've been strafing the beachhead and our front-line columns just before daylight. They hit fast, then run for their hiding place before our planes can intercept them. That may have been one of their hiding places."

Drinks in the club were on the house when a flight destroyed more than four enemy aircraft, and we all drank to Blickenstaff and his impending return to the United States. Every man in the place envied him the trip home, but after a year and a half in the combat zone he certainly deserved a leave. Few, if any, envied the fact that Blick would return for more combat missions when his furlough ended, even though he had been promoted to major and would be promoted to lieutenant colonel on his return.

Blick and I drank our own toast to the day almost two years before when we had walked out of the gates of Luke Field, freed from the iron rules of a cadet system at last. We had been elevated to the status of "officer and gentleman." At the time, I didn't dream that two years later Blick would be my commanding officer and about to become a lieutenant colonel, one of the key personnel in what was fast becoming the hottest fighter outfit in the ETO.

I had been asked to sign up for a second tour and was promised a couple of quick promotions if I stayed on. I gave the idea serious consideration. I wanted to do everything I possibly could to help the squadron. The love of flying fighter planes and the thrill of combat made the idea seem all the more appealing. But on thinking hard, I doubted if I'd get through my first tour alive, much less another one. And Doc gave me the clincher: "Don't be a damn fool, Marv. If you're lucky enough to get the chance to go home, take it!"

That's when I pushed the thought of a second tour out of my mind for good.

Blick lived about twenty miles from Los Angeles, so I asked him to take time to see Harriett and the baby. "Tell her I'm okay and assure her I'll be coming home one of these days. But don't clue her in about what we're going through over here. She would worry herself sick if she found out. She already knows enough from what she hears on her radio."

The rest of the pilots in the squadron wanted Blick to visit or telephone their loved ones if he could. He promised to make contact one way or another with the waiting families at home. Though most of us wrote regularly, that was no assurance to the folks at home that we were still alive. Too often letters continued to come even after the family had been notified that the pilot had been killed or, perhaps worse, was "missing in action." If Blick could talk to them, give them the feeling that we were real, it would be better, much more alive than a letter.

One of Blick's last orders was to keep me on the ground for a few days. He did not want me to finish my tour before he returned from leave.

It was hard for me to adjust to the fact that I had been grounded for the time being. Staying in bed while the other guys got up before daylight to make the briefing did seem like luxury, but the inactivity was making me a nervous wreck.

On August 26, 1944 Doc stuck his head in the door and yelled at me to get out of the sack.

"Hey, Bledsoe, a squadron of P-51 pilots flew in here last night and they'll be with us for a few days. They're part of the Ninth Air Force stationed in France. Their CO asked Rimmerman if there was someone who could fly over to their home base in our transport and get some important papers and supplies. It seems these guys were sent here suddenly and arrived with nothing but their flight gear. Their base is right near Paris, so I volunteered you—and me too. I'm coming along as co-pilot. Get up—their CO wants to see you."

By the time I got up Doc had it all rigged. There was an old single-engine Canadian Norseman on the base, used for general transportation. Doc commandeered it and made plans to get going—and get into Paris. That was the whole idea.

The P-51 outfit was one of the few fighter squadrons that had been moved into France. They operated much like the Germans in those days, off dirt runways near a grove of trees that could hide the tents and planes. Their job was tactical air support of the ground forces: strafing ahead of the troops and keeping the Luftwaffe on the deck. It was a different job from ours; our missions were more of the strategic sort. This P-51 outfit was right up by the front line.

The colonel in charge pointed out his base on the map. "It's just a strip in the middle of a field. There are no buildings, but if you get low enough you can see our tents scattered among the trees. Since you've been over that territory many times, you shouldn't have any trouble finding it."

My heart skipped a beat. "That's awful close to the front, Colonel. I won't have any trouble finding the strip. What I'm worried about is running into EA with that old crate I'll be flying. We wouldn't have a chance if Jerry jumped us. Have there been any bandits in that area lately?" I asked.

"Nope," he replied. "The Huns haven't been operating in that sector for a couple of weeks. You shouldn't have any problem with the Luftwaffe if you stay on course. Here's a list of the stuff we need. Give it to my executive officer and he'll have it loaded on the ship for you. I'll need these things by Saturday night. That gives you three days to make the flight." He laughed; he had read my mind about getting into Paris, which had been liberated by the Allies a couple of days earlier.

Doc was waiting for me outside. "That P-51 strip where these guys are operating is right near Paris, Doc. Gather up all the cigarettes, candy, and K-rations you can get and we'll take them with us. Better get as much cash as you can, too—I don't have much money. We want to be able to trade with the natives. You get the stuff together. I've got to get approval from Rimmerman before we take off."

"Whoopee!" Doc yelled. He made a beeline for the PX.

Rimmerman was ready for me. "I know, Bledsoe. Doc has already briefed me. You've volunteered to fly over to France on an important mission and you need Doc as a co-pilot. It's okay with me.

"But if anything happens while Doc is flying that bucket you'll get all our necks in a sling. Watch your step. I've been told there are plenty of Germans hiding out in Paris and there's shooting still going on in the city, so you and Doc be careful." Even with the warning, I could tell Rimmerman was happy we had the chance to make the trip.

When we crossed the English Channel and arrived over the French coast, we were flying low and slow so we could take in all the sights. Doc was having a ball as I pointed out areas I recognized. "Hey, Doc, there's where we strafed an enemy airdrome while the Germans still held this territory. . . . Over there, by that little railroad siding, is where we shot up three locomotives. . . . Here's where Dewey Newhart and I got bounced by the ME-109s on my second mission." And so it went. God, it all seemed like ages ago.

The countryside was littered with wrecks and military hardware the Germans had abandoned during their retreat, pockmarked from thousands of bombs dropped during the D-Day period. We got a bird's-eye view of bombed cities and villages. On the ground, French civilians waved at us as we flew over.

We located the P-51 airstrip without difficulty. The exec, a major with a sense of humor, laughed as he read the note and list of supplies requested by his CO. The "vital" supplies the colonel needed by Saturday night turned out to be his dress uniform, fresh clothing for himself and his pilots, and three cases of cognac!

"The colonel has a hot date coming up Saturday night and he wants to be prepared. He's looking forward to a great weekend," the major said. "I hope you guys don't mind flying all the way over here just to get this junk."

"We couldn't care less, Major. We're glad to have the chance to get into Paris and look around a bit," I responded.

We bounced down the dirt runway with Doc trying to keep the cognac bottles from breaking. Aloft, in short order we saw the Eiffel Tower. "Thar she blows, off the starboard bow!" Doc yelled.

As we approached Le Bourget Airport, we could see it was a shambles. There wasn't a building that had escaped devastation. The paved runways had been totally destroyed. It had once been the French headquarters for Field Marshal Goering and the elite of his favorite Luftwaffe squadrons—those yellow-nosed 109s we had tangled with in the past. Our bombers had really worked the airport over. We landed on a bumpy dirt strip that had been bulldozed alongside the broken runways. It was so short it could only accommodate light aircraft.

Doc and I made our way over to a tent where we saw a crude handlettered sign saying OPERATIONS OFFICE. We wanted to borrow a jeep so we could ride into Paris in style. The ops officer brought us up short. "What the hell are you guys doing here in the first place? You can't land here without official orders. This is still a battle area. We don't furnish sightseeing tours. Get back in that puddlejumper and head for England, where you belong. Of all the goddamn nerve, wanting to borrow a jeep to ride into town!"

While he was busy chewing us out, the wheels were going around in my head. I thought the lousy weather might be a good excuse for laying over and decided to give the idea a whirl. "We're on a special mission and were on our way back to England. We were forced to land here on account of the bad weather. That's not an instrument ship I'm flying. So we'll have to lay over until we get a break in the weather."

"Bullshit. You know it's bullshit and I want you to know that I know it's bullshit. So don't try to con me. I don't blame you for wanting to see Paris but don't give me no crap. Okay, we'll blame it on the weather. You can wait for the weather to change but don't wait too long. I want you guys and that bird you're flying out of here in the morning. You can catch a ride into Paris on one of our trucks. They leave and come back regularly all day and night so there's no excuse for you not getting back here tomorrow."

As we pulled into the city, we could see that the Parisians were overjoyed at the departure of the Nazis. Groups of people were gathered on the sidewalks waving at the Americans rolling through the streets of Paris on trucks and military equipment.

There appeared to be a mass movement of furniture and goods as the people brought out their coveted personal belongings from hiding places. They were piled high on wagons, handcarts, and wheelbarrows. It was a gay and excited crowd, pleased that they had been able to hide and salvage their personal treasures from their former captors. We were soon to learn they had even hidden their best wines, waiting for the day Paris would be liberated.

Wherever we went, the blessings of the people of Paris were with us. Their happiness at being free again knew no bounds and no attempt was made to hide their emotions or gratitude to Allied forces.

Our driver dropped us off in the center of the city where there were a number of hotels. We checked in as if we were regular tourists in peacetime. The one big difference was that the manager of the hotel asked for payment in cigarettes instead of money. For a few packs of American cigarettes, we were given the royal treatment.

It was difficult to believe that this proud city had been under Hitler's heel for four years. The people looked well-dressed and, on the surface, seemed to have been leading normal lives. But easy or hard, they had not been living free lives and they were bursting with joy at being rid of the Boches.

From all we could gather, visiting Thunderbolt pilots were a novelty in Paris. There had been other pilots around who had been shot down in the area, some of whom escaped the clutches of the Germans with the aid of the French underground and eventually rejoined the Allied forces. But I was evidently among the first to appear as a tourist.

Doc practiced his college French. He never missed the chance to say "My friend is a Thunderbolt pilot" to anyone he spoke to. That phrase seemed to have a special meaning to the French, who had witnessed us down on the deck strafing and crippling the German military. They considered us heroes who had set the stage for their liberation.

As Doc and I made our way around the city, it didn't take long to realize that Parisian shopowners preferred our cigarettes, candy, and K-rations to money. The articles we had brought along were all but nonexistent in France so even the most exclusive shops were eager to barter and trade for the PX items. We ended up with some beautiful gifts to take back to the States. Doc bemoaned the fact that we didn't fill the plane with "trading goods" from the base.

We stopped at a crowded sidewalk café for a glass of wine. Doc ordered "champagne for my Thunderbolt pilot friend." The magic words brought a murmur from the patrons, then a rumble of applause as they toasted "the Thunderbolt pilots." (Including Doc, too.)

· We hated to do it, but we had to leave Paris the next day. The deadline for our return to Raydon was approaching. It was late in the afternoon when we were ready to take off and I knew it would grow dark while we were still over France.

"Shouldn't we have some kind of a password or signal to let the guys on the ground know we're friendly?" I asked the operations officer. "I'd hate to get shot down by one of our own guns." An understatement.

He responded that we definitely should have the code signal of the day, but things had been moving so fast around there that the only code he had was three days old. "You guys were busting your britches to see Paris, now you'll have to take your chances."

"Okay, Doc, you heard what the man said. Let's get going."

"What the hell, Marv, the trip was worth it. We'll make it okay. I'm not worried," Doc replied.

"All right, Doc, we'll shove off in a few minutes. While I'm checking out, round up some flares. Get every color you can lay your hands on. Get an extra flare gun. If we get challenged, we'll start shooting flares. If we make enough of a fuss, the ground gunners will sure as hell know we aren't Krauts."

We took off from Le Bourget and everything went fine until we got near the English Channel. Then someone on the ground picked us up with a huge searchlight. A moment later, two other searchlights zeroed in on us. It was like being alone on center stage. "Start shooting flares, Doc!" I cried. "I'll waggle my wigs and turn on my landing lights. That might help them identify us."

Doc had both pistols ready and started firing different-colored flares with each hand. I rocked my wings back and forth like a seesaw. A moment later the lights were turned off and it was pitch-black once again. The ground gunners were evidently satisfied. They probably thought we were just a friendly transport making our way back to England. How right they were. No enemy pilot would be caught over Allied lines at night in the kind of egg beater we were flying.

Doc breathed a sigh of relief. "Wow, those lights were bright. Did you see where my first flare lit? It caught our tail wheel. I thought it might catch us on fire, but it fell off when you started rocking. I'm beginning to sweat this deal out a little."

"So am I, Doc. If I could find a field and set this thing down, we'd spend the night there and not worry about the colonel and his stuff. Now we've got another problem. We're hitting a bad head wind and if it gets worse we'll be sweating out our gas. Put on your chute."

As we crossed the Channel the weather got soupy. At land-fall in England gunnery units picked us up in their search-lights. Doc shot flares and I turned on our landing lights and rocked the ship, but they weren't taking any chances and let go with several warning bursts of flak that exploded in front of us. "Give 'em more flares, Doc. I'll turn this baby around and we'll make our entry someplace else. They've made it pretty clear they don't want us passing over this area."

I had a good idea where we were. I decided to head for a landmark where the Stour and Orwell rivers ran into the North Sea, creating a Y from the air. Our base was located about twelve miles from the fork of the Y. It was barely light enough over the Channel to see the dark outline of England, but I soon located the two rivers and turned inland.

"Hey, Bledsoe, someone's blinking a signal light at us. Do you think he's trying to send us a message in Morse code, or is that some kind of a challenge?" Doc yelled over the roar of the engine.

"He's wasting his time if it's Morse. I sure can't read it and wouldn't know how to signal him back if I could. Shoot off a few flares, but don't use all of them. We may need more when we get to our own field."

The blinking light stopped and the sky was black again. We never found out who it was or what he was trying to tell us.

The weather had turned bad enough to make me go on instruments. This ship was never meant for serious instru-ment flight. The dials were on the far side of the panel and I had to lean over to the right to read them.

It was time to get a position fix from Raydon and have them be ready to light up the runway. To my disgust, the radio wasn't functioning properly and I couldn't get through. After we crossed the English Channel and entered the British blackout it was too dark to make out any objects on the ground. I would have to do some dead reckoning and sharp figuring. I checked the time and calculated ground speed and distance.

"Doc, check your watch. Let me know when exactly six minutes have passed. That should put us close to home base. Have the rest of your flares ready when I give the word. I can't raise anyone on the radio so we'll have to locate home base on our own. When I think we're close, we'll circle to attract their attention and hope they turn on the runway lights. I can't make out a thing on the ground."

"Okay, Marv, but we don't have a lot of flares left. What're we going to do if they don't turn the lights on?" Doc was sounding nervous.

"If they don't turn the lights on, there's no way we can find that runway. We're so low on gas we may have to point this egg beater toward the Channel and bail out."

We flew on through the darkness in silence. I was kicking myself for not staying the night in Paris or for not leaving earlier. Doc was probably contemplating how he'd react if we had to hit the silk.

"Six minutes on the dot," Doc reported. "What now?"

The blackout below was complete. All we could see was a never-ending black mass. I thought we were close to our base but one could never be too confident with dead reckoning.

"Okay, Doc, I'm starting my circle. Go ahead with the flares."

I advanced the prop pitch to get more noise out of the engine. I goosed the throttle back and forth and turned on my landing lights, trying to attract attention. All the while, Doc was shooting flares out the window.

A full minute went by with no response from the ground. We might not be anywhere near our field. I did some quick calculating to see if we had enough gas to get to the Channel. If we did have to bail out, I didn't want the plane to crash in a populated area.

"Hey, Bledsoe, there goes my last flare! I'll try my flashlight." Doc sounded desperate.

I continued circling. I was about to give up when I saw a ray of light on the ground. It was as if someone had opened and then shut a door to a lighted room. I prayed it was someone at the base heading for the tower to turn on the runway lights.

A row of dim lights came on and exposed the outlines of a landing strip. "Oh, happy day!" Doc yelled. "We've made it, Marv, we've made it!"

"Not yet, Doc. I've still got to get this flying coffin on the ground. It's been a long time since I've made a night landing, so hang on. There's no guarantee we'll set down in one piece." It was my turn to sound nervous.

In a few seconds I was lined up for my approach to the runway. "Tighten your seat belt, Doc. Here goes!" I said as we groped for the ground. I leveled out above the runway and chopped my throttle. I was a little bit high and really dropped the old transport on the ground with a thump.

"There goes the cognac!" Doc screamed.

Moments later, a jeep pulled up in the darkness to pick us up. "Where are we? What field is this?" I asked the driver.

"Raydon," was his one-word reply.

Doc roared with laughter. "What a lousy navigator. Land at your own base and have to ask where you are!"

We were greeted by the colonel of the P-51 outfit. He was anxious to get his so-called supplies and be on his way into town. "I've got a big weekend. Thanks for bringing my stuff back on time," he said nonchalantly.

CHAPTER 14

Just One More Pass

When we got back to our hut, Doc revealed that he had liberated several bottles of the colonel's cognac. Willie Price went to work on the booze while he listened to Doc's story about our trip to Paris. The cognac took its toll. Willie awoke with such a cognac hangover the next morning he couldn't get out of bed.

I was in a hurry to finish up my three hundred combat hours, as planned, but after Blickenstaff went home on leave, I realized that Willie Price was going to give me a bad time about flying so often. Before the Paris trip, when I asked Willie to put me on the next day's mission, he answered in his typical fashion: "Go to hell, Bledsoe. Blick gave me orders to slow you down. He wants you here when he gets back. At the rate you're going, you'll have your tour finished in no time at all."

Willie didn't have the strength to resist my insistence about flying the next mission when I bugged him about taking another pilot's place. He finally agreed. "Okay, but I hope you get your ass shot off, Bledsoe. I'd die right now just to be rid of this hangover. I've got a headache you wouldn't believe. Get the hell out of here and let me die in peace," he groaned. Just as I was going out the door of his Nissen hut, I heard him say weakly, "Take it easy, Marv. Be careful and good luck."

We were on an escort mission to Frankfurt, where military industrial plants made it a number one target for the bombers.

The flak guns were so heavily concentrated that their barrage of steel dirtied up the sky. Our flights were able to avoid the flak, but our Big Friends kept formation and flew right into a barrage so thick that they were momentarily hidden from view by the black smoke. By the time they came out on the other side, their formation had been ripped apart. Planes were staggering all over the sky from the impact of the flak. I saw two bombers explode and disappear without a trace. A flash, a puff of smoke, then nothing but blue sky. Two Flying Fortresses had vanished before my eyes. No pieces, no parachutes.

The radio controller reported many bogies in our area. It was obvious we were going to have a difficult time helping the bombers get home. This was not the usual milkrun by a long shot.

"Jonah here," I heard Rimmerman call. "This is the kind of setup the Jerries are primed for. They'll go after the stragglers and the cripples. Keep your eyes open for EA."

Many of the bombers had one or two engines shot out and were leaving a telltale trail of smoke behind them. I saw crew members throwing everything they possibly could out of the B-17s to lighten their load.

I spotted a flight of bombers high above me and was startled when I saw flashes on one of the ships, the impact of bullets hitting the fuselage. As I watched, a bomber fell off on a wing and started a spin toward earth, trailing heavy black smoke. A P-51 fighter squadron was supposed to be guarding that particular group of bombers. I strained my eyes to see what was taking place and saw a flight of fighters streak through what was left of the bomber formation. Another Fortress went spinning toward the ground, enveloped in smoke. Within moments, it exploded. I counted only one parachute.

"Seldom Leader here, Jonah," I called to Rimmerman. "There's a group of bandits working on that box of bombers at twelve o'clock high!"

"This is Lawyer Leader, Seldom. Those are 51s escorting that group. You probably saw Mustangs."

I cut in on the radio before Rimmerman had a chance to reply. "Seldom here again. If those are 51s they're shooting our Big Friends. I just saw another bomber explode. Jonah, how about me taking my flight and having a looksee?"

"Okay, Bledsoe. But only one flight. Our job is to escort our own group of bombers, so the rest of Seldom Squadron should stick with this bunch. Keep your eyes peeled, men. If those are bandits, they may work their way down to us. Go ahead, Bledsoe."

I signaled the three ships behind me to close up formation and to increase speed. The attacking fighters were a long way off. We would have to hurry if we were going to get there in time to help our Big Friends. "Pour it on, you guys," I called. "Give her the needle or we'll be too late!"

In less than a minute, I counted four more crippled bombers going down in flames. Those German fighter pilots really knew their business. We might be heading into more trouble than our one flight could handle.

"Hurry it up, Bledsoe! Those guys are in deep trouble!" That was Rimmerman.

"We've got everything forward, Jonah. We're at full power and closing fast. Should be in range in a minute or so," I replied.

As we neared what was left of the bomber group, my wingman yelled: "White Two here. EA's are making a head-on pass at the lead bomber. There's two of them. There they go! They're streaking for the deck. Let's get em!"

"Hold it! Hold your position!" I ordered. "There's another group of 109s at one o'clock high. They're just waiting for us to take the bait and head for the deck after their buddies. If we do, they'll attack the bombers again. Stick with the bombers. Don't get sucked down to the ground after a couple of decoys!"

I switched my radio over to the bomber-fighter frequency to try and raise the lead bomber. "Hello, Big Friend. This is the flight of Thunderbolts who just joined you. I don't know who you are, but we're here to help. Where's your escort? Do you read me, Big Friend? Over."

"I'll say we can read you, Thunderbolt. Stick with us, will you? We've been catching hell from these German fighters. They bounced us a few minutes ago and our P-51 escorts took out after them. The last I saw of our escort they were chasing a couple of 109's toward the deck. Stay with us, pal," the bomber leader pleaded. He tried to sound calm. I felt sorry for them.

"You bet we'll stick. You can count on it. In fact, I'll see if we can get some more help up here. Those bandits are still circling upstairs figuring out their next move," I replied. I switched my radio back to our fighter frequency.

"Jonah, this is Seldom Leader. This outfit is all alone up here and there's about a dozen 109s above sizing us up. How about sending the rest of my squadron up here to even things up if the EA decide to attack again?"

"I heard you talking, Bledsoe. The rest of your guys are already on their way. Stay with the bombers. Don't get sucked away like the P-51s did. That was a lousy thing, going after a couple of decoys instead of staying to protect their bombers. I'm going to see to it that someone answers for it." Colonel Rimmerman was having to split up his fighters to do double duty; if the Luftwaffe hit in force now, it could prove disastrous.

"Okay, you guys," I called to my flight. "You heard Jonah. If the 109s attack, let them have it but don't pursue them. Make your pass and then come right back to the bombers. That's an order!" I emphasized.

The bandits were still circling a couple of thousand feet above. They tried to maneuver us into a position where we'd have the sun in our eyes. They were in a perfect attack position to control the next move and call the shots. All we could do was wait.

The rest of Seldom Squadron was near, so I thought we could try some strategy of our own. "Bledsoe here, Seldom Red Leader. Keep the other flights with the bombers. I'm going to take my flight and head upstairs to meet the bandits. No need to let them call the plays. Okay, White Flight, let's go!" I started a climbing turn and headed upstairs for the confrontation.

We were about a thousand feet below the bandits when their leader made his decision. He whipped his ship over on a wing and streaked for the deck. Evidently he didn't want any part of us.

"The sonsabitches," my wingman, a replacement, called after the departing German pilots. "The goddamn cowards are taking it on the lam. They're afraid to face us!" he yelled bitterly.

"Don't you believe it," I responded. "Those guys weren't chicken. Did you see the yellow noses on those 109s? Those pilots are the elite. They probably had orders not to mix it up with fighters unless they had us outnumbered. I'll bet they'd have loved to take us on but their boss wouldn't let them."

We stuck with the bombers until we arrived at the English Channel and then took off for home base. Later, we were questioned at length about the unprotected bombers. Some P-51 squadron leader, eager to make a kill, was going to have trouble for leaving the Big Friends to chase a couple of enemy 109s.

The dawn of a new day found me trying to get on the schedule to fly the next mission. Willie was still a little reluctant to let me fly so often but he had just about given up fighting me about it.

I was trying to work out some way to be a part of the mission when another pilot, Lieutenant John Harper, walked in and said he was too sick to fly. Willie exploded.

"Bullshit. You've found out we're going to have a rough mission and the way to get out of it is to say you're sick."

Willie was no diplomat, but according to Doc he had hit the nail on the head.

"Harper is one of those characters with a yellow streak down his back a mile wide. He aborts on every rough mission and doesn't care what the rest of the squadron thinks about him. He doesn't have the courage to quit combat because he's afraid of what the folks at home will say," Doc said. "He's played sick several times before a mission and then had the gall to show up at the bar once the group is airborne."

I had already formed my own opinion of Harper when we were on that mission to shoot up the German airfield. As his flight leader peeled off to go down to the deck, Harper broke out of formation and headed upstairs. He kept circling around up there until the fight was all over. Back at home base, he claimed he had seen a couple of enemy planes in the air and had pulled out of formation to go after them. "I had a real dog fight with one of them," Harper related. "I was on this guy's tail, ready to blast him to bits when the son-of-a-bitch ducked into the clouds and I lost him."

Blickenstaff had talked about reclassifying Harper as unfit to fly and getting him out of the squadron; he didn't because it would have caused a stink at headquarters. It could only create bad publicity and the brass wouldn't like that. So Blick decided to put up with Harper—but the word was out in the squadron: never count on him when things got tight.

"How about me flying in your place?" I asked Harper.

"It's okay with me. I'm too sick to fly anyway."

"How about it, Willie? Let me fly as your element leader. If Harper can't fly, I'm the one to take his place. All the rest of the guys not scheduled today have gone back to their sacks," I persisted.

"Jesus Christ, Bledsoe. I hope you get your ass shot off! I've never seen a guy so eager to get through his tour and get home. Hell, I flew eight months before I logged as much combat time as you've got in the past six weeks. Okay!"

Harper left the ready room to return to his hut, acting like a man who had been reprieved from the gallows.

Willie had flown bomber escort missions on his first combat tour, but I was still a little surprised when he said to me confidentially: "I'm really glad you're going along. This getting down on the deck is new to me and I'm scared shitless. If you see me doing something wrong, clue me in."

He was modest enough to realize that all of us needed all the help we could get if we were to survive. He also knew that strafing targets on the ground was a lot different from what he was used to.

On the way to the target, I was glad for the practice of flying formation again as a wingman. I found I had grown rusty, although it had only been a month since I was last a wingman.

Suddenly, I saw something below.

"Hey Willie, this is Bledsoe. There's a train at one o'clock. It's just now pulling into that station down there."

Willie spotted the train and turned for the deck to make his attack.

The engineer on the train saw us coming and speeded up in a desperate attempt to pull into the station's repair barn. He made it just as Willie started his pass. The locomotive was inside the barn with the string of boxcars protruding along the track. Willie and his wingman bypassed the engine and shot up some boxcars as they went over. As number three man in the flight, I made a quick calculation as to where the locomotive might be sitting inside the barn, pressed the trigger, and watched a stream of bullets tear through the wooden structure. Seconds later, steam spewed out and the barn burst into flames. My bullets had not only found the locomotive but had also hit something highly flammable.

"Holy cow! Did you see that?" Willie called. It made me grin. It was the first time he had ever seen the results of shooting those 50-caliber machine guns at close range.

Soon after we shot up the remaining cars, we saw smoke curling lazily in the air. It was the telltale sign of another locomotive. Willie and his wingman went to work on it and I followed them down, then peeled off in the opposite direction when I saw another engine hiding under a bridge. We had luckily let down in a busy area. There were plenty of targets.

"Hot dog! There's another one backing into that tunnel at four o'clock. Come on, Seldom!" Willie yelled. He was taking to strafing as if he had been doing it all his life.

The locomotive was securely inside the tunnel. We couldn't get to it with our machine guns, so we lined up to drop our bombs and try to seal up the tunnel. As we were making our run, I spied another locomotive parked among a clump of trees. I made a quick turn, gave the train a short burst, and watched with satisfaction as the steam spewed into the sky. Seconds later, my wingman and I were back in formation.

Willie was having the time of his life. "Man, this is a different kind of war than the one I fought before I went home on leave. I like this shooting back for a change," Willie said. He was dodging the flak as he spoke but there was no quiver in his voice. It explained why Blickenstaff wanted him back for a second tour. Willie was a brave man and a leader.

When we landed at home base two hours later he was still glowing, elated over the results of his first combat trip on the deck. "Jesus, we'd charge down on those characters shooting like mad. What a time we had for ourselves. Those trains went sky high. To hell with the milkruns. I like this getting down on the ground and letting those Krauts get a taste of our lead."

A storm closing on the Continent kept us on the ground for the rest of the day. It wasn't long before Willie Price had a poker game going. It was the first chance I'd had to get in on a game since my arrival in England. I found that Willie's style of poker was right up my alley. He played with a passion.

"Bet 'em wild and sleep in the street," he said, and that was just the way it went. It wasn't long before I had most of Willie's money. He didn't seem to care.

August came to an end. And so did the combat missions of seventeen pilots in our group who were reported missing or killed in action during the month. One of the pilots was killed by the blast from his own bomb when he dropped it while too low to the target. Another failed to return when he flew directly into the remains of a Focke Wulf 190, which he blew out of the sky during a dog fight.

On the other side of the ledger, the group destroyed eighty-three enemy aircraft on the ground and twenty-nine in the air for the month.

It seemed hard to believe that less than three months earlier I was flying my first mission on Blick's wing—green as they come. I had a hard time remembering anything other than combat flying. I had crammed what felt like a lifetime of experience into this short period—but it was having its effect. I didn't realize it just then, but the danger and the continual fear had my nerves very near the breaking point. Since the day I arrived I had steadily been losing weight, and by this time I was looking haggard.

My tail bone was sore. It was not possible for me to sit still for more than a few minutes, but my fanny wasn't the reason: I simply couldn't relax. I tried, but I couldn't discipline myself to take time off and rest, although I knew better than anyone else that I needed a break in the combat routine.

What kept me going was the mania—it was certainly that —about completing my tour. And there was another reason: flying every possible mission without any letup was one way to keep me from going crazy with fear. Continual flying kept me from worrying about being killed on my next mission.

September found me sweating out my war one day at a time, and even though nearly exhausted, I kept pestering Price to put me on every mission roster.

Our mission for the day was to clear one particular area near the German border "of anything that moves." When our regular group briefing was over, Willie Price took the Seldom pilots aside and revealed that upon returning from a prior mission he had seen an enemy airdrome near today's target area.

"We were too low on fuel to attack then but let's try to find that airdrome and knock off some EA after we finish our assigned job. With a few more kills Seldom Squadron can lead the group in victories. How about it?" Willie asked.

It was to be a volunteer effort and Willie was leaving it up to us. Several of us agreed to rendezvous at a spot Willie had marked on his map and go after the enemy aircraft.

I had gotten through the regular briefing with only the normal butterflies fluttering in my stomach. But the thought of going after a German airdrome that would be surrounded by those death-dealing flak guns terrified me. I bolted for the latrine.

The terror passed as I crawled into the cockpit of the Little Princess. We were soon on our way to our assigned area and methodically went about our business. I had not found any moving targets so I chose an important looking railroad junction on which to drop my bombs and was on my bombing dive when a flak gunner cut loose at me. He poured a burst of 20-millimeters right at me and made a direct hit in the center of my tail section. I was in a shallow dive when the shell hit, blowing off my elevator trim tabs and part of the tail section. The Little Princess momentarily lurched out of control and went into a steep vertical dive. I was only a few hundred feet in the air and the ground was coming up fast.

In a second or two, if my ship failed to respond, it would be all over for me.

Come on, baby, help me out of this mess.

I eased the stick back ever so gently in an attempt to break my dive—gently, gently, or the whole tail assembly would come off.

The Little Princess was slow to respond and I thought for sure we were both through flying. But with a little more persuasion she did respond and I managed to level out a few feet above the ground. The large hole in my tail was plainly visible. I could see that the trim tabs on the right side had been shot off. They automatically control the attitude of the ship in level flight. In spite of this the plane seemed to be functioning okay after I made adjustments on the remaining trim tabs.

I skimmed over the tree tops and climbed for another run at the railroad junction. If the target was important enough to rate a battery of 20-millimeters, then it was worth another try.

The flak had split up my flight momentarily so I called over the radio, trying to determine their position.

"This is Blue Two, Bledsoe. I've been hit pretty bad and am pulling out for home base." It was my wingman speaking.

"Blue Three here. My wingman and I have joined Red Flight. We'll try to pick you up later."

That left me all by my lonesome as I turned and started toward the railroad junction. I was able to keep one jump ahead of those white puffs of death and dropped both my bombs right in the heart of the railroad intersection. The tracks raised up in the air and stiffened, as if in mortal pain. Then they dropped back to the ground in a twisted ruin.

"Let's get together for that special target, Seldom," Willie called out to let us know he was heading for the spot he had marked on the map. If enough pilots showed up we'd take on the German airdrome.

I located Willie and his wingman and pulled up above them. "Willie, I took a pretty bad hit. Look at my tail section and let me know what you think about it."

Price pulled in close enough to reach out and grab my tail. "Jesus Christ, Bledsoe, you really got clobbered. Looks like half your tail is missing. How does she fly? I told you you'd get your ass shot off."

"My controls feel a little sluggish, Willie, but other than that it isn't giving me any problem. She seems to be holding to-gether okay. Take another look for damaged controls. I think she'll be all right." I was eager to accompany Willie to that airdrome.

Willie moved back and forth to get a good look and seemed to be satisfied. "But you better take it easy, Bledsoe. That's a goddamn big hole to take along looking for trouble."

We picked up Lieutenants "Ben" Benjamin and Alger Aal on our way to the enemy airfield. Our attack force now numbered five Seldom pilots. We cruised along the deck, destroying several trucks and four trains while searching for the German airdrome. I had gone down to shoot up a locomotive and had gotten a little behind when I heard: "Hey, this is Ben. I'm going down on a 109 parked in the field dead ahead." An instant later, I could see flames and smoke shoot into the sky as he got in a good burst.

"This must be the spot," Willie hollered. "There's a mess of planes under those trees! They're just in front of the one that's burning. Let's go, Seldom!"

At that moment, the sky became alive with flak. This was not going to be any picnic. The air became black with bursting shells from heavy guns, then white puffs of exploding 20-millimeters. Without thinking, I hit for the safety of the deck. Looking around, I saw Ben. Regardless of the flak he was making another pass on the airdrome. Aal was right on his tail, heading down into the thick of things. The flak almost hid them from my view. We'd evidently hit on one of the Germans' more important airdromes.

I was just getting ready to join the fray when Aal screamed over the radio that he had been hit. Terror-stricken I got back down on the deck at the outskirts of the airdrome.

My chest ached from the pressure of the fear and I found it hard to breathe. I shook all over. I'd have given anything just then to be out of that airplane and safely on the ground, even in enemy territory. I made a turn to head out and away from the fight.

Seconds later, the terror subsided. I began to breathe normally and I had control. For the first time, I understood the panic that caused more than one pilot to leave his buddies and run from a fight. I had come within an inch of doing just that.

Calmer, I climbed into position where I would be able to return the Germans' fire. Willie had set up a left-hand gunnery pattern and I fell in behind him. On my first pass I saw several enemy ships parked on the other end of the field and decided it was time to make a change in our setup.

"This is Bledsoe," I called. "There's more EA on the other end of the field. Someone follow me and I'll set up a pattern in the opposite direction and work on them while the rest of you guys shoot up this batch. That way, the flak gunners will have to divide their fire." Without looking to see if anyone was following, I peeled off to the right and started another pattern. It was reassuring to find Aal right behind me as I dove down on a parked 109 and watched it go up in flames.

The flak was more intense than ever but now the gunners had to cover both ends of the field at the same time and were not able to concentrate their fire.

Aal and I were going down on a string of 109s parked behind a cluster of tall trees. I held the trigger and pressed forward with my attack, completely engrossed in making an effective pass. I could see my bullets hitting the enemy aircraft but it did not explode or catch fire, so I kept firing. It was almost a fatal error. I was just a few feet off the ground and tall trees loomed directly ahead. I doubted that I could pull up and get over the trees without ramming right into them. I horsed back on my stick as hard as I could, all the while hoping to God that my ship, with its damaged tail section, could stand the strain. I barely made it over and *through* the trees—I felt and heard the branches scraping the bottom of the Little Princess.

Once again, that good old P-47 Thunderbolt had performed above and beyond reason.

On my next pass, I concentrated on an ME-110 and it burst into flames. It had been parked so close to a 109 that I felt sure both of them would burn, even though I wouldn't be able to claim it as a kill. Smoke and flames prevented me from seeing well and I did not get a good shot on my next pass. When I came around again, I got a long burst into another ME-110. It caught fire and was burning as I passed over it.

I suddenly became aware that Aal was no longer on my tail. I had been so busy with my own problems I never saw what happened to him. I called out, but there was no answer. With a sickening feeling I realized the flak had caught up with him. The gunners could now concentrate their fire on me.

Just then Willie solved the problem: "Let's get the hell out of here! The joint's getting too damned hot to suit me. Come on! Come on, you guys. Everybody pull out!"

The words were hardly out of his mouth when six ME-109s parked on the ground suddenly appeared before my eyes. They were lined up, just waiting for someone to pick them off. I couldn't resist the temptation of at least one more pass. "Bledsoe here. I just located six 109s. Someone want to help knock them out?"

"Forget it, Bledsoe. We're pulling out. We've had enough for one day. Come on, let's go," Willie responded.

"Okay, Willie, I'll meet you in a minute," I replied. Determined to take a shot at those 109s, I charged down on the enemy aircraft. It seemed as if every gunner on the field was waiting for me, but I was going like a streak and all their shots fell behind me. I lined up the EA in my sights and held the trigger down. The smoke from my guns poured back over the wings of the Princess. She bucked from the kick. I could see pieces flying off the first 109 and flashes of fire running up and down the fuselage as I riddled it good. I pulled my sights off this one, kicked a little right rudder, and raked two more of the 109s parked nearby.

The ground gunners were shooting constantly but still were not leading me enough. I decided to make another pass, knowing they would be waiting for me on the next go around. Instead of making the same turn as on my previous passes, I kept on the top of the trees a few seconds and reversed my turn in order to sneak in from the opposite direction.

"Hey, Bledsoe, I told you to get out of there! Come on now, beat it!" Willie yelled.

"I'm coming, Willie, after just one more pass!" It was foolhardy but I couldn't keep myself from taking another crack at those 109s; it was an impulse I couldn't stave off anymore than I could prevent the panic that had gripped me earlier.

I kept low until I was in a position to pop up quickly and fire at the parked EA. Once again, I raced a few feet ahead of the flak gunners. They kept a path of bullets coming at me but they were bursting behind my tail. I blazed away at another 109, trying to set it afire. It danced on the ground as the bullets tore through it but it didn't burn. It was probably out of fuel. In a final effort, I sprayed a burst at the remainder of the parked ships and saw them lurch as my bullets found their mark.

Then I hightailed it out of there. Every flak gun in the area was after me. A few minutes later I joined Willie and the others.

We were at a thousand feet when I spotted a train on the ground. I was just getting ready to go down after it when I heard the crack of bullets. It felt as if the Princess had been hit and I almost went into a snap roll, trying to get away from this new danger. Then I saw smoke curling back over my wings and I realized that my own guns had fired. They had become so hot from the shooting I had done over the airdrome that they were going off by themselves. It shook me up. I gave up the idea of shooting at the train. I had pressed my luck far enough.

When we got to the coast, we closed up in tight formation and waved at each other, drunk with our success. Ben held up five fingers to indicate that he had destroyed five EA. Willie's wingman signaled for two and Willie claimed three. I had definitely destroyed four, had two probables, and had damaged several others. I could also confirm two for the missing Aal. That meant our small force had run up a score of sixteen enemy aircraft destroyed and a score more of probables. It had been a field day for us, except for the loss of Aal. He was listed as missing in action, those all-too-familiar words. Later we learned that he was killed when he crashed on the edge of the enemy airfield.

When we returned to Raydon, Rafferty was waiting and walked up to me as I was parking the plane. He stuck out his hand and said, "Congratulations, Captain Bledsoe, and I do mean Captain." My promotion had come in while I was on the mission; it seemed a reward for a good day's work.

We were routed out of bed at two in the morning. It was September 5, 1944. The plan was to catch the enemy as dawn broke over the Continent. To do this we'd have to take off in total darkness and not use our lights at all. We did not want Hitler warned that we were coming so early in the morning, and we had been told that Britain was awash with German spies. It would be ticklish just getting the forty-eight Thunderbolts off the ground and into formation in the dark without an accident.

I was flying as leader of Seldom Squadron again that day, and the Little Princess would be the first plane to take off. This was a break for me. It meant that I could be clear of the churning propellers as pilots taxied their planes out to the runway.

It was pitch black except for the bright glow of the fiery exhaust from our ships. I roared down the runway with my head down in the cockpit, relying on my instruments for direction. It was impossible to see anything more than a few feet away. The ships behind would take off by following the flashes from my exhaust.

As I picked up speed, the wheels of the Little Princess left the ground. I wanted to increase speed to maintain better control, so I quickly retracted my landing gear. It was then I thought I'd had it for sure.

The cover had fallen off the warning light that came on when the landing gear was not fully retracted or locked down. The light was normally very dim, similar to that of a dash light indicator on an automobile. But with no cover, in the blackness it had become a blazing light that flooded the entire cockpit. It completely blinded me. I desperately looked over the side, trying to pick up some kind of a reference point on the ground. All I saw was total darkness without so much as a glimmer. I cursed the effectiveness of the English blackout.

I was flying blind a few feet off the ground, loaded down with bombs, ammunition, and extra gasoline. I was piloting the Princess by feel only. If I made even the slightest wrong move, I would plow into the deck and be blown to bits.

I rammed the throttle as far forward as it would go, poured on emergency power, and gently eased the stick back. I was attempting to judge my climb by the sound of the engine and the feel of the back pressure of the stick. It was a classic case of flying "by the seat of your pants."

When the wheels were sucked up into the belly of my ship, the warning light automatically flashed off. Though the entire episode had taken no longer than fifteen seconds, it had seemed interminable. The experience left me wringing wet from the sweat that had poured out of my body. Back on my instruments, I headed upstairs.

Our Thunderbolts were floundering in all directions, frantically trying to line up. The darkness prevented us from getting in formation so we headed for Germany helter skelter. An hour later at twenty thousand feet the first streaks of light appeared in the sky, although it was still dark on the ground. We were finally able to assemble.

It was still fairly dark when we arrived at our target area, but our eyes had grown accustomed to the blackness and we were able to make out various objects on the ground.

Dawn broke quickly and activity over Jerry land got into high gear. Our radios crackled. "Get that train! There goes a soldier on a motorcycle. Must be a messenger, so shoot the son-of-a-bitch. See that group of trucks? Watch it, watch out! Here comes the goddamn flak!"

My wingman was Lieutenant Marvin Albertson. I was making a pass on a locomotive when he called, "Hey, Bledsoe, there's a JU-88 on the deck just to your right. It's going like hell, down on top of the trees!"

The Junkers-88 was the finest twin-engine fighter-bomber in the world. It had inadvertently flown directly underneath our gunnery pattern. My wingman was after him and I followed in hot pursuit. He was traveling at full speed and it was going to be difficult to catch him.

Albertson was startled to see me fly past him. He had forgotten to salvo his belly tank. "Drop your belly tank. You'll never get any speed if you don't," I called.

The Luftwaffe pilot really knew his business. He dropped down to a foot above the tree tops, making it impossible for us to get a good pass at him. He kept twisting and weaving among the trees and buildings on the ground. He operated that bomber like a single-engine fighter. I stayed right on his tail, blazing away with my guns at every opportunity. He was probably surprised to find me right down among the trees with him. But like him, I'd been on the deck so many times before it didn't bother me to make a tight, twisting turn a few feet off the ground.

My bullets knocked pieces off the JU-88, but I couldn't get straight and level enough to get in a good burst. In the murkiness of dawn, the tracer bullets from the twin machine guns in the 88 flashed by me like shooting stars. There was the strange sensation that if I opened my canopy and stuck my hand out, I could catch some of the bullets, they were passing so close. Instinctively, I tried to draw myself down into the cockpit to keep my head from being shot off. That German gunner, as well as his pilot, sure knew what he was doing. Seems as if I had run up against a couple of real experts here.

Moments later, we were over open country and the enemy pilot started a wide circle.

That's your first mistake.

I tightened up my circle, trying to get a proper lead on him. It looked as if my angle of deflection was about right. I squeezed the trigger, felt the Little Princess buck as the smoke from my guns curled back over my wings.

More fragments of the JU-88 flew into the air as some of my

bullets found their marks. At that moment, his ship came alive with flashes of fire. I thought for sure I had him. Not so. He was trying to turn the tables on me. The flashes of fire were flares he had released from underneath his cockpit. It confused me momentarily. Then it dawned on me that he was signaling to ground gunners ahead!

The German pilot led me into what was to have been a neat little trap. He flew directly over a flak nest. The gunners held their fire until he passed over and then let me have it full force. I found myself flying through a cloud of small-arms fire. The white puffs of 20-millimeter shells were exploding all around me.

To get me into the flak trap, the German bomber had straightened out for just a moment. It proved to be a mistake. Though I was catching a lot of the ground fire, I managed a good, solid burst right into the ship's tail. I silenced the tail gunner. Now, if I could just avoid that flak coming up at me from below, I'd have him.

The pilot made another turn to lure me back to the flak nest. I had two choices. I could pull away and detour around the field, or I could go through their field of fire again. If I tried to avoid the flak I'd lose him. I hated to give up on the EA at this stage. I took a deep breath and pushed forward on the stick to get down as close as possible to the ground. I got so low I felt sure that if the ground gunners on one side of the field shot at me, their bullets would ricochet into their own gunners on the opposite side of the field.

"Poor Little Princess," I shuddered as I felt my plane lurch with the impact of a direct hit. But still in pursuit, I passed over the flak nest and we were out in the open again. I held my fire, waiting until I could get closer to the German ship, and then got in some good hits with my next burst. I could see little red and white flashes appear on his left wing. I fully expected the JU-88 to blow to bits, but the plane just kept on flying, weaving and dodging just on top of the trees as the pilot struggled to get away.

I maneuvered closer. I no longer had to worry about the rear gunner. I was right on the German's tail when he straightened out again for a brief instant.

This should do it. I squeezed the trigger and the guns fired. But to my complete rage I squirted out only a bullet or two before running out of ammunition.

The enemy pilot must have realized what had happened. He eased up on his turn and pulled a couple of hundred feet up in the air. He was looking over his shoulder. I thought he was looking at me. But in the excitement the German pilot and I had both forgotten about my wingman. He had kept us both in sight by flying above us and cutting the corners. Now he moved to finish off the JU-88. As the pilot straightened out the plane, Albertson dove on him. Once again pieces began flying off the German plane, but that JU-88 kept right on flying!

To my surprise, Unangst, my element leader, came in for a pass. I thought my flight had been separated during the wild chase, but they had remained above me. He fired a concentrated burst at the German ship. That did it.

The bomber started a gentle climb to the left, pulled up about a hundred feet and then fell off on a wing, and plummeted. It hit the ground with a splintering crash.

The JU-88 burst into small pieces and scattered over the countryside. Flames swept the open field where a gallant pilot had gone down. He had put up a magnificent fight.

War is crazy. Seconds before, I had been trying to shoot the plane down. Now, I felt sorrow at the death of a competent pilot and his gunner.

Our mission had been successful. Several locomotives destroyed, the railroad tracks blocked with broken boxcars, tracks at important railroad junctions bombed into twisted steel, and scores of trucks and tanks damaged beyond repair: it was not a bad score for one day.

We were still excited and heady at debriefing, all talking at the top of our voices when Harper burst in. "Boy, oh, boy!" he yelled! "Did you see me knock that JU-88 out of the sky after Bledsoe missed it?"

I thought he was pulling my leg because I hadn't been able to bring the German bomber down. I was wrong. Harper was serious. He declared, "I was flying on Unangst's wing and fired a long burst over the top of his ship when he made his pass. I saw my bullets rip the canopy off the top of the 88. I must have killed the pilot instantly. But anyway, I'm claiming a kill!"

Other pilots reported that Harper had made fake claims in the past, and we were inured to it. This time, however, he had gone too far. He was trying to take credit for a victory that belonged to Unangst and that several pilots had seen.

Rafferty was the first to jump on him. "Harper, knowing you like I do, I'd bet my last dollar you were lagging behind and protecting your ass when the shooting started."

Unangst's face had turned beet red. "You're a liar, Harper. I looked around to check my tail before I made that pass on the 88, and although you were supposed to be on my wing, you weren't anywhere in sight," he exploded. "I think Rafferty is right. You were hiding out somewhere, waiting for things to cool off."

"There was no doubt about it," I broke in. "It was Unangst who brought the German down. Albertson and I got in some good hits but Unangst finished him off. He should be credited with the kill."

That seemed to convince the debriefing officer.

"Well, maybe I did miss and Unangst shot him down," Harper replied lamely. Then he left the room fast.

Rain and fog kept us on the ground for the next two days. This gave Swanson time to patch up the Little Princess and get her back into operation again. It also gave my sore fanny a rest and my jangled nerves a chance to simmer down. Thanks to the weather and Willie Price's love of poker, I won a fistful of money while waiting for the next mission.

CHAPTER 15

Operation Market-Garden

By September 10, 1944, I had passed the 200-hour mark —more than two-thirds of my 300-hour combat tour. If I could keep up the pace, I would finish before the winter weather set in. Home sweet home for me before Christmas.

I was getting a lot of satisfaction out of being assigned a leadership position in the squadron and in being promoted. I enjoyed the responsibility that came with it. My locomotive score had passed Parker's twenty-five, and I had the distinction of having destroyed eight locomotives on a single mission. In fact our whole group was going well. We were becoming recognized as the top fighter outfit in the Eighth Air Force.

The Nazis were retreating rapidly into their father-land—and the Allied fighter planes were helping speed them along. We took off each day at about an hour before dawn to catch trucks, tanks, and troops moving along the roads. We shot up everything that moved. We had to be on the lookout constantly to avoid strafing our own troops and equipment. It did happen, but not often. The teamwork was generally good between the fighter pilots in the air and the foot soldiers on the ground.

The action on the ground was moving so rapidly the Germans ran right off the combat maps posted in our ready room each day. General George Patton's Third Army armored columns covered ground so fast we had some difficulty finding the "front." Our ground forces had swept through France and were deep into Belgium. The Thunderbolt pilots were to keep one jump ahead of the infantry and armored columns. This was not easy, because the retreating Germans managed to move most of their antiaircraft guns with them. The more we pushed them back and the more concentrated their flak guns became, the tougher our missions were and the more losses we suffered.

When the Germans were chased out of France, they relocated their buzz-bomb sites further north. The result was that our field at Raydon was in a direct line between the buzz-bomb launch ramps and their major target: London. We began to hear the flying bombs over our base on their way to London almost nightly. The flashes from their exhausts lit up the sky, and those of us watching would hold our breaths until the bombs passed us by. Field Marshal Goering had made a personal threat that he was going to wipe out "Colonel Zemke's butchers and the murdering pilots" of Colonel Duncan's group; Axis Sally let us know about it in her daily broadcasts. We thought Goering was serious enough to make our base or Zemke's 56th Fighter Group nearby a target for buzz bombs. To make things worse, sometimes a bomb's engine quit prematurely and it could fall almost anywhere between the North Sea and its target.

Those missiles scared me especially. Their arrival was heralded by a rumbling roar similar to the sound of a diesel truck. When I'd hear them coming, I'd hide my head under the covers. But after a while I got so I could tell by the sound that there was no danger—as long as I could hear that characteristic roar. If the engine stopped, my heart leaped into my mouth. That meant the bomb was on its way to the ground.

Whenever one landed anywhere near, our hut shook from the concussion. A bomb hit the runway not far from the hut. That time I really cowered in fear, waiting for the explosion. The seconds moved by like years. Nothing happened.

"Go off, you son-of-a-bitch!" someone shouted from a bunk nearby.

But that bomb didn't explode. Goering hadn't gotten us that time, either accidentally or on purpose.

September 14, 1944, brought an unusual type of mission. I was ordered to take the squadron over to a clandestine air base in northern England and pick up a pair of B-17s flying into Holland on a special mission.

One of the bombers would be loaded with high explosives. A pilot would get it off the ground, head it toward the English Channel, and while still over England but just before he reached the coastline, he was to bail out. The bomber would then be guided to its destination by radio control from the other B-17. The target was a German ammunition dump in the northern part of Holland, far from the active war zone.

The radio control plane that was to guide the "flying bomb" to the target would be manned by high-ranking officers in charge of the project who wanted to see how it would work out. Our job was to ward off enemy fighters.

The weather officer predicted clearing skies by the time we arrived at the secret airfield. As usual, his professional prediction wasn't even a good guess. When we got there and were ready to land, ground fog covered the place like a blanket. We circled for thirty minutes, but the fog still clung to the ground. We could see tops of the cars parked at the base and could make out the heads of people walking around below us. The runway itself was invisible.

I raised the control tower.

"Seldom Leader here. We're circling your field but can't find the runway. How about parking a few trucks alongside it?"

"Roger, Seldom Leader. Hang on a few minutes."

We saw the trucks move, lined up with flags atop them to designate the runway, and we landed without ever seeing the ground. It was a weird feeling. My wingman and I made it on the first pass. Several other of our pilots had to go around again a time or two, but they all got down safely.

We had been awake since three o'clock that morning and had not had anything to eat, because we were supposed to have breakfast at this field. Then we were told upon arrival there would be no time for breakfast because the mission was ready to roll. My guys got good and sore. Frayed nerves, of course. They bitched at me to get them something to eat, and as the minutes passed the complaints got louder and longer. Finally I went to the operations officer and asked about it.

"There won't be time now, Captain. The ship will be ready any moment. As soon as you're ready, I'll advise the colonel."

I told him we were ready when they were.

An hour later we were still standing around. Rafferty sounded off. "If the brass is in such a goddamned hurry, why don't they get their asses out here?"

No one would have dreamed of arguing.

When more time passed and we were still standing there, I knew that if this went on much longer I would have a mutiny on my hands.

I went looking for the operations officer again. This time a flunky told me he was too busy to talk to me. That did it.

"He'll be a damned sight busier if this goes on much longer!" I yelled—loud enough so that the enlisted man found him for me. I didn't beat around the bush. "Major, my people have been up since before daylight horsing around on this deal, and here we are still horsing around. I wouldn't be surprised if half my pilots abort and go home as soon as they are airborne. If the brass isn't ready to go, you'd better get these guys some breakfast."

The major was a typical poopsheet artist.

"You and your men will have to follow orders like everyone else and don't you forget it. The colonel will let you know when he's ready to go."

"Look, Major, I know these guys. If they decide to abort, just what the hell are you going to do about it? Are you going to get them sent home to the States? There's nothing any one of them would like better. Where's the colonel?"

"The colonel's in a briefing and doesn't want to be disturbed. If you want to take the chance . . . . " He showed me the briefing room door.

I knocked, waited a moment, and then entered without invitation. The room was full of bird colonels. I came to attention in front of one of them who appeared to be in charge of their meeting.

"Captain Bledsoe reporting, sir. I'm the squadron leader for your mission. I want to inform you that my pilots have been waiting to take off for more than two hours. They haven't had anything to eat this morning, sir. I'd suggest you feed them before we take off."

"I'm afraid there won't be time for a proper meal, Captain," the colonel replied, reasonably enough. "We'll be ready to take off in a few minutes now. The operations officer should have taken care of your boys a long time ago. Tell him I said to rustle up some hot coffee and sandwiches—on the double."

He looked squarely into my eyes and smiled slightly. "None of us has seen combat. We certainly need all the help we can get from your squadron. Frankly, most of us are scared shitless."

At least he had the good grace to be candid.

"Welcome to the club, Colonel. I'm scared every time out. I'll get my pilots together and we'll be waiting for you." The colonel had turned out to be a lot better guy than the people around him seemed to be.

After I delivered the message to a not very happy operations officer, hot coffee and baloney sandwiches soon appeared and we wolfed them down. They tasted good, but they sure gave us trouble later at high altitude: my stomach got so bloated I thought I was going to explode. We'd have been better off going hungry.

When the brass was finally ready, we took off and circled the field, waiting for the two B-17s. Then we headed toward the English Channel. Just before we got there the pilot and co-pilot of the "flying bomb" hit the silk. Their parachutes floating lazily toward the green fields below looked so peaceful. The pilotless flying bomb was now under the control of the colonel in the radio-control ship.

The plan called for the radio ship to maintain an altitude of ten thousand feet. Any higher than that would make it impossible to guide the flying bomb to a target on the ground.

We would be a long way from the active war zone, so I wasn't anticipating any problems from the Germans. About ten minutes before we were scheduled to arrive over the target, a lone flak gunner started shooting at us. His exploding shells began making those familiar dark blossoms in the sky. He must have been a real novice. He was missing us by a mile.

The crew of the radio-control bomber had obviously never been around flak before. They started climbing, not realizing that the gunner on the ground was absolutely no threat to any of us. By the time we got to the target area the radio-control ship was at well over fifteen thousand feet and still climbing. The colonel would never be able to guide the flying bomb into the ammunition depot from that altitude.

A regular bomber crew would have been thoroughly disgusted at that performance. On every mission the B-17s pressed on to the target without deviation from course. They did not break formation no matter how thick the flak became but this outfit had panicked at the first shots. The other guys flew through real concentrations of flak every day, lucky to make it through the exploding steel all around them, and all they could do was grit their teeth, say a prayer, and proceed full speed ahead. It was no wonder the regular bomber crew's tour of duty was only twenty-five missions.

"Seldom Leader here," I called over the radio to the squadron. "White Flight will drop down closer to the target so we can see what happens when the bomb hits. The rest of you stay with the control ship. Okay, let's go White Flight."

I peeled off on a wing with three other ships following me down. At five thousand feet, we could see the explosive-laden B-17 headed toward what appeared to be an ammunition dump. I got in radio contact with the control ship and attempted to help it steer the bomb into the target. "Hold it up! Hold its nose up! You're letting the bomb dive too fast. It will hit the ground long before it gets to the target!" I yelled.

The ammunition depot was protected by several flak positions, and they started letting us have it. Flak was popping in the area of the radio-control ship, and the colonel seemed more intent on gaining altitude and getting out of range than he was on hitting the target. There was a tremendous flash. The flying bomb hit the ground—a full mile from the target. The colonel was too high to see well enough to guide the flying bomb on target. The show was over. We had spent five hours in the air for naught.

When we got home, the boys bitched and bitched. Rafferty said it for everyone. "I felt like shooting that radio ship out of the sky. That goddamn colonel ought to be court-martialed!" he ranted. "That chicken was so high, it was a wonder he could even see the target. Man, what an explosion when that bomber hit the ground! If he had stayed at ten thousand feet, they could have steered that thing right into the mouth of that ammunition dump. We'd have seen some real Fourth of July fireworks."

Most of the guys blamed the colonel, but I blamed the cloak and dagger boys. They were so determined to keep their "secret weapon" under wraps, they didn't use common sense. They should have assigned an experienced bomber crew to run the radio ship, not a junior birdman even if he was a colonel. A real crew would have considered the mission a milkrun.

Winter was raising its head. By September 17, 1944, the days were getting noticeably shorter. Hitler and his military had more hours of darkness to cover their movements, and they were taking full advantage of it to move men and equipment without fear of fighter pilots knocking them out. Perhaps because of this, the Allied advance bogged down near the Siegfried Line.

I was racing the winter weather, trying to push my time up to that 300-hour mark. Once winter socked in, there would be many days when operations were impossible and we would sit on the ground. Doc told me that the group had flown only two missions a week at the outside the winter before, and that would mean months to finish up the combat hours I needed to finish my tour. I didn't want to wait six months for the rest.

Headquarters also must have had winter in mind when they gave us a brand new assignment: locate and track antiaircraft gun positions along the route to Holland. We couldn't figure out why. It had all the makings of a suicide mission. Rimmerman nailed it down in his report to the brass: "We won't have any trouble finding the flak. Living through it to tell anybody, that's going to be the problem. But, 'ours not to reason why. . . .' "

So we went out every day, shot up antiaircraft positions, and got shot up in turn. We finally learned the reason for it in one of the most solemn briefings I ever attended.

"Men, Operation Market is on, and this is the most important mission since D-Day," our CO explained. "Today there will be an armada of Allied ships in the air to make an airborne invasion of Holland! Two thousand American and British transports and gliders will carry a whole army into the Arnhem area. The idea is to split the Germans. Paratroopers will be dropped to join the Underground forces, and the gliders will come in with ground troops after they have established a foothold."

The success of the daring move would depend in part on the fighter pilots. The transports and gliders could be torn to shreds if we did not neutralize much of the flak.

"Our job today is to keep one jump ahead of the air armada. We'll fly ahead of them and do our best to draw the fire of the flak guns. It's hoped we can wipe out the flak nests before the unprotected troop planes fly over," Jonah said. "Remember, those guys will be helpless while they're in the air. There is no way they can defend themselves until they make that landing. They'll be depending on us to look after them. Thousands of lives are going to depend on us finding those flak nests. Regardless of losses we're going to knock out those flak positions."

We synchronized our watches to the same time that thousands of pilots throughout England would be using this morning. It gave me a deep thrill to know I was involved in an historic event. Tough as the mission was going to be, not a single pilot in the group complained. As for me, for once I was resigned to whatever fate had in store. I did not even have to make the usual dash for the latrine!

In the few minutes between briefing and takeoff, I wrote another long letter to Harriett and put it in my foot locker, just in case. This job was going to be extremely dangerous and every one of us knew it; there wasn't even any of the usual bickering as we got ready for takeoff.

Swanson and the rest of my ground crew were hovering around the Little Princess like bees. They too obviously felt the tension, and they responded by making sure my equipment was in tiptop shape. Swanson had been given the additional job of installing a pair of experimental rocket launchers on the Little Princess. Headquarters had asked for a flight leader volunteer to give these a try, and I was willing. They were placed under the wings, between the bombs and the exterior gas tank. With them I was really loaded. My P-47 would take off so heavily laden that I wondered what the designer would think if he could see it.

I climbed into my ship a full five minutes early and sat, watching my watch, waiting for the exact second when I was to start my engine and take off. My mind raced back over the missions I had flown these past three months and I had a clear picture of Harriett and our Little Princess at home.

God, help me make it.

When our group was airborne and began moving south, we could see planes of all descriptions so thick in the sky that I couldn't begin to count them. British bombers and gliders led the way. They were trailed by two thousand American aircraft.

If this invasion succeeded, the airborne troops would divide the Nazi forces in the west and let Patton, Bradley, and Montgomery start moving to Berlin again.

We flew by the gliders and transports as we headed toward Holland. We were close enough to see the faces of the soldiers in the planes; they gave us the thumbs-up salute, and we returned it.

The enemy coast loomed. We had made our first checkpoint exactly on time.

We cruised at a thousand feet, less than three minutes ahead of the air armada. The battle with the flak gunners was about to begin. At that altitude we were perfect targets. I visualized the gunners licking their chops.

Lord, stay with me.

Suddenly flak filled the sky around us and steel ripped through the Little Princess. Instead of breaking formation and getting away from the flak positions, our normal plan of action, we lazily circled and returned in an effort to locate the flak nests on the ground. The Krauts must have thought we were crazy. They kept blasting away, which was what we wanted them to do—that was the only way we could find them to knock them out.

"I've got the bastards spotted. Follow me!" an angry pilot called on the radio. We were right on his tail as he did a wingover and headed for the deck. We were shooting back now and it felt good to be returning their fire, bullet for bullet. A moment later, those particular guns were silent.

"Jonah here. Good job, boys. That takes care of that bunch. Let's pull on to our next contact point," Rimmerman called.

Just as we finished, the air armada pulled into view. They didn't draw a shot as they passed over the area. We had lost two pilots. It was a price that had to be paid to make sure that those thousands of paratroopers would not be shot out of the sky.

When we reached the next contact point I fired my rockets at a gun emplacement, but they didn't even come close. The rockets wobbled crazily and went astray. Later I was told it was the first time rockets had ever been fired at the enemy from a fighter plane in the ETO. It turned out to be a dismal failure, as I learned beyond doubt on my second pass. I tried the rockets again and cussed them as they lurched off course. I was already annoyed because the rocket tubes caused excessive drag and the plane was hard to maneuver.

That does it.

I salvoed the rest of the rockets and launchers. The Little Princess seemed to sigh with relief at losing all that excess baggage.

The same routine—get shot at, spot the guns, then attack —was repeated several times until we reached the areas near Arnhem where the British paratroopers were dropped.

Although it cost us dearly, our part of the job was a resounding success. We silenced every flak gun on our route and made the way safer for the transports and gliders who followed in our wake.

In the drop zone, we saw several buildings blazing. The Dutch underground had struck at a prearranged time. We could see vehicles dashing to and from the nearby village. The cars carried orange flags, which identified them as friendly. We had orders to shoot up any vehicle that did not carry the orange marker.

The paratrooper drop zone and the glider landing areas had also been marked by advance troops who had been dropped during the night, with colored-smoke pots and orange flags. Suddenly, the transports arrived and paratroops came tumbling out of them; the sky was filled with parachutes, a positively dazzling sight. White silk and the orange of supply chutes were everywhere, so many parachutes that some of the troops landed on top of others. I watched with amazement as paratroops bounced off and away from each other.

Good luck, you guys. Give 'em hell!

We watched with equal awe as the gliders came in for landings. What a way to fly! Hundreds of them came down in a field far too small for them. They hit the ground from all angles and all directions. They rammed each other, fences, trees, and anything else that got in the way. We couldn't tell how many casualties the British suffered in the landings, but I could see soldiers piling out of the gliders, ready to fight.

During the landings we searched the outlying area for enemy, on the ground or in the air. Although we moved around the drop zone as long as our gas held out, we did not see any movement. Right on schedule, other fighters arrived to take over, and we headed toward home base.

As we made landfall out, we saw several wrecked gliders that had gone down in the cold waters of the English Channel. They were being torn apart by the waves. Even though we were short of gas, we swept back and forth, searching for survivors. We did not see any. All we could hope was that English patrol boats had found them earlier.

A sad Seldom Squadron pulled into home base at Raydon. There was no buzzing the field. We had taken a beating, as we knew we would. The group had lost several men and many of those who did return were flying badly damaged planes. We were lucky to be back from this mission, but for once I and the others felt more concerned about someone else: those paratroops and glider men that we had left behind enemy lines. Their job was to break out and head for Berlin. There would be no rest for them this night.

That evening, the group had a message from General

James Doolittle, Chief of the Eighth Air Force, congratulating us for an outstanding performance in what seemed to be a very successful accomplishment.

That night I had trouble sleeping, thinking about the losses we had suffered and about the paratroopers who would die or wind up in the hands of the enemy. I had a nightmare I didn't remember, and woke up in a sweat to find out I wasn't the only one having trouble; the glow of burning cigarettes from several nearby bunks flickered in the darkness. It seemed hours before they were put out and I could finally drift away to sleep, exhausted from this day's extraordinary ordeal.

The Eighth Air Force spared no effort to assist the airborne invasion. Hundreds of transport planes and bombers carried reinforcements and supplies into the areas that our forces in Holland now held. Our job on September 18 was to be a repeat of the mission on the day before. Keep the flak away from the planes.

After our losses on the seventeenth, the assignment brought a feeling of impending doom to the squadron. Some pilots kidded lamely that if they got out of this alive they would join the Japanese kamikaze force. I was so sick that I spent nearly an hour in the latrine, just waiting for my gut to calm down.

Our orders once the gliders and paratroops reached the drop zone were different for this mission. We were to scout the area for German ground forces, being extremely careful to make positive identification before shooting military rolling stock or other targets.

"Don't shoot anything on the ground if it doesn't shoot first or unless it fails to carry proper markings," the briefing officer emphasized. "We've got a lot of support from the underground forces working with us on this invasion, and they'll be active. Their equipment will be marked with a broad orange stripe or carry an orange flag. Our own stuff that landed with the gliders will have the white star."

We took off and rendezvoused as we had before, and again

watched wave after wave of bombers and transports roar across the channel a few hundred feet above the water. Many towed gliders that carried more troops, field guns, antitank guns, and ammunition.

We dipped our wings to salute them. We kept one step ahead of the air armada to neutralize the remaining flak positions before our Big Friends came within range of the deadly guns. The drop seemed better organized than yesterday's initial attack.

"Bledsoe, there's a big truck racing down the road at six o'clock!" Rafferty shouted. We were outside the drop zone, but the truck could be a friendly.

"Hold your fire, Seldom, until I can make an identification," I called. I made a pass over the large truck that was going full speed down the paved road and looked for friendly markings. It did not carry the orange insignia or a white star. "Okay, Seldom. He's all yours. Let him have it!" I shouted.

The truck was going top speed when Rafferty let fly with a burst of bullets. It burst into flames. It was loaded with fuel. The flames set trees on fire on either side as the burning truck careened down the road. It spread fire for hundreds of yards before it finally piled into a tree and exploded.

We continued to move around the area, ready to take on the enemy wherever we found him.

We were flying over an innocent-looking field when a 20-millimeter shell came tearing through my right wing. I couldn't figure out where it had come from and decided to take another look at the haystacks below. On closer inspection, I could see radio equipment not quite hidden by the stacks. We had run across some sort of military installation. When I looked over the ground, it seemed to be a radar station.

"Seldom, fall back while I check out this radar station and see if it's in friendly hands," I called.

I got the answer fast enough: one of the haystacks parted and the snout of an antiaircraft gun came out. I zoomed out of range, white puffs of 20-millimeter shells running right behind my tail. Several of the haystacks held antiaircraft guns.

"Bledsoe here. We're going to destroy this radar station. We'll bomb it first and then strafe it."

The overcast was solid at eight hundred feet and our bombs were fused to go off on impact. It was going to be difficult to drop our bombs without getting our fannies busted. I kept my dive as shallow as possible and as I released my bombs I gave the ship full power. The Little Princess jumped away. Even at that I felt the concussion. It brought to mind what had happened to one pilot on the mission the day before: he blew the tail off his own ship with his own bomb and went straight in.

As I veered away, the ground gunners zeroed in on me and the flak came up fast.

"Seldom, don't get too low when you drop your bombs. Put them anywhere in the field. Just get rid of them so we can work this place over."

Within a few minutes, our flight of eight Thunderbolts had strafed every haystack on the field. My gas gauge indicated it was time to head for home.

"Okay, Seldom. That takes care of that! Let's pull out and go."

Just then I had a call from First Lieutenant Robert Alansi.

"Hello, Bledsoe. This is Alansi. I'm hit bad. Don't think I can make it back. I'm pulling out."

"Okay, Alansi, we're on our way too. Anything we can do to help you?"

"No, I don't think so. My engine is missing and losing power. I can't hold altitude. I'll have to set down soon."

A couple of minutes later I could hear Alansi talking to his wingman. His ship was cutting out on him and he had the choice of going over the side or making a forced landing in some farmer's field. He decided on the latter. He picked a small field near a cluster of farmhouses. My flight flew over him just as he made a wheels-up landing.

Alansi jumped out of the ship the moment it stopped skidding along the ground. He started running as fast as he could toward the houses. Chances were the Dutch farmers would be friendly and he could count on their help. But it suddenly looked as though he had forgotten something. He turned around, ran back to the ship, reached into the cockpit for a small bundle, retraced his steps, and disappeared into the yard of one of the houses. We shot up his ship and headed for home base. We never could figure out what was in the bundle he retrieved, but it could have been supplies for just such an occasion.

When we got back to Raydon the pilots in Alansi's flight were joking about his misfortune. It brought a laugh throughout the ready room when someone suggested he had probably run back to his ship to pick up his medals. Most of the pilots in Seldom Squadron considered Alansi some kind of a character. He was often the butt of jokes because of his wild imagination. He would claim all manner of heroic feats that could not be confirmed by other pilots on that particular flight.

One day Alansi came back with a real humdinger claiming he had shot up a boxcar that held vital airplane instruments. Then someone asked: "Hey Alansi, how'd you know they were airplane instruments?"

Alansi didn't crack a smile. "I saw the labels on the cartons," he explained.

"I hope I'm not around to listen to Alansi's exploits in Holland when he gets back," Rafferty said. "He'll have wild and wooly tales to tell. The trouble is there won't be anyone around who was there."

It seemed bizarre that the pilots could pass off so lightly what had happened to one of their own number just a couple of hours earlier. But that was the war.

We were still talking about Alansi when Willie Price yelled for me.

"Hey Bledsoe, Colonel Rimmerman wants to see you—on the double!"

That "on the double" had an ominous ring.

The colonel didn't mince words. "Jesus Christ, Bledsoe, what's this about you shooting up a radar station in Holland? Goddamnit, man, British paratroopers were ordered to take that radar station as their first objective. Headquarters was advised that the raid was successful. The last they heard it was in the hands of the British. Then some triggerhappy American pilot attacked the station and the British troops who were holding it!"

Rimmerman was doing something unusual for him: he was chewing me out in front of a flock of pilots in that room. He was furious; the brass had unloaded on him and he was getting to the source. I waited for him to finish. I was thinking about all the holes in my ship made by the gunners in that hayfield.

"Sir, I don't know who had control of that radar station, but we had good reason to destroy it. I was checking the place over when they opened fire and almost blew me out of the sky. I'd like to hear headquarters convince the rest of the guys in my flight that the place was in British hands. While we were shooting it up, I saw several soldiers run out of one of the gun emplacements and they didn't look British to me! Furthermore, there wasn't a sign of an orange flag or anything else to show they were friendlies."

"Are you sure they were shooting at you, Bledsoe?"

"I don't know who the hell they were shooting at, Colonel, but I know they sure as hell hit me."

Rimmerman looked relieved. "Something's gone wrong, then. Intelligence reported the Dutch underground and the English paratroopers had captured the place. Maybe the Germans made them hand it back. Screw headquarters! It doesn't matter who had control of the station. When they cut loose on you guys it's open season."

Rimmerman became absolutely jolly, thinking over the report he was going to make to headquarters.

"They were really upset. The guy who chewed me out said you boys really worked over this place. I was ordered to get to the bottom of it and report back. Now I can. I'm really going to rub it in. You're doing a good job, Bledsoe. Sorry I let loose on you, but the brass made it sound like you were really getting us involved in something sticky with the Limeys."

I left Rimmerman's office aglow. When I told Doc about the encounter he said he had been putting the bug in Rimmerman's ear about the good job the instructors were doing for the squadron.

It was true, and it showed. We lost seven pilots but as bad as our losses on the two flak-busting missions had been, we were shocked to learn that our neighboring fighter group had lost sixteen pilots that day.

It was a crazy kind of war. The next day we would be out looking for the enemy again. Any one of us might have our number come up and every one of us knew it. I had never seen a drop of blood shed in this war, and yet death rode with me every day. The big question was, could I last out the course?

CHAPTER 16

The Process of Elimination

There was good news and bad news for the fighter pilots on September 21, 1944. The good news was that some ground-pounder at Eighth Air Force Headquarters, God bless his soul, had sharpened his pencil and figured out that at the going rate of loss, fighter pilots had one chance in a hundred of living to finish a 300-hour tour. The reason for the low odds was the sort of war we were fighting—strafing on the deck. The new statistics showed that the only way any reasonable percentage of us could survive would be to drop the tour requirement by at least fifty hours. Henceforth, he indicated, the combat tour ought to be 250 hours.

But tactical headquarters yelped; they needed every fighter pilot to help bring the Germans to bay, they said. So the brass compromised, and the news came down: the combat tour had been shortened to 270 hours.

I was elated when I heard the wonderful news. It was like a gift from heaven. One more mission would take me over the 250-hour mark.

But the bad news we had from headquarters that day was very bad. Operation Market-Garden had become an utter disaster, at least for the moment. The troops in Holland were up to their necks in Germans. They needed help from us in the worst way. The weather was socked in tight at first, but when it cleared for a few hours, our guys were told to seek out targets of opportunity in the drop zone. I wasn't scheduled to fly that day, but I heard later that the group found plenty of trouble. Goering had plans of his own for a Luftwaffe air drive. He sent up every fighter plane he could muster to shut off the Allied escape route. Our group's forty-eight Thunderbolts were jumped by twice that number of ME-109s. We claimed fifteen enemy aircraft destroyed and another fifteen probables, at a cost of a dozen planes damaged and three planes and pilots lost.

Merchant, one of our instructor group, also failed to return. With his loss, Rafferty and I were the only instructors left—two of seven who came to the squadron in June. Following the statistics of the efficiency expert at Eighth Air Force, either Rafferty or I would get it on the next mission or two. It was simply a process of elimination. I had only a few more combat hours to complete my tour, but poor Rafferty had nearly a hundred left.

We talked over how to survive.

"Hell, Marv," Rafferty argued, "you've got some leave coming and you ought to take it. By the time you get back they'll probably drop the tour to two-fifty and you'll be practically through. Don't be a damned fool. Keep your ass on the ground for a few days."

It was tempting, but I had my own theory. "The hole in your argument, Raf, is that I might sit around here a month waiting for them to drop the tour requirement, and then they'll decide not to do it. Next thing you know, I'll be facing the winter weather and it could take weeks to fly my remaining missions.

"Anyhow, Raf, in a few weeks the war might come to an end and I'll find myself sitting here, wondering what they're going to do with superfluous fighter pilots. They might even raise the tour back up to three hundred hours—or more, if things calm down a bit. No thanks, Raf, I'll fly every mission until I'm through, if Willie will put me on the schedule."

Rafferty was plainly worried about me coming out alive since the odds were against either of us finishing our combat tour in one piece.

Doc took the attitude that the war was just too damn big for any one pilot to make the difference and that is why he argued against the idea of me signing up for a second tour. Doc agreed with Rafferty. "Stay on the ground for the time being, Marv, and see what happens," was Doc's advice.

When it became obvious I was not going to heed their warnings, Doc and Rafferty got together and reminded Willie Price, who was in charge of scheduling, that Blickenstaff had left word to "keep that Bledsoe from flying so many missions as I want him here when I return." Blick figured on getting me to sign up for a second tour of combat duty to help run the squadron until the war came to a successful conclusion.

Willie waxed hot and cold on the issue. He really didn't care one way or the other, but this time he was going along with Doc and Rafferty. "You're going to keep your ass out of that airplane for awhile and take it easy whether you like it or not, Bledsoe," he said.

I made a big to-do, but secretly I was relieved. Besides I knew I could wear Willie down and get back on the schedule if I argued long enough. I was too tired to think straight. I felt completely pooped out. In the past three months, I had flown well over 300 hours, most in combat with flak busting so close by I could reach out and grab it. The Little Princess had suffered so much battle damage she was carrying dozens of patches and scars on those parts that had not been replaced entirely. I had scars, too. My nerves were on edge, I was fidgety, eating little, and not getting enough sleep. My butt was killing me from sitting on the hard raft. I was hollow-eyed and weak from the diarrhea that hit me after every briefing. My weight was down from my normal 160 pounds to about 130. I was really in no shape to keep on flying combat. Staying on the ground for a while might be my last chance to get out of this war alive and back to Harriett.

For a few days storms over the Continent prevented everyone from flying. That hiatus just about finished off the airborne invaders. The grand plans had not materialized as the Germans captured most of our troops in the area.

During the break in missions, Rafferty and I flew to a nearby base to see some of the former instructors from Luke Field who had volunteered for combat when we did. We were shaken by more grim reports.

Jack Shively had been killed on his first strafing mission when he went down to get a train and flew into the ground. He must have been hit by flak.

Gene Wagner's life had run out the following day when his outfit ran into a large gaggle of enemy aircraft. He was on his second mission.

Ward and Benton had been killed over Germany a few days later on the same mission.

Mytte was the only one of the Luke Field crowd not finally accounted for. He had been shot up and seen to bail out over enemy territory. His chute seemed okay and his flight leader saw him come down. But later information came to headquarters that Mytte had fallen into the hands of German civilians and been killed. Rafferty and I had heard about that sort of thing; we had all been warned to surrender to the German military and at all costs to avoid the civilians, but this was the first direct knowledge we had of what could happen.

Rafferty and I headed back to Raydon in a state of shock, chilled by the realization that we two were among the last survivors of our Luke Field group.

It may seem odd, but I never knew the first names of Ward, Benton, and Mytte—just as I never knew the first names of most of the pilots who filtered in and out of our squadron. The turnover was enormous; men were constantly coming in and going out, lost on missions or rotated home. The only people a pilot really knew were his CO and a few friends. I had become friendly with Doc, and Blickenstaff and I went back a long way, as did Rafferty. But dozens of others came along—mostly nice guys—and I never got to know them. Too often a man was in the squadron, up in the air, and dead before most of us knew anything about him.

Rafferty decided he was long overdue for a binge. It would help to drown his sorrows, he figured. That night he and Hedler broke open a quart of Scotch. They were hitting the bottle when the rest of us left to hit the sack. Doc and I took off for our own hut next door.

We were soon awakened by a loud crash and a blood-curdling yell. Next thing we knew, Rafferty came running into our hut.

"Hey, Doc! Wake up. Wake up, Doc," he was hollering as he tried to rouse Doc in the bunk next to mine. "That goddamn Hedler ran into the stove and knocked it all over the hut. One of the stovepipes fell and cut a big gash in his leg." Rafferty was half-drunk and laughing so hard he could hardly get the story out. "Funniest thing I ever saw. Hedler was on the floor, tangled up in that hot stove and getting the hell burned out of his fanny. Come on, get out of the sack, Doc. Hedler needs you."

"Beat it, Rafferty. Serves the idiot right. Horsing around in the middle of the night," Doc grumbled as he rolled over to go back to sleep. He didn't intend to have his sleep disturbed by a pair of drunks.

"Come on, Doc. Get out of bed. Hedler will bleed to death. Hey, somebody turn on the lights! I can't find my flashlight," Rafferty crawled under Doc's bunk looking for the lost flashlight.

By this time all in the hut were awake. Some of the guys were rolling around in their bunks, cursing Rafferty and yelling at him to get the hell out and let them get some sleep. If Hedler bled to death, that was just fine.

"Doc, you might as well get up," I said, giving Doc's bunk a kick. "Rafferty will have everyone on the base awake in a few minutes."

"Okay, okay. Give me a second to get my eyes open," Doc yawned. He rolled over again. He finally pulled himself out of bed, groaning all the while, and got dressed.

"Come on, Doc. I can just see Hedler bleeding to death while you're looking for your socks," I said.

"Who cares?" he replied. "Serve the damn fool right for horsing around this late at night while sane people are trying to get some sleep."

Doc was still muttering when he left the hut. In a couple of minutes he was back. I figured it was a false alarm. "How was he, Doc?" Has your patient died? You sure weren't gone very long."

"I forgot my pipe. I haven't seen Hedler yet." Doc was still half-asleep as he rummaged about his bunk until he found his pipe.

An hour or so later, Doc was back. He was wide awake, a glow on his face, and in good spirits.

"Everything all right, Doc?" It seemed to me he had been gone a long time.

"Yeah, everything's okay. Hedler had a bad cut from the edge of the stovepipe. Damn fool. I had to clean it out. Then sew it up with some nice stitches." He grew very clinical as he described the stitches. Obviously the incident had given the medical man in him a lift; it was the first time in months, he told me, that he had done anything but dish out pills for headaches, colds, and constipation.

The next day, with even more gusto, Rafferty described the operation in great detail.

"You should have seen old Doc. You'd have been proud.

We took Hedler over to the hospital and Doc went to work. He didn't bat an eye. He washed away the blood and sewed up Hedler's leg. After that, he had to treat Hedler's burned butt. That crazy Hedler was still loaded and was accusing Doc of being a horse doctor. He kept demanding that Doc produce his license to prove he was a medical doctor. After it was all over, Hedler said he'd probably die of hydrophobia from Doc's last patient. It made me sick when I saw Hedler on that table with the blood spurting out. It sure sobered me up in a hurry! I wonder if they'll award old Hedler a purple heart?"

The patient was up and around in a couple of days, and pretty sheepish over the ruckus. By the end of the week he was able to fly again, although his leg was still a little stiff. On that mission he was badly shot up by flak, parachuted out, and was never seen again. The process of elimination was at work.

I had found it unbearable to stay on the ground, waiting for the combat tour to be reduced to the 250-hour mark. By constantly bitching at Willie, I had managed to put in more time by taking the place of other pilots who were happy to avoid the next mission. Fortunately, my last two missions had been escorting bombers over Germany and with the Luftwaffe choosing to stay on the ground, I brought the Little Princess back unscathed.

I had reached the point where I had but one more combat flight to complete my tour. I began to sweat this out as a thousand pilots had before me. I wouldn't be the first pilot shot down just as he was getting ready to go home.

The Jerries had pulled back and the Americans were reaching deep into Germany. Enemy lines were now so far away it was taxing the gas supply of our Thunderbolts. By the time we got to enemy territory, we had used so much gas to get there that we couldn't stay long enough to do much good.

Our group was ordered to switch over to P-51 Mustangs for the time being. It was a sleeker, lighter ship and it didn't gulp gasoline at the rate the seven-ton Thunderbolt did, so the P-51 could stay in the air much longer than our P-47s.

But what a job the Thunderbolt battlewagon had done! The German position attested to the fact that it was more difficult to knock down this fighter than any of the other fighter aircraft. Thunderbolts could sustain battle damage that would almost surely have felled just about any other airplane. Major General William E. Kepner, commander of the Eighth Air Force, declared: "It was the P-47 Thunderbolt that broke the back of the German Luftwaffe."

Our squadron was scheduled for what looked like an easy escort mission on October 3, 1944. I was surprised when Willie Price had me down to fly as his wingman. He explained, "Headquarters predicts we're going to have a milkrun today, Bledsoe, so this is a good time for you to finish up. You're my wingman, so stick close. I don't want your ass shot off on your last mission. Have you been checked out in the 51 yet?"

I lied. "Sure." I had flown a P-51 only once before, back in the States a million years ago.

My crew chief was shocked. Swanson would be sweating out my last mission, too. "Captain, you're not going to try finishing your tour in that P-51 sewing machine, are you? You ought to wait until they try another mission in the Thunderbolts and then take the Princess. She's ready!"

I knew it was foolish not to have a few practice runs in a new ship or else to wait for another Thunderbolt mission, but I wanted to finish my tour. I would have liked to do it in the Little Princess, but I was so edgy I couldn't have sat still and waited. I was so jittery I felt as though I would jump out of my skin. I had to get this last mission over with. Besides, since this was going to be a milkrun it would be almost like a practice flight. Since I was flying on Willie's wing, I wouldn't have other people depending on me as their flight leader, so I wouldn't be sticking anybody's neck out but my own.

As we took off I thought of Swanson's comment. The P-51 did sound like a sewing machine compared to the roar of the Little Princess. The engine popped away . . . pop . . . pop . . . pop; the steady hum of the radial engine in the Thunderbolt was always a reassuring sound. I was glad it was an escort mission. I'd hate to get down on the deck and battle the flak gunners in this peashooter.

When we were deep in enemy territory one of our newer pilots started having trouble with his cooling system. It was Jerry Devers. He always got excited at any sign of a problem and had been chewed out many times, cautioned over and over again to take it easy when he talked on the radio. Here he was again.

"Hey, this is Jerry!" he shouted at everyone in general. "My coolant is haywire. The indicator is in the red. What'll I do? This thing is liable to quit on me any minute! Where are we? What'll I do if my engine quits?" He kept the radio tied up for a full minute with this chatter before he took his thumb off the radio control button and gave someone a chance to answer.

"Goddamn you, Jerry!" Willie roared. "Stay off this radio. If you're having trouble, turn around and go home! I've told you before about chatter on the radio. Bledsoe, take that screwball home, will you?"

Under normal circumstances an experienced pilot would not have been sent home as an escort. But today everyone in the group was sweating out the pilot flying his last mission. It was being made too easy for me, I decided. "That's okay, Willie. I'll stick with you. Let one of the wingmen escort him home."

"Jonah here. Get back to the field, Bledsoe, and take that guy with you," Rimmerman interrupted.

I was not going to bust my luck. "Roger, Jonah," I replied. I sighed with relief.

"What'll I do, Bledsoe? Will this thing fly with the coolant needle in the red? What are we going to do?" Jerry implored.

"We're going home, Jerry. Now, take it easy. Stay off the radio. I can't help you. You're in that cockpit by yourself. Keep going as long as you can. If your engine quits, it'll be up to you, just you, to decide whether you want to bail out or try to make a forced landing. Come on now, and not another word on the radio!"

The thought of heading home and the prospect of not having to face death again had made me so excited I could hardly contain myself. My mouth was dry and I was breathing heavily. I felt like a green pilot on my first mission instead of an old hand on my last one.

Later, when we were out of radio range with the group, Jerry reported that his coolant needle was out of the red and his ship was normal. We were abreast of each other a few hundred feet apart when we hit the overcast and started our letdown. He elected to fly with his own instruments rather than close up on my wing and follow me through the overcast. That was okay with me, because I was having a hard time adjusting to the P-51 instrument panel. The gun sight was directly in the way and I had to lean forward and bob my head back and forth to see the instruments.

While flying in the dark clouds, I saw my airspeed indicator drop slowly from 220 miles an hour to the 190 mark. I thought I must have started climbing. But on cross-checking my altimeter, I could see the ship was still losing altitude and not climbing at all. I figured the engine must be losing power and that was slowing down my airspeed. As I watched the airspeed indicator keep falling off, I was drenched in sweat. My tachometer showed I had plenty of power and my altimeter was reacting normally. It had me completely baffled.

If my airspeed indicator was correct, I was moving slowly toward the stalling speed. I'd soon fall off on a wing and into a spin.

When the airspeed indicator dropped below the stalling point and my altimeter showed I was still in a shallow glide, the light suddenly dawned; being on my last flight and in a strange ship on instruments must have fogged my thinking. The Pitot tube, which registers air speed, had gradually iced over, showing a false reduction reading of air speed. It had never happened to me before and had caught me by surprise. I knew what to do now—disregard the malfunctioning airspeed indicator until I could thaw it out with the Pitot tube heater. The heater would melt the ice formed over the tube's opening, which was located on the wing. I searched for the switch to turn it on but couldn't find it. I was still looking for it when my radio fairly bounced as I heard Jerry scream.

"Bledsoe! Help! I'm stalling out! I'm on instruments in the clouds and I'm going into a stall. What'll I do? I'm down to a 150 and losing speed. What'll I do, Bledsoe? Why don't you answer?"

That was almost the last straw. How could I answer while he was still yelling? He finally let me get in a reply.

"Take it easy, Jerry. Your Pitot tube is frozen. Turn on the Pitot heater and you'll be okay. While you're waiting for it to thaw out, hold your course and altitude with your altimeter and the needle and ball indicators. Don't pay any attention to your airspeed," I instructed. I was pointing out things that had to do with basic instrument flying, things he should have learned in flying school. Even now, in the soup, I thought of my supervisors at Luke Field telling me to pass the students whether they were proficient or not. They ought to be listening to Jerry.

"Where's the heater switch, Bledsoe? My God, where's that switch? I'm in a spin, I think. What'll I do? I can't find that switch and I'm in a spin!"

"Forget the heater switch, Jerry. I don't know where it is. Here's what you have to do. Center your needle and ball. Cross-check with your altimeter—it'll tell you whether you're diving or climbing. You've got to use rudder and stick to get your needle and ball under control. That'll take you out of the spin. While you have your needle and ball centered, control your airspeed with your altimeter." I knew it was a lot harder to do than it sounded, but the airplane could be flown through the clouds with those basic instruments. I tried to sound calm, hoping to transmit the feeling, but it didn't work. Jerry kept screaming until he fell out of the overcast in a spin. He survived—fortunately he had enough altitude to regain control of his ship a few hundred feet above the ground—but he was lucky to come out alive.

By this time we were out of radio range with one another, so I continued on course, breaking through the overcast over the English Channel. Now that I could take my eyes off the instrument panel I tried to find the Pitot heater switch, just to satisfy myself. I never did find it aloft, which shows what a fool I was for flying a combat mission in an unfamiliar airplane.

On arriving at home base, instead of giving the field a final buzz I made a gentle peel-off and a careful approach to the landing strip. Once on the ground, I made for the parking revetment where I immediately had the crew chief point out the Pitot heater switch. It was placed behind an unmarked protective cover.

In a daze I walked to my Nissen hut. My combat tour was over. For me, the shooting was done. I had come through hell and I was alive. My only worry now was getting out of England before my luck ran out and one of the buzz bombs found me. I thanked God for getting me through and prayed for the day I'd be holding Harriett in my arms again.

PART III

Home

CHAPTER 17

Flak Happy

I walked around in disbelief. I wouldn't be shot at anymore today. My combat tour was complete and I was still alive. When I hit the sack, bone weary, I thought how, for the other pilots, tomorrow would bring another mission, another brush with death, and more empty bunks. But I wouldn't be there.

As I awoke in a strange, new world the next morning, the sun was streaming through the dirty windows of the Nissen hut. The thought of not having to face flak any longer suddenly made me feel strangely old and drained of strength, like a tired, worn-out old man. I was twenty-eight years old.

I found it hard to adjust to its being all over. It had been a terrible ordeal. There wasn't a scar on me, but I had battle wounds, the images of all the pilots I had known who had lost their lives. The seconds on combat missions that had stretched like hours had taken their toll, too. We had all been surrounded by so much death and destruction it had become almost commonplace. I had lived on death's threshold each day these past few months. The fear and the possibility of dying had accompanied me on every mission and returned with me to my Nissen hut every night. Now the haunting whisper was gone! I was a free man. I had been released from bondage.

Swanson and the rest of the ground crew slapped me on the back and pumped my hand until it hurt. They had sweated out that last mission along with me, a worried lot when I took off in that P-51 sewing machine. But I had made it. Tomorrow they'd have a new pilot to look after, a new name on their ship, and the "sweating 'em out" would start all over again for them. They had been in England for two and a half years and didn't know when they'd get home.

For the other pilots in the squadron, the war was still terrible and real. But they were equally glad I had made it. Every man in the squadron shook my hand and wished me well. I was a symbol of hope for all of them.

The weather was beautiful, and I began getting ready to leave the base and report to the point of embarkation at Stone, England, where I would take a ship for the U.S. and start the rest of my life.

I packed a few belongings and gave the rest of them away. The guys in my hut drew lots for my warm bunny suit and my innerspring mattress. As I packed, I thought of the three and a half months so crammed with action. I had completed seventy combat missions, almost every one amounting to a major confrontation with the enemy, in a period of just a little over a hundred days. I had destroyed thirty-five German locomotives and seven enemy aircraft. An administrative officer told me some time later that completing the mission in such a short time had set some kind of record and the destruction of thirty-five locomotives was still tops in the ETO.

As I picked up my gear the other pilots were waiting in the ready room, all set for a mission. To the last man, they gathered around, shook my hand again and again, and wished me luck. I was going home, they were waiting to hit the "wild blue yonder" and the flak-infested sky once more, and they wished *me* luck. I felt like a brother to the older pilots and like a father to some of the younger kids. One of the newest replacements, barely nineteen years old, reminded me of Kid Novak.

I realized I would remain concerned about all of them, even though I was leaving. Many of these pilots wishing me well would never finish their combat tour alive. Tears were in my eyes when I boarded the transport plane that was to take me to the debarkation point.

When I arrived at the port on October 9, 1944, I found a strange lot of Air Corps men waiting to be shipped home. They were a different breed of men from the shipload who had accompanied me overseas a few months earlier. We were excited at seeing a new country, charged up at the thought of combat—disciplined military men, ready to carry out orders from our superiors. But this ship was filled with combat-weary veterans who wanted only one thing: to get home fast. They didn't care how many regulations had to be broken or how much red tape needed to be cut.

My problems began on the boat.

In the past three months, I had become accustomed to bouncing out of bed before daylight. Three or four hours sleep had seemed sufficient. Now that I was on the ship and could sleep till noon if I wanted, I found it impossible to rest after the first crack of dawn. I had to get up and get going. My nerves were so taut I couldn't sit back and take things easy. I spent my time pacing back and forth on the deck, restless, waiting for the crossing to be over. I felt like a caged animal. Packing the seventy missions into such a short time had made a wreck of me. The two weeks it took to cross the Atlantic seemed like two years.

We finally got there. "Hey, Bledsoe. There she is! Come on, let's get on an upper deck where we can get a good look," one of my shipmates shouted. He had been peering through the haze for hours, waiting to catch a glimpse of the lady in the harbor. He had finally spotted the Statue of Liberty.

I went back to my bunk, not wanting to be so near and yet so far from Harriett and the Little Princess. And I was afraid I might not be able to control my emotions at the sight of the United States.

The past two weeks had been hell. I seemingly couldn't adjust to the fact I was no longer flying missions. I had developed a very bad case of nerves. Doc would have diagnosed my situation as "flak happy" and would have sent me to the "flak home."

Night and day I relived my war—the tension of instrument flying; friends piling into the ground; bombers exploding in air as if they were made of tissue paper; and the agony each time one of the bunks in our hut was empty because a pilot failed to return.

"Relax," I said over and over, trying to discipline myself. "Take it easy, or you'll wind up in the hospital!"

Before going through combat, I could accept anything, come what may, with a free and easy attitude. But now there had to be a tight schedule or I'd start coming apart. Time had to be clocked off, every second accounted for, just as it had been in the briefing room and on a tough mission. Every tick of my watch had to have some meaning. I was wound up like a taut spring.

Maybe I was in shock. I didn't know. All I knew was that I just had to get home and let Harriett take care of me.

We pulled into New York harbor. All of us were ready to bolt ship when the gangplank was lowered. Instead everyone held himself in check and tried to act nonchalant in front of the cheering crowds who met the ship. We made our way slowly, ever so slowly, onto U.S. soil, which many of us had never expected to feel again.

The train ride from New York to California was a nightmare. We made so many stops along the way, I wanted to get out and run. I had telephoned Harriett and she would be waiting for me. When we pulled into the Union Station at Los Angeles, my trip was finally at an end. In a few moments I'd have Harriett in my arms and everything would be okay.

The anticipation of the meeting made me weak in the knees. After the train had stopped I remained in my seat for a short time just to get my nerves under control. It was like the last minute in the briefing room before a tough mission. I had butterflies in my stomach and my head was swirling. But I was soon caught up in the swarm of passengers hurrying down the ramp, where an anxious crowd waited at the other end of the gates. Inexplicably, I felt so scared I wanted to run the other way. Then I saw her! She was beautiful and the baby with her was walking around, just as big as you please. Why that's gotta be our Little Princess!

Oh, thank God, I made it back! I'm home at last!

Harriett slipped under the rope that separated the crowd from the arriving passengers and raced into my outstretched arms. It was some time before either of us said a word. I don't know who was more happy, or who shed the most tears. But it was wonderful. I held her so tightly she couldn't breathe.

The process of elimination had skipped me. We had beaten the odds. At last, we were together again.

The Army Air Corps had given me a month's recuperation leave and would soon notify me of my next assignment.

After a few days of visiting relatives and well-wishing friends, I experienced a tremendous letdown. Few civilians seemed to realize that a brutal war was raging and that day after day, week after week, young men were dying in combat. Some of the people, deprived of such things as butter, were complaining loud and long about it. Others raised their voices because gasoline rationing curtailed their driving.

I became bitter and frustrated that I was unable to make them understand what English civilians went through, when the German Air Force and then the buzz bombs made their relentless attacks. I wanted these Americans to visualize the killing going on overseas and have them pitch in to help our combat-weary men in every possible way. But the shooting and the bombing taking place were elsewhere and they were too far removed from the battleground to comprehend the horror.

I found myself ready to pick an argument at the drop of a hat. No one could understand why I was so touchy. There was no way they could know of the pictures and memories that had scarred me deep inside. Only those who had been there really knew what went on in the combat zone. I tried to tell people about the war and what it was like overseas; they looked at me as though I was a fanatic and shrugged. "Yeah, we saw that in a newsreel," was about all I could get out of them. It was somebody else's war.

If it hadn't been for Harriett and the Little Princess, I would have returned to Seldom Squadron and the war. I felt guilty being home when I knew the guys in the squadron were still in the fight. Everytime I heard or saw an airplane, I thought of them facing those Nazi flak gunners. Sometimes my mind would drift back to those paratroopers and I once again saw them dropping into Holland, fighting to stay alive.

It took Harriett a few days to figure out my trouble, and then she was wonderful in her understanding. I had become truly terrible to live with. When we planned to go anywhere, I stood over my little family like a tyrant with a whip—only the whip was the second hand on my watch. I was continually fighting time, back on an imaginary schedule, and determined that there should be no wasted moments. I was still sweating out that gasoline over the English Channel, dodging flak over Germany, landing a crippled airplane.

In spite of loving my family, I was glad when my leave was over. Once I got back into the cockpit of an airplane, I thought I might get over my case of nerves. I was eager to push the throttle wide open on a Thunderbolt.

But I still wasn't prepared for my orders. I couldn't believe my eyes when I read: "Captain Marvin Bledsoe, combat re-

turnee, will report for immediate active duty to the commanding office at Luke Field, Arizona."

The possibility of being returned to Luke Field had never
crossed my mind. But I knew that when I did return this time
things were going to be different. My life at Luke Field
wouldn't be the same, and not because I had been promoted
to captain. Neither was it because I was the first instructor on
the field to return to Luke from a combat assignment. My life
there would be different simply because I wasn't going to put
up with any of the old crap. I'd been through too much these
past few months to be concerned with the pettiness of Luke
Field. Anyone who gave me trouble over trivial affairs or poop
sheets was going to be straightened out in a hurry. The worst
thing anyone could do was kick me out of the military. In my
frame of mind, I could not have cared less.

But I discovered Luke Field had changed radically. The
former commanding officer had been replaced by a maverick
who had rolled up many hours of combat time and was not
much for shuffling papers and handling red tape. Before the
United States entered the war, he served with the Royal Air
Force during the Battle of Britain; later he was transferred
into the U.S. Army Air Corps when the first American combat
groups arrived in England. Being an experienced combat
fighter pilot, he was invaluable to the new Eighth Air Force
Fighter Command. He became a group commander and full
colonel. At the end of his second combat tour, he was sent back
to the States to be promoted to brigadier general and to take
over a training command. He had been at Luke Field for less
than a month when I arrived. His forte was shooting, cussing,
and sweating out combat missions, not filling out poop sheets.
The operation of a training field the size of Luke was big
business and took plenty of paper work; the new colonel was
trying to fill the bill, but he was having plenty of problems. My
orders were to report to him immediately.

He greeted me warmly. "Glad to meet you, Bledsoe. I knew
Duncan and Rimmerman well. You were in a good outfit.
How in the hell did you ever get sent to this place?" He

expressed surprise when he learned I had been stationed at Luke Field earlier as an instructor. "But that's great. Since you've been a part of this rat race before you can be a lot of help to me. I just can't talk the same language as these guys who've sat out the war here. I've got to get rid of them. They've been sitting here on their butts for the past four years. It's time they turned their jobs over to a few of the boys who've done some fighting and need to get away from the flak. I've shipped off a couple of the supervisory sports already and I'm looking for ways to get rid of more. By God, maybe they'll learn there's a war going on!"

He made me think of Kid Novak lambasting the instructors.

In no time at all, the news was out that of the thirty-five instructors who left for combat, Bledsoe was back. Everyone was hungry to hear how it had been. The new CO had let it be known there were going to be transfers to combat and the instructors and key personnel were anxious about what they would face. I was welcomed like a hero by the old instructors and the brass. Things were different for me at Luke Field. They wanted to hear how the other thirty-four men who had left with me had made out; they were shocked to learn that most of the original number had been shot down, and the war wasn't over yet for those remaining.

No longer were these instructors bemoaning the fact they weren't being sent out to combat. They knew they were finally on their way.

The fact that I had once been considered the prime troublemaker of the field had been completely forgotten. To them now I was a brother instructor who might reveal information that could keep them alive. They hung on every word when I answered their questions. They winced when they learned of the deaths of so many acquaintances, instructors they had known personally. Year after year at Luke Field, they had been removed from the realities of war; at last they were finally aware there was something more important to learn than filling out poop sheets.

Many of them seemed terrified at the thought of being shot. I felt sorry for some of them. But along with the pity, I felt revulsion toward those officers who had previously treated me like dirt and now were trying to cozy up to me.

The colonel assigned me to work in the air inspector's office. What irony! The previous air inspector was none other than the major who had chewed me out in front of all the instructors at that meeting so many months before. I could still hear him. Now he had been shipped off to combat. I wondered how well he'd be able to fly on the deck and how he'd like the flak.

My job was a great one. Air inspector personnel were supposed to see that the field was operated in a smooth and efficient manner. We were responsible only to the commanding officer. Even though we might be dealing with officers who outranked us, our authority exceeded theirs.

During the next few weeks, I took delight in checking students on their flying proficiency, helping them in every way I could, and making suggestions as to the general training program. When I would see some of my suggestions put into operation by the brass I was as pleased as if I had just shot up a dozen enemy locomotives. Yes, Luke Field had changed.

It was during this time that Rafferty arrived at Luke to report for duty. I was elated. Good old Raf! He had gotten out alive! Of the original instructors who had been assigned to the 350th Fighter Squadron in England—with the exception of Ray, who had quit—Rafferty and I were the only ones who had not been shot down! Even at that we had beaten the odds.

Rafferty broke into a loud laugh when he first spied me. "Jesus Christ, Bledsoe, the last place on this earth I expected to see you was at Luke Field. How long have you been here? How come they haven't kicked you out yet? I'll bet you've been giving them nothing but trouble."

He was surprised to learn about the changes at Luke, and it amused him to think of me checking up on some of the old instructors and the brass in my new role.

As soon as we could, we had a great bull session and he brought me up to date on life overseas.

Colonel Rimmerman had almost finished his second combat tour when he hitched a ride in a converted two-seater P-51. Captain Bret Thompson, the pilot, got fouled up on instruments, the plane crashed, and they were both killed.

Colonel Duncan made it back okay. When he made the forced landing in enemy territory, he joined up with the French underground. In a couple of days he was helping them blow up bridges and doing as much damage as ever to the Germans.

Blickenstaff returned from leave to take the squadron, sporting the silver leaf of a lieutenant colonel. Blick chewed Willie Price out when he learned Willie had let me finish my tour so quickly.

Alansi had the good fortune to land on the farm of a friendly Dutchman when he got shot down during the airborne invasion of Holland. "He came back with some of the wildest tales you ever heard," Rafferty said. "We never did know why he returned to his ship after his belly landing." landing."

So that was the squadron.

Raydon seemed a long time ago.

A short time later a report came through that because the war was winding down, there was a surplus of combat returnees and those wanting to get out of the service could be discharged through a point system.

I was anxious to resume civilian life and eager to settle down in a small southern California community. I wanted to raise my family and go into business for myself. An opportunity was waiting for me in Riverside, California, to enter the real estate business through an established broker there. I was confident that in a short time I could run my own business and make it successful.

There was a special sort of chemistry between Harriett and me. Her support, her love, and the fact that we both wanted the same things out of life would make it easy for me to embark upon civilian career.

I would miss flying military aircraft but that was secondary to getting on with my life. My nervous system was almost back to normal and with my bright future I knew I could put Luke Field, the combat and the war into a proper perspective. In short, I was ready to make the change from captain in the Army Air Corps to the rank of civilian.

I met all the requirements for the point system. I was older than most pilots, had been awarded several medals in combat, was married, had a child, and wasn't in a critical assignment. When I applied for discharge I was told I'd be among the first to go. It was hard to believe that in less than a week I would be out of the Air Corps.

I had two regrets. I was sorry I had not been able to make people more aware of the battle overseas; and I bemoaned the fact that my days of flying fighters were at an end.

My three and a half years in the Air Corps seemed to center around those hundred days fighting the Germans. My thoughts and, yes, my heart and soul, were with Kid Novak and the others I had known who had been killed over enemy territory.

I packed my uniform and silver wings and took them and my memories with me.

As I walked out the gates of Luke Field for the last time I didn't look back.

It was August 20, 1945.

Index

INDEX